KU-535-161

4238

MI5
MI6
Britain's Security and Secret Intelligence Services

MI5 MI6

Britain's Security and Secret Intelligence Services

R. G. GRANT

BISON GROUP

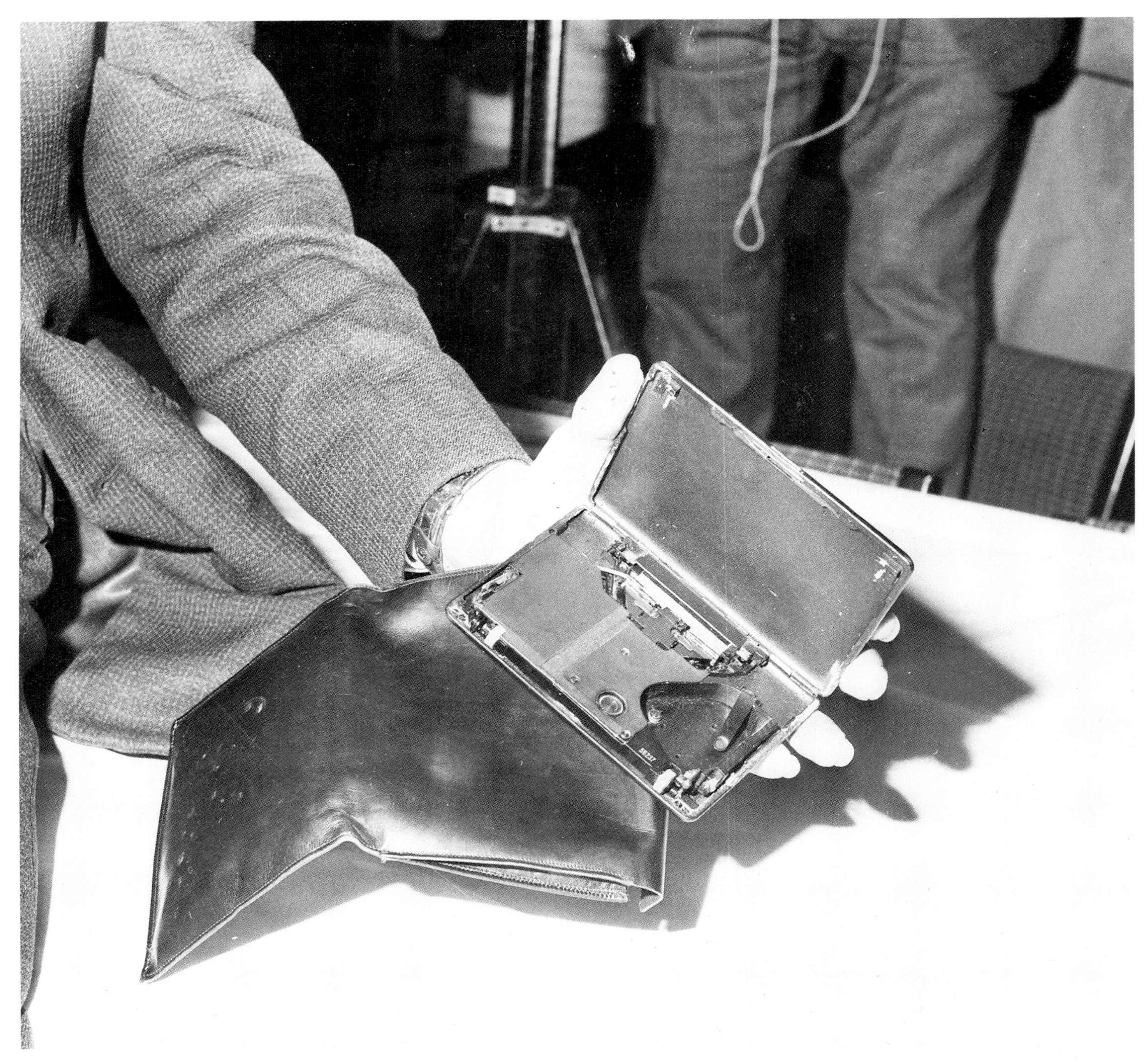

First published in 1989 by
Bison Books Ltd
Kimbolton House
117A Fulham Road
London, SW3 6RL

Copyright © 1989 Bison Books Ltd

All rights reserved. No part of this publication may be reproduced, stored in a retrieval system or transmitted in any form by any means electronic, mechanical, photocopying or otherwise, without first obtaining the written permission of the copyright owner.

ISBN 0-86124-542-3

Printed in Hong Kong

10 9 8 7 6 5 4 3 2 1

PAGE 2: Sir Maurice Oldfield, head of MI6 1973-78 (bottom left); IRA terrorist; Sir Percy Sillitoe, head of MI5 1946-53 (top right).
PAGE 3: The Berlin Wall looking east (left); Anthony Blunt, the Soviet spy who was a friend of the Queen.
THIS PAGE, ABOVE: A miniature camera concealed in a cigarette case, used by KGB spy Douglas Britten, an RAF technician.

CONTENTS

INTRODUCTION

In 1989 the British security service MI5 (Military Intelligence 5) and MI6, the secret intelligence service, celebrated their eightieth anniversaries. They are the oldest of the great intelligence bureaucracies that now span the globe, though no longer the most important. Two of the most secretive organizations in the world, they have ironically had to learn to live with a high level of public interest and media investigation. Their very secretiveness has stimulated curiosity and provoked sensational revelations by former officers – from Harold 'Kim' Philby, the Soviet mole in MI6, to Peter Wright, disgruntled molehunter turned Tasmanian farmer. Without these leaks, it would have been impossible to write a history of either MI5 or MI6.

Now that the two services have been dragged out of the darkness into the limelight and many of their secrets exposed, their story can be told with at least a degree of confidence. It is an extraordinary tale, full of convoluted plots and intrigue, blunders and triumphs. But it is also a story that poses some extremely serious questions about the ultimate worth of the secret services. Just how good is the intelligence they have provided over the years? Have they tended to pursue their own interests – and their own political line – independently of the government they are meant to serve? Is secrecy a cloak for incompetence and illegality?

One point must always be born in mind. Even today, our knowledge of the activities of MI5 and MI6 remains very imperfect. Many of the stories about them are uncheckable and different accounts of the same events are often contradictory. Revelations have always come from people who might well have an interest in distorting the facts. Espionage and counter-espionage exist in what CIA officer James Angleton called 'a wilderness of mirrors'. Truth is elusive in this secret world.

BELOW: An SF (Special Facilities) microphone designed to fit into a telephone handset. MI5 operatives have sometimes disguised themselves as telephone repairmen to install SF in a building under surveillance. This bugging device is not used to listen in to phone calls – that can be done in much easier ways – but to pick up conversations in the room where the telephone is placed.

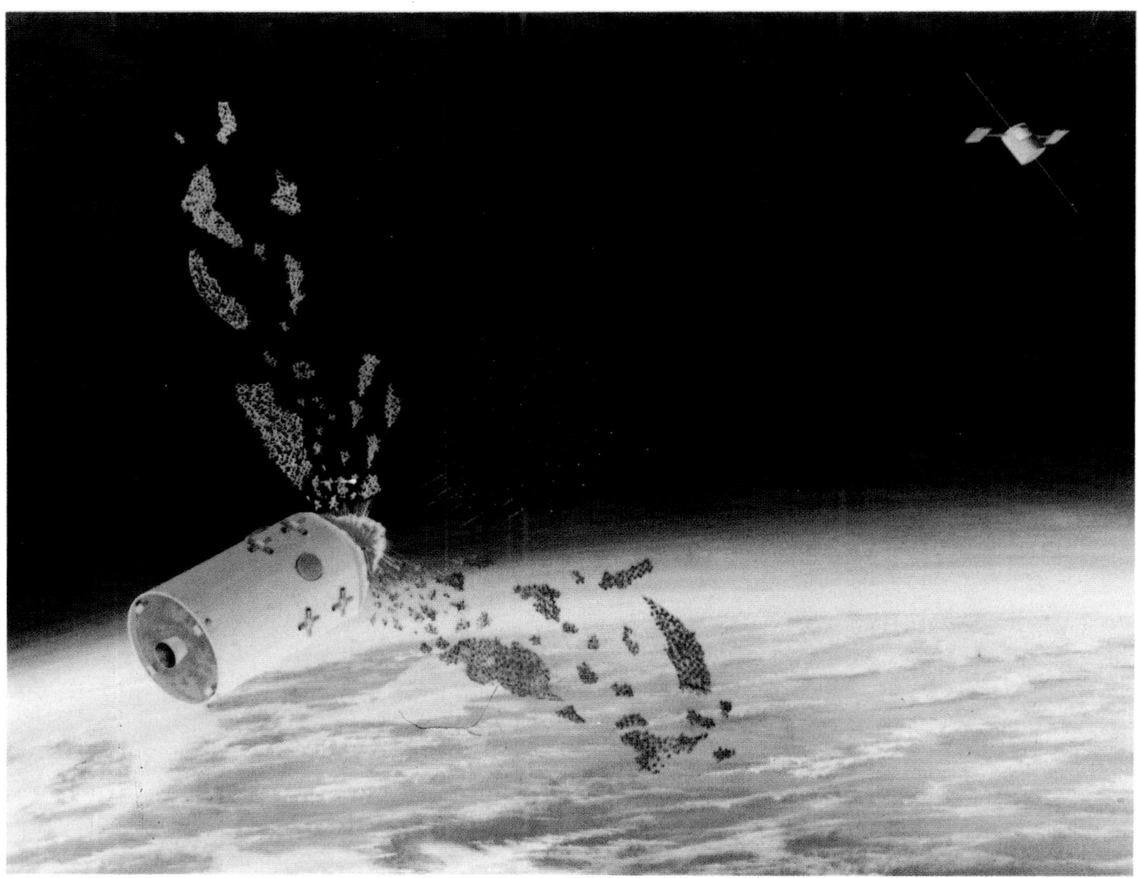

Over the last two decades the work of the field agent has been supplemented by new airborne devices for the gathering of intelligence. They range from the relatively simple pilotless drone (above) to laser-armed satellites capable of destroying other information satellites (left).

CHAPTER ONE

ORIGINS

BELOW: The disasters of the Boer War, such as Spion Kop pictured here, shook the British military establishment out of its Victorian complacency and stimulated a search for ways of improving intelligence and counter-espionage.

The history of the secret service in Britain is usually traced back to Queen Elizabeth I's secretary of state Sir Francis Walsingham, who set his agents to uncover Catholic plots against the throne in the late sixteenth century. Regular finance for covert activities began in the reign of Charles II with the instigation of a Secret Service Fund, later transformed into an annual Secret Service Vote by parliament. The money was used as much for political bribery as for payments to informers at home and abroad, but this shadowy side of the British state was reasonably effective. Radical political groups were plagued by government agents provocateurs and spies, and all Europe acknowledged the long arm of British covert influence.

During Queen Victoria's secure and peaceful reign, however, the secret service tradition almost died out through disuse. On the domestic front Charles Dickens could boast in the 1850s: 'The most rabid demagogue can say in this free country what he chooses. . . He speaks not under the terror of an organised spy system.' Intelligence work abroad also declined.

By the end of the nineteenth century, the army and navy had responded to alarms about lack of strategic and tactical intelligence by setting up their own intelligence divisions, but there was nothing covert about their activities. They relied on reading foreign newspapers or other published material, the reports of attachés at British embassies, or the observations of officers travelling abroad. As for domestic security, in 1883 the Special Irish Branch of the Metropolitan Police was established in response to a series of Irish Fenian bomb outrages. It soon became simply the Special Branch, with general responsibility for the surveillance of political undesirables. Still, only in India and Ireland, two countries with restive and potentially rebellious native populations, did the British authorities run clandestine networks of informers.

The start of the twentieth century ushered in a new era of insecurity. The Boer War of 1899-1902 revealed startling deficiencies in Britain's military organization. At the same time, the expanding military and industrial might of Germany seemed to threaten Britain's long-established supremacy. In 1905, the British government set up a Committee of Imperial Defence to oversee strategy and push through new policies that would improve the organization of the services in peace and war. The state of British intelligence and counter-espionage soon came under close scrutiny.

A joint services conference in 1906-7 concluded that the existing situation was unsatisfactory, but doubted much would be done to change it. Spying abroad was regarded with distaste by the British Foreign Office, which disliked being tainted with any underhand or ungentlemanly behaviour. And anything that smacked of a secret police at home was anathema to the custodians of the British liberal tradition. For example, the sanctity of private correspondence – always one of the first victims in a counter-espionage war – was held in the highest esteem. It would take a well-mounted campaign, both in Whitehall and in the country at large, before Britain would get its first modern secret service organizations.

The leader of the campaign in the corridors of power was Lieutenant Colonel James Edmonds. In general, the Boer War had been a disaster for British intelligence, but Edmonds had attracted very favourable notice. Put in charge of 'Section H', a unit

During the Boer War (below), the standard of British intelligence was generally very low. An exception was 'Section H' run by James Edmonds, later to be knighted as a brigadier-general (left). Edmonds laid the foundations for MI5 through his credulous compilation of material on German espionage in Britain.

entrusted in particular with the inspection and censorship of cables and mail to and from South Africa, he had provided a steady flow of useful information. In 1907, he was given control of MO5, the small 'special section' of the War Office Directorate of Military Operations responsible for counter-espionage. He soon set about gathering alarming details on German spies in Britain and framing recommendations as to what should be done about them.

At the same time, forces were at work shaping public opinion. Britain had long taken pride in its openness to foreigners of all political complexions, making the country a traditional haven for political refugees from Europe. But a newly strident nationalism was breeding xenophobia as the rising might of Germany, and in particular that country's expanding naval power, undermined national confidence. Lord Northcliffe's *Daily Mail* and other right-wing newspapers found a wide audience for their argument that national security was threatened by the presence of large numbers of Germans resident in Britain. By 1907, propagandists had focussed popular anxieties on to a precise scenario: Germany, it was argued, intended to invade Britain. To support the invasion, the Kaiser's secret service had clandestinely installed a vast underground army in the country, carrying out reconnaissance and espionage to prepare the ground, and ready to spring to arms the moment war began. The letter pages of the newspapers revealed mounting paranoia. A certain Lieutenant Colonel Heath wrote to *The Globe* in April 1907:

> The streets of London swarm with Germans. Where do they go? What do they do? They appear in no hurry. They are comfortably dressed and well nourished. Undoubtedly soldiers.

The idea of the Kaiser's hidden army gained very wide currency. Two years later, Edmonds himself would solemnly reassure Lord Esher that he need not suspect German waiters in London 'of being in any way organised for offensive action.'

Despite his relative moderation on that occasion, Edmonds was in fact totally convinced of the reality of the supposed vast German espionage network in Britain, and he produced an official report fully endorsing popular fears. The network was, he claimed, made up of 'mobile agents' roaming the country and 'local agents' in perma-

BELOW: HMS *Dreadnought*, one of the powerful battleships that were the focus of the arms race between Britain and Germany before World War I. The fear of a surprise naval attack was the prime motive for espionage by both countries.

nent residence, orchestrated from a central control in London. In all, its agents numbered many thousands. Edmonds did not have any solid evidence for the existence of such a network, but he believed in it most firmly and convinced his superior, the Director of Military Operations, Major General John Spencer Ewart. General Ewart was more interested in arranging for espionage against Germany than in counter-espionage in Britain, but these two lines of thought ran easily together. He concluded that 'we must have a proper secret service of our own . . . a regularly organised bureau.'

The Secretary of State for War, R B Haldane, and many other senior figures in the defence establishment were still highly sceptical of the need for such a secret service, or for any tightening of the Official Secrets Act. But in 1909 spy fever mounted. The serial publication of the novel *Spies of the Kaiser* in the *Weekly News* created a popular sensation. The author of this fiction, William Tufnell Le Queux, claimed that his James-Bond style accounts of the fight against German espionage in Britain were all based on fact, and the newspaper offered a £10 prize to any reader who wrote in claiming to have seen a spy. Not surprisingly, re-

LEFT: The neurotic Kaiser Wilhelm II, ruler of Germany from 1888 to 1918, in the uniform of a naval officer.

BELOW: British author and adventurer William Le Queux (centre), whose exuberant but unconvincing tale of espionage, *Spies of the Kaiser*, ignited popular spy mania in 1909 and helped convince a sceptical British government of the need for a secret counter-espionage service.

ABOVE: A pre-World War I British torpedo boat in harbour. The small network of German spies operating in Britain at this period concentrated on ports and dockyards, observing movements of Royal Navy vessels and hoping to pick up technical details of their armour and weaponry.

ports of spy-sightings increased through the year. Most amounted to nothing more suspicious than a man with a foreign accent noticed to be wearing a wig, or a German tourist spotted studying a map. But the accumulation of such trivia carried weight with those who were already predisposed to believe the realm at risk from the Kaiser's spies.

Against this background of popular concern, a sub-committee of the Committee of Imperial Defence, chaired by Haldane, sat to consider the whole question of foreign espionage. The sub-committee showed a certain amount of common sense. It was not altogether convinced by Edmonds' large body of circumstantial evidence for German espionage and did not share his vision of the scale of the alien threat. But the sub-committee did believe that the Germans had plans to invade Britain and sensibly concluded they probably were conducting espionage. Also, it was felt that some action had to be taken to restore public confidence. So, in July 1909, the sub-committee put forward a series of recommendations that were to be quickly implemented. It suggested increasing police powers, especially with regard to aliens, and defending possible targets against sabotage. Most important of all, it accepted Ewart's suggestion for the setting up of a Secret Service Bureau: 'to deal both with espionage in this country and with our own foreign agents abroad'. Here lay the origins of both MI5 and MI6.

Since lack of cooperation or even downright hostility between MI5 and MI6 has sabotaged British security operations on a good number of occasions over the years, it is to be lamented that the original plan for a single bureau was not adhered to. There seems to have been an intention to form a military and naval section within the same organization, but by 1910 the present-day division had emerged, with the military section becoming a security service concerned with counter-espionage at home (and in the Empire) and the naval section turning into a secret intelligence service running agents abroad. For convenience, we will refer to the security service as MI5 and the secret intelligence service as MI6, although they underwent several changes of designation over the years. In the trade, MI6 has more commonly been known as SIS.

The first head of the counter-espionage organization, initially known as MO(t), was

a 35-year-old asthmatic, Captain (later Sir) Vernon Kell. A friend and colleague of Edmonds, Kell had to retire from the Army to qualify for the new post; a considerable risk to his career under the circumstances. The risk turned out to be worth taking: he was to remain head of MI5 for 30 years. Kell's only qualifications were a limited experience of intelligence work, partly in China, a knowledge of foreign languages, and a firm conviction that German spies were a menace to the safety of Britain. To combat this threat, the British government allotted Kell a single room in the War Office, a desk, a filing cabinet, and a budget of £7000 a year. Yet, rather unexpectedly, this junior officer turned out to have a brilliant gift for bureaucracy, and soon began to expand his tiny empire.

Kell's brief was to follow up the thesis of Edmonds and Le Queux that the Germans had established a substantial network of agents in the south and east of England, primed to carry out acts of sabotage in support of an invasion force. He was to uncover this network by a concentrated surveillance of the 30,000 Germans resident in Britain. All were suspect and a proper object for investigation. Kell's first major objective was to compile an 'Alien Register', a huge card index listing all aliens in the country and noting any suspicious facts about them. Chief Constables were required to provide Kell with 'Special Alien Reports' every three months covering their area of Britain, along with details of any possible suspects among them. By 1914 MI5 had details of about 16,000 resident aliens on its files, around 11,000 of them Germans. In a way, this was no mean feat for an organization which, even by July 1914, employed a staff of only seven people, although, of course, it was the police who did most of the work.

The major obstacle to Kell's investigations was simple but fundamental: the network he sought to uncover was a figment of the imagination. We now know that German military intelligence ignored Britain before the Great War. The German Army had no plans to invade the island and, indeed, believed the British Army would play no part in the coming European war. The accumulation of files did nothing to apprise Kell or the British authorities of this vital fact, which could have made a considerable difference to strategy and the allotment of resources. In this sense, the pre-1914 intelligence effort was irrelevant.

Yet Kell did discover spies and greatly enhanced the prestige of his organization in the process. For, although German military

BELOW: Sir Vernon Kell, the creator of MI5, who headed the security service from its foundation in 1909 through to 1940. A man of severe intellectual limitations, unimaginative and chauvinistic to the point of racism, he nonetheless possessed a great gift for bureaucratic manoeuvre and steered his organization from tiny origins to a position of very considerable power.

ABOVE: Gustav Steinhauer, ex-Pinkerton detective and bodyguard of the Kaiser, was the German spymaster who ran a network of agents in Britain from his base at Potsdam.

ABOVE RIGHT: Gustav Neumann, a German waiter resident in London, one of the men who acted as intermediaries, forwarding letters from spies in British ports to Steinhauer in Germany.

FAR RIGHT: The German secret agent Max Schultz on trial at Exeter in August 1911. It was through the interception of Schultz's correspondence, forwarded by Neumann, that MI5 identified Steinhauer as a spymaster and unravelled his British network.

intelligence was concentrated on France and Russia, German naval intelligence had a lively interest in Britain. A naval confrontation between the two powers was widely anticipated. Both technical information about the Royal Navy's ships and news of fleet movements could be of great value to the German naval authorities. At the time MI5 came on the scene, Gustav Steinhauer, a former Pinkerton detective and one-time bodyguard to the Kaiser, was running a small but significant espionage operation around Britain's naval ports and dockyards. Historian Nicholas Hiley has recently published interesting details of their activities and how their network was cracked.

Steinhauer ran the operation from Potsdam in Prussia. The agents were either German residents in Britain, German visitors or, occasionally, British naval personnel. Information from these agents had to be sent to Steinhauer by post, but mail to Germany from a port town would have attracted attention, so the letters were relayed via a series of forwarding agents in London. So an agent in, say, Plymouth sent a letter to a German hairdresser or a German waiter in London, who then forwarded the letter to a fictitious individual, c/o Steinhauer, Potsdam.

MI5 got on to the Steinhauer operation in 1911, when a German journalist, Max Schultz, living on a houseboat in Exeter, attracted the attention of the police. A check on his correspondence carried out by the Special Branch and the GPO revealed that Schultz was sending reports on the Royal Navy to Steinhauer, via a forwarding agent in London. Schultz was arrested and convicted of spying – despite his defence that all the information he had transmitted was freely available in the press – and MI5 arranged for all letters addressed to Steinhauer, from whatever source, to be opened and copied. By this simple device, they soon identified a considerable number of spies and forwarding agents.

MI5 handled this fortunate situation quite competently. A series of agents were picked up – Heinrich Grosse in Portsmouth, a stoker on board the destroyer HMS *Foxhound*, Dr Armgaard Graves in Glasgow – but even when arrests were made, care was taken not to alert Steinhauer that the whole operation was blown. The climax came after George Parrott, a Royal Navy gunnery officer, was arrested in November 1912. The man who had recruited him, Karl Hentschel, demanded money from German intelligence to keep his mouth shut, but finally agreed to tell all he knew to Kell and his MI5 colleagues for the sum of £30.

TOP: Two portraits of the eccentric founder of Britain's secret intelligence service, Captain Sir Mansfield Cumming.

ABOVE: Admiral Alfred von Tirpitz, the eventual customer for Steinhauer's intelligence.

Kell's personal prestige and the standing of MI5 were greatly enhanced by this counter-espionage success. It was, of course, small beer, and in no way justified the fantasy vision of a German espionage threat that had led to the foundation of the secret services. But it pleased the politicians. At the outbreak of war in 1914, Kell was able to advise the immediate arrest of 22 identified German agents (one in fact escaped capture) and the surveillance of 200 other suspects. The only one of the 21 arrested agents to be actually tried for espionage was a hairdresser from the Caledonian Road who had earned the princely sum of £1 a month forwarding letters to Steinhauer. Still, MI5 had made its mark. Kell knew how to get the credit for an operation. When Prime Minister Herbert Asquith visited Kell's office for a briefing on the state of the counter-espionage campaign at the start of the war, he was so impressed by a map he was shown, purportedly pinpointing all the German spies operating in Britain, that he declared the operation 'a major victory'.

The nascent MI6 (first known as MI-1C) got off to an altogether shakier start. Its first chief was Commander Mansfield Smith-Cumming, a retired officer of the Royal Navy – the head of the service has been known as 'C' ever since. Cumming was 50 years old and had been on the Retired List for over 20 years. Chronic seasickness had ruined his chances of a career afloat, but he had remained in touch with the Navy, performing the occasional useful service on the intelligence side.

Cumming took to his new job with enormous enthusiasm. An astonishing character, he set the tone of rather boyish irresponsibility and eccentricity that was for long to prevail in MI6. He regarded espionage as 'capital sport' and played the role of a spy with great gusto. According to one of his colleagues, Cumming's office in Whitehall Court could only be entered after 'C' had operated a system of levers and pedals to move a false wall, revealing a hidden staircase. The man himself wore a monocle and only wrote in green ink. As with most of the great breed of English eccentrics, it is very difficult to say exactly what was concealed under Cumming's sometimes bizarre self-presentation, but he certainly won the loyalty and affection of those who worked for him.

His air of eccentricity was exaggerated after 1914 by a wooden leg – the limb was lost in a car crash outside Paris in which his son was killed. The account of this event that was current among Cumming's MI6 colleagues is worth quoting because, although almost certainly exaggerated, it shows what they believed him capable of. Sir Compton Mackenzie gives the standard version in his memoirs:

> The car, going at full speed, crashed into a tree and overturned, pinning C by the leg and flinging his son out on his head. The boy was fatally injured and his father, hearing him moan

something about the cold, tried to extricate himself from the wreck of the car to put a coat over him; but . . . he could not free his smashed leg. Thereupon he had taken out a penknife and hacked away at his smashed leg until he had cut it off, after which he had crawled over to his son and spread a coat over him . . .

Cumming was quite undaunted by this tragedy and mutilation. He continued for the rest of his life to be a very fast and dangerous driver – his Rolls Royce was a noted hazard to London pedestrians. At work, he would whizz around corridors with his wooden leg balanced on a child's scooter, propelling himself with the other leg, and frequently disconcerted visitors by absent-mindedly tapping his wooden leg in the middle of a conversation.

Despite Cumming's individual energy and enthusiasm, however, his department did not at first flourish. Whereas MI5 came under the aegis of the War Office, MI6 was placed under the Admiralty, traditionally responsible for overseas intelligence. Like its German counterpart, British naval intelligence was quite active even before World War I, and it overshadowed the new secret service, struggling with limited resources to establish some foreign networks. When a naval officer, Captain Trench, and a Royal Marine, Lieutenant Brandon, were arrested for espionage in Germany in May 1910, they were operating for the Naval Intelligence Division, not Cumming's service.

Apart from taking a few trips to the Continent himself – adopting a series of disguises of which he was inordinately fond – Cumming enlisted the occasional services of businessmen in the arms industry who could gather information or make contacts through their dealings with German clients. In at least two cities, Rotterdam and Brussels, the beginnings of a network emerged. In Rotterdam, operations were conducted by a retired naval officer in the shipping business, Richard Tinsley, while in Brussels an engineer, Henry Dale Long, ran a number of informants. It is not reported, however, that any information of great moment was delivered by Cumming's men, and on at least one occasion there was an embarrassing blunder. The tendency of the unscrupulous and mercenary to exploit the financial opportunities of espionage has always been a hazard of covert intelligence gathering. Through his Brussels network, Cumming was offered a German codebook for the then substantial price of £600. He paid the money, but the product proved to be a worthless forgery.

Still, Cumming had the embryo of an organization implanted by the outbreak of war in August 1914. He was therefore ready to join Kell in exploiting the spectacular opportunities for intelligence and counter-intelligence operations that total war provides.

BELOW: First Sea Lord Admiral Sir John Fisher, a supporter of good naval intelligence.

CHAPTER TWO

WAR AND REVOLUTION

BELOW: In August 1914 British hatred of Germany, reflected in this cartoonist's jibe at Prussian atrocities, excited public fears of the hidden enemy in their midst.

Not surprisingly, the outbreak of war with Austria and Kaiser Wilhelm's Germany vaulted British spy mania to new heights. The public flooded the police with false accounts of German sabotage – some quite bizarre, such as the rumour that the pier at Walton-on-the-Naze had been blown up by

THE TRIUMPH OF "CULTURE."

the hidden enemy – and the authorities themselves were nervously on the look out for suspicious foreigners. Possession of pigeons was regarded as an especially significant mark of the spy, since it was widely believed that the Germans would employ these useful birds to send messages home. Sir Basil Thomson, head of the Special Branch at that time, commented:

> In September 1914 . . . it was positively dangerous to be seen in conversation with a pigeon; it was not always safe to be seen in its vicinity. A foreigner walking in one of the parks was actually arrested and sentenced to imprisonment because a pigeon was seen to fly from the place where he was standing . . .

MI5 and Special Branch had to steer a very canny course in their relations with their political masters. If they rejected the scare-stories as baseless, they could be accused of complacency; but if they accepted the existence of a vast network of undetected spies in the country, they faced the alternative accusation of incompetence. Pre-war propagandists such as Le Queux kept up their work throughout the war, making sure that both MI5 and the politicians had an uncomfortable time of it. Yet in reality the German espionage effort against Britain during the war was feeble, and the British response totally effective.

MI5 began to expand the moment war was declared and never stopped growing until the Armistice over four years later. By then, Kell was in control of a staff of 844 (compared with 14 at the outbreak of war) and had at his disposal an annual budget of around £100,000. It was during this time, incidentally, that the department took on the designation MI5, after a spell as MO(g) and MO5. Kell's staff spread to Europe, carrying out intelligence work on the Western Front and vetting visa applications at British embassies. They also ran the Military Port Control Service, which checked people attempting to enter the country, and compiled a massive information bank known as the Registry. But it was the triumph of the MI5 Detection Branch in its counter-espionage role that raised the organization's reputation to new heights.

The key to MI5's success lay in postal intercepts. At the start of the war there were elaborate plans for the interception and censorship of cable communications, but none for opening private mail. One solitary MI5 censor was appointed to keep an eye on possible indiscretions in soldiers' letters arriving in Britain from overseas. The in-

LEFT: Carrier pigeons were highly suspect as possible vehicles for sending secret messages out of the country, although in reality German spies never used them.

BELOW: The Kaiser inspects the Kriegsmarine on manoeuvres. Intercepted naval radio messages provided Britain with some of its best intelligence during World War I.

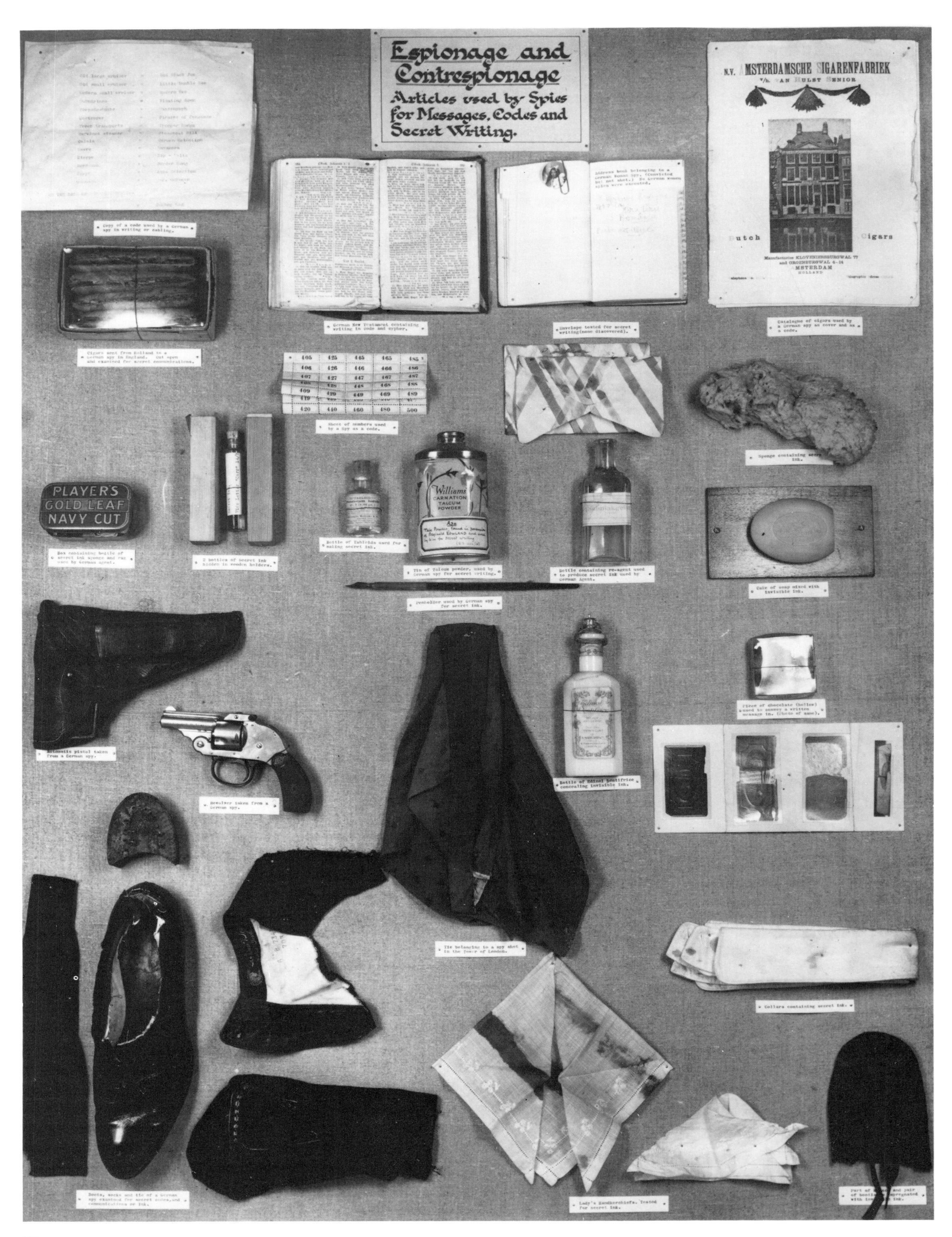
Espionage and Contrespionage
Articles used by Spies for Messages, Codes and Secret Writing.
N.V. AMSTERDAMSCHE SIGARENFABRIEK
Dutch Cigars
PLAYER'S GOLD LEAF NAVY CUT
Williams CARNATION TALCUM POWDER
Sheet of numbers used by a spy as a code.
Cake of soap mixed with invisible ink.
Revolver taken from German spy.
Tie belonging to a spy shot in the Tower of London.
Collars containing secret ink.
Lady's Handkerchiefs. Tested for secret ink.

telligence services soon impressed on the government the importance of the surveillance of foreign mail, however. By the end of 1914 there were 170 postal censors at work and over the next four years their numbers would swell to almost 5000.

The few German agents infiltrated into Britain had little choice but to use either telegrams or the post to send back their reports. The wirelesses of the day were too cumbersome for clandestine use and they could hardly enter the country with a basket of homing pigeons. In an attempt to evade the censors, they resorted to codes and invisible ink, methods which might have stood some chance of success were it not for a high quality counter-intelligence effort which, rather untypically, saw MI5 co-operating successfully with MI6.

As we have already seen, the pre-war German espionage network had been unravelled through MI5's knowledge of the address in Germany to which intelligence reports were being sent. Under wartime conditions, agents would have to mail their reports to safe 'postboxes' in neutral countries for forwarding to the German spymasters. If MI5 could identify these postboxes, they would know individuals sending mail there were hostile agents.

The most strategically placed neutral state was the Netherlands, which became the spy centre of Europe during the war. MI5 employed its own agent there, James Dunn of the *Daily Mail*, but he was arrested by the Dutch authorities in 1915. Thereafter Cumming's MI6 Rotterdam bureau, headed by Tinsley, did the work, compiling a list of local German agents and their addresses. This 'Black List' was constantly updated as the German network developed, and was passed on to the postal censors via Kell's office in London. Any letter to one of these addresses, however innocent-seeming, would be examined for a possible coded message or handed over to chemists trained in the mysteries of invisible writing. If the agents were obliging enough to include their name and address in Britain in the letter, as they often did, it was an easy matter to pick them up.

In all 31 German agents were brought to trial in Britain during World War I. Their quality was not high. The first to be arrested, Karl Lody, was an officer and a gentleman, much admired by his British captors for his high patriotic principles, but he was a hopeless spy. Infiltrated into Britain with a stolen American passport, he toured the country exhibiting a striking curiosity about harbours and anti-aircraft defences. Even had MI5 not identified him by the normal means – his correspondance with a known German agent in Sweden was opened – his behaviour would have attracted public suspicion. On 6 November 1914 he was shot by a firing-squad in the Tower of London, one of 12 German agents executed in the course of the war.

Subsequent agents showed less principle – most did it for the money – but little more competence. Dutch travelling salesmen like Haicke Janssen and Willem Roos were seduced by offers of £250 plus £3 a day expenses to attempt intelligence-gathering on their trips to Britain, only to end up in front of a firing squad (their code for communicating with their German controller resulted in business telegrams so odd they attracted the attention of the cable censors). The unfortunate Robert Rosenthal was identified because a letter he had written from Copenhagen to his German controller, giving full details of his imminent mission in

LEFT: An exhibit of espionage equipment taken from German agents captured in World War I. Because radios were too bulky for concealment, they had no choice but to communicate by post using invisible inks and codes. But few messages escaped the vigilance of the postal censors.

ABOVE AND BELOW: External and internal views of the rifle range at the Tower of London where nine of the 12 German agents executed in the course of the war were shot by firing squad.

The last of Scharnhorst and Gneisenau
W L Wyllie

ABOVE: German spy Robert Rosenthal leaves court under armed guard; his cover had been blown by an unlucky postal error.

ABOVE RIGHT: A British firing squad despatches a German agent on the Western Front.

RIGHT: Wartime Prime Minister David Lloyd George, the object of a rather improbable alleged assassination plot involving the use of an air rifle and a poisoned dart.

PREVIOUS PAGES: An artist's impression of the sinking of the *Scharnhorst* and *Gneisenau* at the first battle of the Falklands in 1914. The successful efforts of the Admiralty's Room 40 codebreakers put the German Navy at a serious disadvantage, although the intelligence the cryptographers provided was not always well exploited.

Britain, was included in the wrong postbag and sent to London by mistake. When he arrived by sea in Newcastle, masquerading as a commercial traveller in cigar lighters, he was promptly arrested. Janssen, Roos and Rosenthal all gave MI5 their full cooperation after their arrest, providing important details of German espionage techniques and offering to be 'turned' – to work for Britain instead. But MI5 was apparently not keen to fish in such murky waters. Perhaps given the quality of the agents involved – Rosenthal was an ex-forger and addicted to cocaine – MI5's disdain was not misguided.

So efficient was the British counter-espionage effort that by mid-1916 the Germans had virtually given up the quest for secret intelligence. There were only five arrests for espionage from then until the end of the war. It should be noted that none of the cases involved Germans already resident in Britain. Yet despite the lack of any evidence to connect alien residents with espionage, sabotage or subversion, popular opinion demanded strong measures. Eventually all 'enemy aliens' of military age were interned for the duration of the war. Many other restrictions were imposed on where aliens could live and work.

Kell continued his pre-war work on the Alien Register, but vastly expanded its scope. By the end of the war there were files on 137,500 individuals, including not only aliens but people who had come under suspicion 'by reason of any act or hostile association'. Indeed, MI5 sat at the hub of a vast information-gathering network, recording facts contributed by all the British ministries and by the Dominions as well as the police and its own informers. Useful material was distributed when appropriate to French, American and Italian intelligence services, and the French Deuxieme Bureau responded fruitfully with gems from their brilliant cryptographers who were deciphering wireless intercepts. Staffed by a growing army of clerical personnel, the Registry was the central focus of MI5 operations. It took on an almost mystical prestige as a repository of secret knowledge, and therefore a source of power.

Many people whose names appeared in MI5 files were in no way associated with Germany. Officially, MI5's remit excluded the surveillance of 'political subversives'. But with the decline of German espionage after 1916, Kell shifted his attention to groups who were seen as disrupting the war effort. These included strikers, especially in the munitions factories where the introduction of unskilled labour was causing resentment, and left-wing groups such as the Independent Labour Party (ILP), which were making propaganda for peace negotiations to be opened immediately. MI5 justified its new field of action by claiming, quite wrongly, that both strikers and the ILP were

financed by 'German gold'. An MI5 officer gave a perhaps more candid version of the rationale behind this move into political surveillance when he said of peace groups:

> If they are not for the success of our country it is not unreasonable if they are classed as pro-German. That, at any rate, is what the mass of the public consider them.

The ILP had its letters opened by the censors and its telephones tapped. No evidence of German links was ever found, but a campaign of systematic harassment by the Special Branch – raids on premises, the seizure of leaflets and newspapers, organized attacks on pacifist meetings – continued into the last year of the war.

It was the Special Branch which effectively resisted any wholesale development of MI5 into a political intelligence service. In February 1916, MI5 drafted some of its officers to create a secret intelligence department within the Ministry of Munitions, designated PMS 2, to investigate labour unrest in the arms factories. With a network of informers and *agents provocateurs*, PMS 2 was soon producing alarmist reports of German influence amongst the radical shop stewards. It also spread its net wider, claiming to uncover a plot to assassinate the Prime Minister, David Lloyd George, by shooting him with a poisoned dart from an air rifle while he played a round of golf. The Special Branch chief Basil

ABOVE: Admiral Sir Reginald 'Blinker' Hall, head of wartime naval intelligence and a notable figure in the secret world for many years afterward. His work with the Room 40 cryptographers laid the foundation for all Britain's future triumphs in signals intelligence.

Thomson was contemptuous of the intelligence provided by this MI5 offshoot and determined to keep it off his patch. After a brief bureaucratic contest, in April 1917 PMS 2 was closed down and the Special Branch was formally confirmed in its monopoly of political surveillance. As we shall see, this was the beginning of a serious power struggle between Thomson and MI5 that would carry on into the post-war era.

On the whole, MI5 had a good war and its reputation tended to improve. Cumming's fledgling MI6, on the other hand, produced a patchy performance in a crowded field. It had to compete with the Naval Intelligence Division (NID), operating after November 1914 under the inspired leadership of Captain (later Admiral Sir) Reginald 'Blinker' Hall, and with the army's Intelligence Corps attached to the British Expeditionary Force on the Western Front. When Cumming's department was shifted from the Admiralty to the War Office at the start of 1916, it was only one of four units in the special intelligence section, with the designation MI1(c).

The NID undoubtedly put in the best intelligence performance of the war, largely through their grasp of signals intelligence (Sigint). Provided almost at the outset of the war with a German naval signal book, found by the Russians on the body of a petty officer from the German cruiser *Magdeburg*, Captain Hall assembled a motley collection of academics, clerics and publishers in Room 40 of the Admiralty and set them to breaking German codes. Working on telegrams and radio intercepts, they could soon read almost all enemy messages. Although the information so obtained was not always well exploited by the Royal Navy – partly because excessive secrecy inhibited the flow of intelligence from Room 40 to naval commanders – it led to at least one major diplomatic coup. In January 1917 a telegram from the Kaiser's Foreign Minister, Arthur Zimmermann, to the German ambassador in the then still neutral United States was intercepted and decoded. It contained a suggestion that Mexico be encouraged to join the war on Germany's side, in return for a promise of territory to be taken from the southern United States; and that the German Navy intended to adopt 'unrestricted warfare', implying attacks on neutral shipping. The contents of the Zimmermann telegram were made known to President Woodrow Wilson and almost certainly hastened his decision to enter the war against Germany.

With 'Blinker' Hall well in control of naval intelligence, Cumming was forced to concentrate his efforts on the land war in Europe. Radio communications were seldom used on the Western Front, so signals intelligence had little role to play. The interrogation of German POWs provided important information, as did the debriefing of escaped British POWs, and aerial reconnaissance of the battlefield made a vital contribution. But networks of agents in the rear of the enemy lines had an important intelligence function, especially in observing the movement of troop trains which could indicate the time and place of an offensive. Since the German Army had overrun Belgium and part of France, the population behind the lines was well disposed to provide intelligence, but it was almost impossible to contact them directly across the trenches (although occasional successful communications were achieved by pigeon and by balloon). So networks of agents had to be run out of the neutral Netherlands into occupied Belgium. Any information gleaned was passed laboriously back to Holland, then by boat to England and on to military headquarters in France. The

ABOVE: A British intelligence officer interrogates a German prisoner of war. The questioning of PoWs was an important, if unspectacular, source of military intelligence.

LEFT: On the Western Front in February 1918, aerial reconnaissance photographs are assembled into a mosaic on top of a map to the same scale. It is a basic principle of intelligence work to use as many different sources of information as possible in building up a picture of the enemy's actions and intentions.

ABOVE: General Cockerill, head of the War Office special intelligence section in 1916.

BELOW: A hollow Dutch coin used by British networks for smuggling messages out of German-occupied Belgium.

Netherlands was also the main base for infiltrating agents into Germany from the north; in the south, Switzerland performed the same function as a neutral stage for espionage.

The Intelligence Corps attached to the General Staff was theoretically responsible for 'tactical' intelligence and MI6 for 'strategic' intelligence, but both organizations ran networks from the Netherlands and Switzerland, with more emphasis on competition than cooperation. The Intelligence Corps itself ran two distinct operations in Holland, one controlled by Captain Cecil Cameron from Folkestone and the other by Major Ernest Wallinger from London. Relations between these two were not always friendly, but certainly better than either maintained with Cumming's chief man in the Netherlands, Tinsley, who reported back to 'C' through the British military attache at the Hague. The bureaucratic struggle for overall control of intelligence-gathering in Holland and Belgium was never resolved and there was often bitter acrimony. Like so many men attracted by the secret service, Tinsley was neither likeable nor particularly honest. His behaviour towards officers of the Intelligence Corps in Holland was outrageously uncivil, and they countered by accusing him of exploiting his position for personal gain – accepting bribes from Dutch companies to keep their names off the black list of firms not permitted to trade with Britain. These accusations were never proven, but did nothing to encourage good relations between the intelligence organizations.

While British intelligence officers squabbled, patriotic Belgian and French civilians risked their lives to provide information on troop-train movements. Until the summer of 1916, a network of between 20 and 40 train-watchers, codenamed 'Frankignoul' after one of its leading members, operated on behalf of MI6 in Belgium and northern France. Intelligence reports were carried across the frontier into Holland on a tram that still ran into Maastricht. The Germans may have got wind of the network when they seized some of Tinsley's reports on their way to England on board the steamer Brussels, captured in the North Sea in June 1916. Certainly, the network was too centralized for security. Once the Germans had a lead, they soon wrapped up the whole ring. Ten of its members were executed the following December.

The collapse of Frankignoul left Cumming largely bereft of good intelligence to offer his customers. GHQ in France complained in late 1916 that they were receiving 'no information of value' from MI1(c). Cumming responded by a transfusion of new blood into his Dutch operation. A South African officer in the Royal Field Artillery, Captain Henry Landau, found himself precipitately transferred to the secret service and sent off to Rotterdam after a morale-boosting interview with 'C' himself. With his assistant Lieutenant Hugh Dalton, Landau achieved a notable degree of success, first recruiting a series of agents among Belgian railway workers and then taking over the 'Dame Blanche' train-watching network originally run by Cameron's branch of military intelligence.

Dame Blanche was by general accord the best source of information from occupied Belgium and France in the course of the war, running 51 train-watching posts. Landau and Dalton proved expert at handling their informants and won the respect and trust of the network's leaders. It was the British intelligence officers who came up with a simple solution to one of the major problems Dame Blanche faced – how to get messages out of Belgium into Holland once the Germans had built an electrified fence the whole length of the frontier. Crossings were perilous, so the British suggested that peasants whose fields bordered the fence on the Belgian side should be co-opted to throw bundles of messages across at prearranged points. Surprisingly, this worked perfectly. By the end of the war, only 35 out of more than a thousand civilians who took part in Dame Blanche had been arrested, and the ring was still in excellent working order.

Apart from the train-watching networks, it is not recorded that Cumming's organization made any striking intelligence contribution to the war on the Western front. According to author Nigel West, about 55 of the 235 Allied agents arrested in Germany between 1914 and 1918 were working for Cumming, but we are not told what secrets they uncovered. There was a considerable secret service contingent in Cairo, keeping an eye on the Mediterranean theatre, but their deeds also seem to have made little impact on the progress of the conflict.

Further north, however, British agents participated in spectacular fashion in world-shaking events. Cumming appointed his first station chief in Petrograd, the capital of Britain's wartime ally Imperial Russia, just after the start of the war in September 1914. Major Archibald Campbell arrived with ambitious plans to improve the Russian Army's signals intelligence and develop his own network of informers. Within less than a year he was back in Britain, having been

ABOVE: Demonstrators flee under fire on the streets of Petrograd during the Russian Revolution of 1917. The British secret service became deeply involved in Russian politics throughout the period of revolutionary upheaval, shifting from their proper role of intelligence-gathering to a policy of covert action against the Bolshevik regime.

driven out by the British military attaché at the Petrograd embassy, Colonel Alfred Knox, who fancied his own talents in intelligence work and wanted no interlopers. The next man Cumming sent out, Major C J M Thornhill, soon fell under Knox's control and ended up as a second military attaché. His successor Sir Samuel Hoare (a future foreign secretary) fared somewhat better, feeding back to London sensible reports on the rapid disintegration of the Russian war machine and the Imperial government. At the end of February 1917, Hoare returned to England ill and exhausted, leaving control of the secret service station to his deputy Major Stephen Alley.

Despite the evident difficulty of getting into the action in Russia, 'C' remained determined. In March 1917, the long-predicted collapse of the Russian Imperial regime at last came to pass, followed three months later by the accession to power of a liberal socialist government led by Alexander Kerensky. Cumming decided it was vital for Britain to back Kerensky against the revolutionary Bolsheviks, who were calling for an end to the war. If Russia made a separate peace with Germany, the whole of German military might would be turned against British and French troops on the Western Front. So the Bolsheviks must be stopped from taking power.

Apparently expecting little of Major Alley, his man on the spot, Cumming sought a new agent to bring support to Kerensky. The British secret service chief in New York, Sir William Wiseman, happened to know a person with recent experience of military intelligence who was in the United States at the time, the famous novelist William Somerset Maugham. Since Maugham also spoke Russian, he seemed the ideal man for the job. In June 1917 he was dispatched to Petrograd via Japan and Vladivostok, authorized to spend $150,000 of British and American money to prop up the Russian government.

Maugham did not receive a warm welcome from British officials in Petrograd, such as Colonel Knox, who were backing the right-wing General Kornilov against Kerensky – a British armoured car squadron actually participated in Kornilov's abortive attempted coup in September. But Maugham quickly achieved an entrée into government circles and spent his money wisely on anti-German propaganda. His in-

RIGHT: Tsar Nicholas II, his wife Alexandra and his heir, the Tsarevich Alexev. The overthrow of the Russian Imperial dynasty by a popular uprising in March 1917 opened the way for revolutionary leaders to seize power.

BELOW: A Soviet poster of Vladimir Ilyich Lenin, the eventual winner in the revolutionary power struggle. MI6's initial motive for opposing Lenin was the fear that he would make a separate peace with Germany.

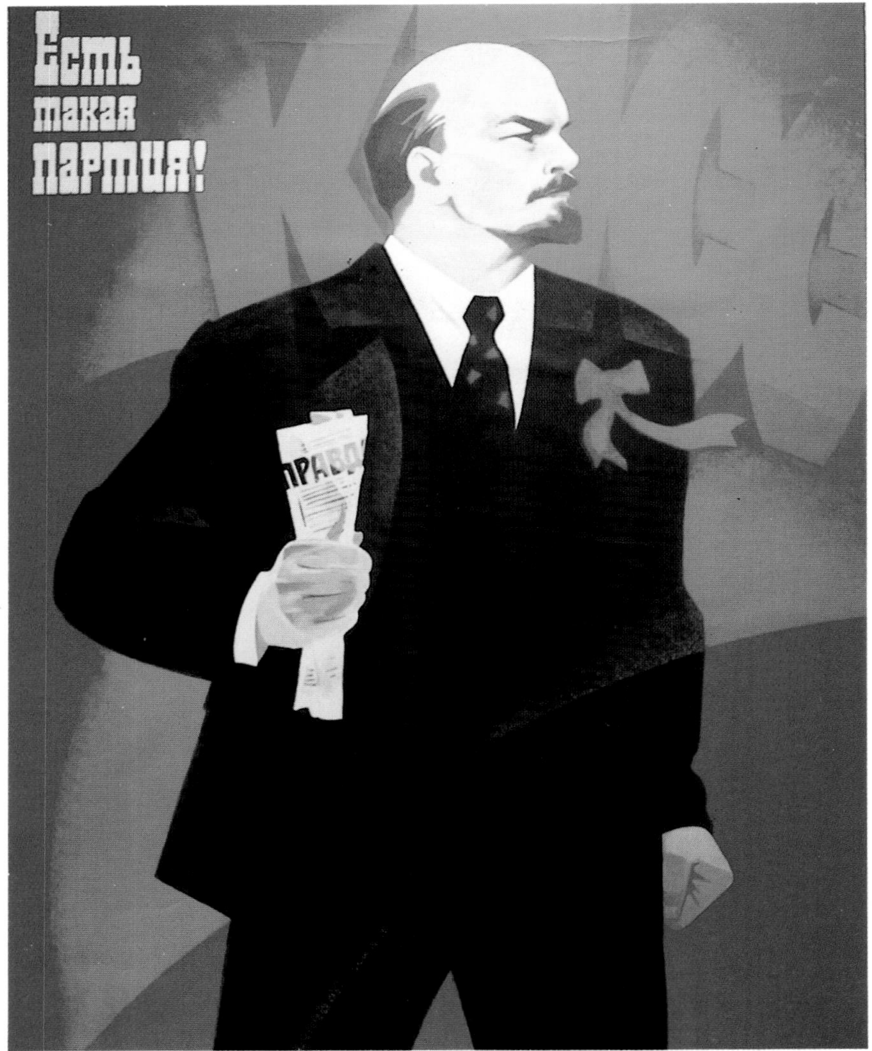

telligence reports quite correctly noted the decline of Kerensky's power, informing Wiseman in September that the prime minister was 'losing popularity' and that 'the murder of officers continues freely'.

On 31 October Kerensky summoned Maugham to a meeting and asked him to take a personal message direct to the British prime minister, Lloyd George. The message was a desperate appeal for supplies of guns and ammunition to defend the regime and continue the war. Maugham left the same evening, rendezvoused with a British destroyer in Oslo, sailed across the North Sea to Scotland and was at Number 10 Downing Street the following day. Maugham's efforts came to little, however, for Lloyd George's answer to Kerensky's appeal for help was a curt 'I can't do that'. A week later, on 7 November, Kerensky was overthrown by Lenin's Bolsheviks. Maugham did not return to Russia.

As the Bolsheviks consolidated their precarious hold on power and pursued a separate peace with Germany, British policy veered toward subversion of the new Soviet government. By March 1918 official British diplomatic representation had been withdrawn from the new capital, Moscow, and only an unofficial mission remained, headed by Bruce Lockhart, who began funding anti-Bolshevik groups. In Petrograd, a representative of British naval intelligence, Captain Francis Cromie, was still in place, soon

In June 1917, MI6 sent the famous novelist William Somerset Maugham (left) to Petrograd on a mission to keep in power the Russian liberal socialist leader Alexander Kerensky (far left). Despite Maugham's best efforts Kerensky was overthrown by the Bolsheviks (below).

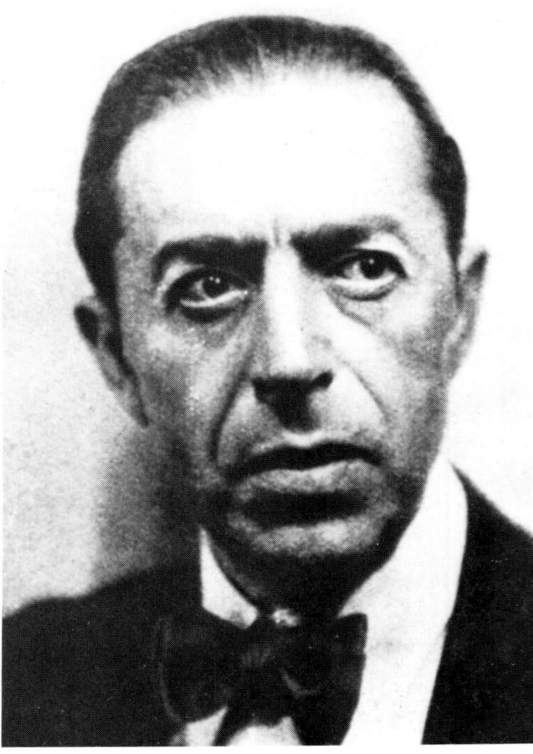

British agents in Russia: Bruce Lockhart (above), the head of the British mission in Moscow; and Sidney Reilly (right), a man of many aliases and several wives, described by the head of MI6 as 'sinister' but a 'genius'. Both Lockhart and Reilly conspired with anti-Bolshevik Russians to overthrow Lenin's government and were implicated in the abortive 'Latvian plot' of summer 1918.

joined by a replacement for Major Alley as head of the MI1(c) station, Commander Ernest Boyce. The role of Boyce in subsequent events was to be subdued, however, in comparison with that of two more flamboyant British secret agents, Captain George Hill and Sidney Reilly.

George Hill had been invalided home from Ypres and found himself working for MI5 in London during 1916. By the following year he had taken up aviation, transferred to intelligence work abroad and was flying agents into the Balkans. His knowledge of Russian made him an obvious choice to send to Petrograd in the immediate aftermath of the Bolshevik Revolution. Russia was still technically Britain's ally and Hill was officially sent as a member of the Royal Flying Corps to advise Trotsky on setting up an air force. Unofficially, he was sending intelligence reports back to London and doing everything possible to counter German influence and keep Russia in the war.

It is hard to distinguish fact from myth in Hill's own account of his exploits in Russia. One of his more fantastic personal intiatives was apparently to seize the foreign reserves and crown jewels of Rumania, which were being held in Moscow, and secretly transport them back to Bucharest – straying rather wildly from the objective of his mission. He also claimed to have helped the Bolsheviks set up both a secret police, the Cheka, and a military intelligence organization, so that he would have up-to-date information on German military formations on the Eastern Front and on German agents inside Russia which could then be transmitted to London. After the Bolsheviks at last concluded their peace with Germany in March 1918, Hill increasingly co-operated with Cumming's station chief Boyce. He turned to running his own agents and saboteurs, operating against German forces in occupied Russia, and created a courier service to London via Archangel so that his communications would not be read by the Bolsheviks.

Sidney Reilly, meanwhile, arrived in Russia on a mission for Cumming in April 1918. Reilly was even more of a mythmaker than Hill, and most of his wilder tales about himself have been successfully dismantled. Born in Russia in 1874, he was not, as he always claimed, the son of an Irish sea captain. In reality, both of his parents were Russian Jews and his original name was Sigmund Rosenblum. The fictional Irishness he adopted much later in a chequered career; only the most durable of his many aliases, which included 'Comrade Relinsky', 'Georg Bergmann' and 'Monsieur

Massimo'. In the early years of the war Reilly was living in New York with his second wife Nadine (whom he had married bigamously), making a fortune buying arms on behalf of the Russian government. He was known to Cumming's representative in New York, Sir William Wiseman, and by 1917 had been recruited by MI1(c). Cumming described Reilly as personally 'a sinister man who I could never bring myself wholly to trust'. As an agent, however, Cumming thought Reilly 'a genius' – a view with which Reilly himself, never a modest man, would certainly have concurred. His own version of the objective of his mission to Russia was pitched high enough for any ambition: 'Surely a British espionage agent . . . could make himself master of Moscow,' he wrote.

Along with Lockhart, Reilly was soon deeply embroiled in plots to overthrow the Soviet government, while simultaneously maintaining close relations with leading figures in the Bolshevik regime. British and French money was flowing through Lockhart to an anti-Bolshevik underground organization, the National Centre, led by Boris Savinkov. As a revolutionary in the days of the Tsar, Savinkov had reputedly been reponsible for several assassinations. He now convinced his foreign backers that he could get rid of Lenin and Trotsky in the same manner. Lockhart and Reilly were also approached, via the naval attaché Cromie, by two Latvian officers of the Kremlin guard who claimed their troops were ready to mutiny and overthrow the Bolsheviks. Reilly

The Russian ruling family were victims of the Bolshevik triumph, first exiled to Siberia (above) and then massacred (left, the place of the shooting). The ruthlessness of the Bolshevik terror made it virtually impossible for MI6 agents to operate inside Russia.

ABOVE: American troops march through Vladivostok in 1918. The intervention of foreign armies in the Russian civil war allowed the Bolsheviks to win popular support as the champions of Russian patriotism.

concocted elaborate plans to use the Latvian guards to carry out a coup that would coincide with an Allied invasion through Archangel. He intended to arrest Lenin and Trotsky and parade them trouserless through the streets, before installing his own favourite White Russian general in power.

It is now known that the Latvian officers were agents of the Cheka, the new Bolshevik secret police. The Soviet secret police chief Feliks Dzerzhinsky was informed of every British move, but neither plotters nor police could control the rapid development of events. In July 1918, a first attempt to assassinate Lenin failed, and the subsequent repression forced Reilly into hiding. At the start of the following month, a force of British, French and American troops under Major General Frederick Poole landed at Archangel, intending to suppress the revolution. On 30 August Dora Kaplan, a Socialist Revolutionary, shot Lenin twice from close range. Once more Lenin survived, but this time the Cheka moved to close down the British conspirators. Captain Cromie was shot dead as the Bolshevik police forced their way into his office. Lockhart and Boyce were arrested; Reilly fled the country on a false passport aboard a Dutch freighter. In an early version of a 'spy swap', Lockhart, Boyce and other officials were returned to Britain in October in exchange for the Bolshevik representative in London, Maxim Litvinov, and his colleagues. Hill left Russia too, after one last sabotage mission. In December, Reilly and Lockhart were sentenced to death in absentia by a Moscow court.

A postlude to these dramatic events was provided by a young English musician, Paul Dukes. A student at the St Petersburg Conservatoire before the war, he pursued a musical career in Russia until the worsening political situation gradually sucked him into intelligence work. In August 1918 Dukes was called to London for a briefing from Cumming and sent back to Russia as an undercover agent. Infiltrated across the Finnish border, he established himself in Petrograd, using an array of disguises and false identities to avoid detection. Remarkably, one of his aliases was as an office clerk in the secret police, Josef Ilytch Firenko. Dukes had a hard time of it in a city ravaged by starvation and civil war, often going short of food and sleeping rough in a cemetery. Yet for almost a year he channelled funds to the anti-Bolshevik National Center, liaised with the White Russian armies and kept up a valuable flow of very accurate information back to London. His reports were written in

RIGHT: British spy Paul Dukes as his real self (centre) and in four of his Russian disguises. The first of these (top left) was for the role of 'Josef Firenko', a clerk working for the Soviet secret police. Dukes was arguably the most successful of all British agents in Russia.

tiny handwriting on tissue paper and entrusted to some Russian contact who had decided to flee to exile across the Finnish border, or else carried there by Dukes.

It was apparently information from Dukes which enabled another of Cumming's agents, Lieutenant Augustus Agar of the Royal Navy (secret service designation ST 34), to achieve remarkable successes against the Soviet Navy. Sailing up the Baltic in a patrol boat, Agar sank a cruiser and two battleships in two separate encounters during the summer of 1919, exploits for which he was later awarded the VC.

By September 1919, Dukes's position was becoming untenable. The leaders of the National Center had been rounded up in a Cheka crackdown and his own current cover as a driver in the Red Army was threatening to backfire for his unit was about to be sent into frontline service in the Civil War. With three Russian colleagues, Dukes made a perilous journey to Riga and from there shipped home to be granted a flattering audience with the king and, the following year, a knighthood. No more British secret service agents of note remained inside Bolshevik Russia.

Two observations about these events are worth making. Firstly, the intelligence assessments provided by Reilly and his colleagues (with the honourable exception of Dukes) were often worse than worthless. Misled by their own anti-Bolshevik prejudice – Reilly described Bolshevism as 'this foul obscenity' and 'a hideous cancer striking at the very root of civilization' – and also misled by their biassed informants chosen among the enemies of the regime, Britain's agents in Russia presented a mistaken picture of a feeble government lacking in popular support, awaiting only a gesture of military intervention from the capitalist powers for it to collapse altogether. Consequently a small intervention force was sent, which proved totally inadequate to trouble the Bolsheviks, but was a profound political embarrassment to the participants. Instead of concentrating on accurate intelligence, British agents became involved in sabotage and

BELOW: A British patrol boat commanded by an MI6 agent, Lieutenant Augustus Agar, sank a Soviet cruiser and two battleships in the Baltic in the summer of 1919. Agar worked in close liaison with Paul Dukes.

subversion – a constant temptation for secret services the world over. But the indulgence in covert action was useless because it was based on a mistaken analysis of the political situation. The CIA would learn the same lesson at the Bay of Pigs.

The second observation concerns the contrast between the infant Soviet secret service and its British opponents in this first of many confrontations. Dzerzhinsky's Cheka, the ancestor of the KGB, was grafted on to a long Russian secret police tradition. The Tsarist police had harried the revolutionaries with agents, double-agents, informers and *agents provocateurs*. After 1917, the Bolsheviks had these weapons in their own hands, and they knew how to use them. Reilly always believed in the genuineness of his Latvian officers; it was not until the 1960s that the Soviets revealed how the plot had been managed from the other side. In comparison with the Cheka, the British agents appear amateurish – courageous figures of romance, masters of disguise, but hardly serious professionals at their business. Sir Samuel Hoare described his own sketchy induction course to the secret service provided by one of Cumming's instructors in London. 'One day, it would be espionage or counter-espionage, another coding and cyphering, another war trade and contraband, a fourth postal and telegraphic censorship.' Yet he received more training than many who were to serve MI6 between the wars.

One aspect of the work of the old Tsarist police is especially worth noticing. They were experts at inserting long-term agents into revolutionary organizations, what we would now call 'moles'. The leader of the terrorist wing of the Socialist Revolutionary Party in the 1900s, Yezno Azeff, was an agent of the police, as was the head of the parliamentary wing of the Bolsheviks in 1914, Roman Malinovski. Long-term penetration was a tactic the revolutionaries had learnt to fear and respect. When the Soviet secret service turned its attention to Britain in the 1930s, this is the technique it would use to achieve its ends.

BELOW: Feliks Dzerzhinsky, the wily and ruthless founder of the Soviet secret police, the Cheka. The professionalism of Dzerzhinsky's force, largely recruited from former agents of the Tsar, contrasted embarrassingly with the amateurism of the British secret service.

CHAPTER THREE

A GENTLEMAN'S PROFESSION

BELOW: Winston Churchill (right) as Secretary for War in 1921. Always fascinated by secret intelligence, Churchill proposed a merger of MI5 and MI6 in the interest of economy and efficiency.

In the wake of the Allied victory over Germany in November 1918, both Kell and Cumming were rewarded with knighthoods. But cost-conscious politicians saw little need for secret services in peacetime. By 1921 MI5's budget had been cut from a peak of around £100,000 in 1918 to £25,000, and MI6 (or SIS as it was from this time forward most commonly known) faced a similar reduction, from £240,000 to £65,000 a year. Most of the staff taken on during the war were paid off.

Yet through some tough bureaucratic infighting, MI5 and MI6 succeeded in preserving their independence and extending the scope of their responsibilities. Kell first resisted a proposal, supported among others by Sir Winston Churchill, to create a

unified intelligence service. He also triumphed over Sir Basil Thomson of the Special Branch. In 1919 a government committee authorized Thomson to run a Directorate of Intelligence with overall responsibility for combatting civilian subversion. This was a snub for MI5, which found itself restricted to countering foreign espionage and tackling subversion in the armed forces. But the Directorate proved shortlived. In 1920 Thomson showed his generous understanding of the scope of his responsibilities by sending a 15-man team to Poland. The following year, however, accused of overspending and duplicating the work of other agencies, his Directorate was closed down. Kell's victory was not completed until 1931, however, when MI5 absorbed the Special Branch department responsible for intelligence on civilian subversion.

MI6 achieved what would prove in the long run an even more important coup in 1923 by wresting control of the Room 40 cryptographers – renamed the Government Code and Cypher School (GC&CS) – from the Admiralty. Along with GC&CS, MI6 received a new chief, a former Director of Naval Intelligence Admiral Sir Hugh 'Quex' Sinclair, who took over on Cumming's death that same year. Sinclair moved into a flat in 21 Queen Anne's Gate, backing on to 54 Broadway, and these two buildings became the home of MI6 and GC&CS. Henceforth loosely attached to the Foreign Office, MI6 continued to be responsible for intelligence-gathering outside Britain and the Empire, although each branch of the armed forces still ran its own intelligence division.

While MI5 and MI6, like all bureaucratic organizations, fought to defend their budgets and promote their own self-aggrandisement, if necessary at one another's expense, they nevertheless shared a common view of intelligence priorities in the post-war world. As early as 1918 the head of naval intelligence, Admiral Hall, had set the tone:

> Hard and bitter as the battle has been, we now have to face a far, far more ruthless foe. A foe that is hydra-headed and whose evil power will spread over the whole world. That foe is Soviet Russia.

The assumption that Bolshevism constituted a devilish threat to civilization and the British Empire (no distinction between these two concepts was readily admitted) was an article of faith for the intelligence community between the wars. In its paranoid simplicity, it corrupted their political assessments and misdirected their energies in an increasingly complex world. But the Red Menace had just enough reality to be

LEFT: The doorway of 21 Queen Anne's Gate, the unobtrusive entrance to the headquarters of the secret intelligence service between the wars. It was from here that Admiral 'Quex' Sinclair (below) ran his network of European stations under the cover of 'Passport Control Offices'. Sinclair was head of MI6 from 1923 until his death in 1939.

LEFT: Sir Basil Thomson, the ambitious Special Branch officer who aimed to take over responsibility for tackling political subversion and restrict MI5 to counter-espionage duties. His Directorate of Intelligence proved short-lived, however, and he was disgraced by a sex scandal in the mid-1920s. MI5 eventually absorbed the Special Branch intelligence department.

ABOVE: A Communist speaker addresses a peaceful crowd in Trafalgar Square. Members of the Special Branch or MI5 were present at all meetings of this kind during the 1920s and 1930s, masquerading as left-wing sympathisers. In addition, Communist meeting places were bugged and agents were infiltrated into their organization.

worth countering – MI5 and MI6 were not entirely tilting at shadows.

As we have seen, at the end of the war MI6 was actively involved in covert operations against the revolutionary regime in Russia. These did not suddenly come to a halt, despite moves by the British government to regularize relations with the Russian government in 1920. According to Bruce Lockhart, Cumming's successor Sinclair was 'a terrific anti-Bolshevik'. MI6 stations were set up in states bordering on the Soviet Union, attempting to keep in touch with opposition elements inside the country. Also, Sidney Reilly still maintained a semi-official relationship with MI6 and was active among Russian exiles in Europe, who were seething with largely futile plots against the Soviet regime.

Unfortunately for the British secret service, the exiles were an extremely unreliable source of intelligence and had been extensively penetrated by agents of the Cheka (in 1923 renamed the OGPU). But Britain did possess one totally reliable intelligence source on Bolshevik subversion. GC&CS had cracked the Soviet diplomatic cyphers and for most of the period from 1920 to 1927 was able to read all the messages flowing between Soviet representatives in London and government offices in Moscow. It was thus revealed that Russian assurances of non-interference in the internal affairs of Britain and its Empire were to be taken with a pinch of salt. The Russians were doing what they could – which was in fact very little – to encourage a communist revolutionary movement in Britain and India. The Communist Party of Great Britain (CPGB), set up in 1920, was receiving covert financial backing and instructions from Moscow.

The more extreme anti-Bolsheviks of MI5, MI6 and the Special Branch were not satisfied with this evidence of limited Soviet subversion. They wished to uncover the hand of Moscow behind all the unrest of the times and relished any material that might be used to convince government of the wide ramifications of the Bolshevik plot. This led to embarrassing errors. In 1920 Lieutenant Colonel Ronald Meiklejohn, the MI6 station chief in Estonia, was offered what purported to be paraphrases of telegrams from the office of Deputy Commissar for Foreign Affairs Maxim Litvinov. To the joy of the British intelligence community, these documents showed that the Bolsheviks were financing Sinn Fein in its revolt against British rule in Ireland. MI6 were later forced to admit that the telegrams were fakes; they had believed the information because it told them what they wanted to hear.

Another instance of MI6 credulity led to serious trouble with the government in 1921. The Berlin Head of Station Major Timothy Breen sent London documents supposedly stolen from the office of the Soviet representative in Germany. They appeared to offer conclusive proof of Soviet subversion in India. But when the British government confronted the Soviets with this evidence of their turpitude, they calmly pointed out that the documents were an obvious forgery, concocted from material previously published in a German right-wing newspaper widely read in Russian emigre circles. The government was furious at this humiliation, and MI6 lost much credibility. It made immediate efforts to introduce a system for grading intelligence reports by reliability of source.

Even faked documents can have their uses, however, as was proven by the 'Zinoviev letter' affair which was described by writer Phillip Knightley as 'the greatest communist scare in British political history.' The background to the affair was the election in January 1924 of the first ever Labour government, led by Ramsay MacDonald. For the intelligence services this posed serious problems of loyalty. If only a few extremists regarded the Labour Party as a subversive organization, it was nonetheless generally believed in the intelligence community that a Labour government could not be relied upon to protect the country against Bolshevism. Almost without exception, officers of MI5 and MI6 were personally opposed to socialism in any form. There had been many private discussions of what action to take if Labour were elected. Toward the end of the war, there had even been a proposal to establish a covert source of finance for the intelligence services so they could continue their activities if a Labour government cut off their funds.

The assumption that Labour would be hostile to MI5 was not unreasonable, given that many of its leaders were undoubtedly on Kell's files. But Labour was in reality quite ready to back action against the Communist Party, which, apart from anything else, threatened its power base in the working class and the trade unions. As a consequence, Labour's working relationship with MI5 and the Special Branch went surprisingly well. With MI6 it was a somewhat different story. The new government was keen to establish friendlier relations with the Soviet Union, a direct affront to the policy of the secret service. MI6 withheld intelligence it considered 'too sensitive' from a government it did not trust, and the government developed plans for a thorough critical examination of the secret service: its operations were to be suspended and its files subject to independent scrutiny.

ABOVE: Ramsay Macdonald, Britain's first Labour prime minister. The secret services distrusted the Labour government and their 'dirty tricks' contributed to Macdonald's election defeat in October 1924.

To the Toiling Masses,

Of France, Britain, America, Italy & Japan,

Appeal of the Russian Workers' and Peasants' Soviet Government.

Your entire Capitalist Press is howling like a vicious, unleashed
dog, for your governments to intervene in Russian affairs. The hireling
newspapers of your exploiters, shouting "Now or Never" have dropped
their masks and are openly clamouring for an advance against the
workers and peasants of Russia. But even at this moment they lie
unscrupulously, and shamelessly attempt to deceive you, for whilst they
threaten intervention in Russian affairs, *they are already conducted milit-*
ary operations against the Russia of the workers and peasants.
Anglo-French bandits, who have seized the Murman railways, are
already executing Soviet railway workers. In the Ural mountains, the
Allied governments are using Czecho-Slovak troops, maintained at the
expense of the French people and commanded by French officers, to
break up the workers' Soviets and shoot their elected representatives.
By order of your Governments, Allied troops are cutting off the
bread supplies of the Russian people, in order that the workers and
peasants may be compelled to put their necks once more under the
yoke of the Paris and London Stock Exchanges. The open attack
which Franco-British capital is now making on the workers of Russia
is only the completion of eight months long underground struggle
against the Soviet power.
From the day of the October Revolution, from that moment when
the workers and peasants of Russia declared that they would no longer
shed either their own blood, or that of other peoples, in the interests,
either of Russian or foreign Capital, international capital declared war
on us. From the day when we threw to the ground our exploiters and
appealed to *you* to follow our example, to join us in putting an end
to international slaughter and exploitation, from that moment the
capitalists of your countries have sworn that they would demolish
Russia, because the workers had dared, as workers had never done in
the history of humanity, to overthrow the yoke of capitalism, and to
free their necks from the noose of war.
Your governments supported the *Ukrainian Rada* in its struggle

ABOVE: A Soviet appeal for worldwide support from the working class to stop foreign military intervention in the Russian civil war. British intelligence officers gave far too much importance to Soviet attempts to promote world revolution, and failed to make a realistic estimate of the power and influence of the British Communist movement, which was in fact very weak.

ABOVE RIGHT: Zinoviev (far right), the Soviet leader whose so-called 'letter' was used by MI5 to discredit Britain's Labour Party.

RIGHT: A scene from the General Strike of 1926 – mounted police disperse demonstrators on the streets of London.

But before this planned attack on MI6 could be implemented,in November 1924 there was a further general election, as MacDonald struggled to achieve a workable parliamentary majority. At this point, Sidney Reilly once more enters on the scene. One of the central issues in the election was the Conservative allegation that Labour was secretly pro-communist. What the Conservatives needed was some documentary evidence of communist subversion and Labour connivance. Either by coincidence or design, Reilly came up with just the right material, a letter from Gregori Zinoviev, head of the Third Communist International (Comintern), to the British Communist Party, urging preparation for red revolution. It made specific reference to the value of communist sympathisers within the Labour Party.

Obtained for MI6 by Reilly from a Russian emigre source, the letter was almost certainly a fake. But various intelligence experts in London, including MI6, vouched for the document's authenticity, either taken in by the fraud or, more probably, deciding it would serve their purposes in either case. As Reilly is reported to have said: 'They maintain it's a fake, but it's the result that counts.' After much backstairs manoeuvring, the deputy head of MI6 Colonel Frederick Browning released the text of the letter to the newspapers in the week before the election. It is generally agreed that its publication contributed very significantly to the landslide defeat of Labour.

Subsequent attempts to investigate the origins of the Zinoviev letter were not helped by the final disappearance of Reilly the following year. For some time, Reilly had been held at arm's length by MI6, alarmed both by the unreliability of his Russian emigre contacts and by his flamboyant lifestyle. But he was still in close touch with Ernest Boyce, MI6 head of station in Petrograd in 1918 and now station chief in Helsinki. Both Boyce and Reilly, with their old ally Savinkov, had been drawn into support for 'the Trust', purportedly an anti-Bolshevik organization operating in the Soviet Union. In reality, the Trust was a front run by the Soviet secret police, who had 'turned' several of Savinkov's agents and were using them to lure more emigre enemies of the regime back home to prison or death.

Savinkov fell into the trap in August 1924. Crossing the border to make contact with the Trust, he was immediately arrested and died in custody the following year. Reilly was the next target. With the encouragement of Boyce, he accepted an invitation to meet the leaders of the Trust in Moscow. On 25 September 1925 he crossed the border from Finland; his companions on the journey, supposedly members of the Trust, were OGPU agents. Two months later, after arrest and a lengthy interrogation, Reilly was shot by a Soviet firing squad.

Publicly, MI6 wanted nothing to do with Reilly's last adventure. One of his widows wrote to a number of people in authority to inquire about her husband's disappearance. The reply she got from Winston Churchill's secretary was typical:

> . . . your letter . . . appears to have been written under a complete misapprehension. Your husband did not go into Russia at the request of any British official, but he went there on his own private affairs.

This was more than an example of the principle of 'deniability' – that all covert operations may be disowned by the government if they go wrong. It was rather a sign that the days of active subversion of the Soviet regime were officially at an end.

But there was no abatement of the campaign against the Red Menace in Britain and its Empire. The labour unrest of the mid-1920s, culminating in the General Strike of 1926, was widely, if mistakenly, blamed on the Communist Party. The hand

FIRE
PHOENIX
LIFE
MARINE
ASSURANCE COMPANY
ACCIDENT
C. MISTLIN DENTIST
Dunn & Co Hat Makers
Dunn & Co Hat Makers
Dunn & Co Hat Makers

ABOVE: Commander Alastair Denniston, head of the Government Code & Cypher School.

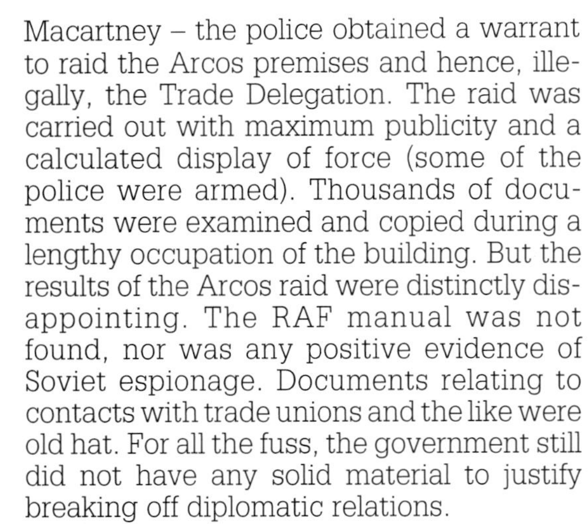

RIGHT: One of MI5's most successful officers, Maxwell Knight, in his later incarnation as a TV animal expert.

BELOW: Captain Guy Liddell was one of the most renowned of MI5's intelligence officers.

of Moscow was also detected behind the rise of nationalist agitation in India. By 1927, the Conservative government was very keen to have some intelligence of Soviet activities that would justify a breach of diplomatic relations with Moscow. Fortuitously, MI5 stumbled upon a minor case of espionage at just the right moment.

The culprit was Wilfred Macartney, a rather unstable ex-Army officer who had actually held a minor intelligence post in the eastern Mediterranean during the war. After a brief career as an extremely inept thief, which landed him for a time in Wormwood Scrubs, Macartney had become a convert to communism, and had been recruited as a Soviet agent. In March 1927 he approached an acquaintance, ex-officer and Lloyds underwriter George Monkland, and invited him to provide information for the Soviet Union. Rather foxed, Monkland reported the approach and was soon playing the double agent, feeding Macartney false information from MI5 to see what happened. To their delight, MI5 found that Macartney was passing on material to the Soviet Trade Delegation in Moorgate.

The Soviet Trade Delegation enjoyed diplomatic immunity, but it shared a building with Arcos (the All-Russian Cooperative Society) which did not. Once MI5 were sure the Trade Delegation was in possession of a classified document – an RAF training manual that had been fed by Monkland to Macartney – the police obtained a warrant to raid the Arcos premises and hence, illegally, the Trade Delegation. The raid was carried out with maximum publicity and a calculated display of force (some of the police were armed). Thousands of documents were examined and copied during a lengthy occupation of the building. But the results of the Arcos raid were distinctly disappointing. The RAF manual was not found, nor was any positive evidence of Soviet espionage. Documents relating to contacts with trade unions and the like were old hat. For all the fuss, the government still did not have any solid material to justify breaking off diplomatic relations.

There followed an intelligence disaster. Determined to go ahead with the diplomatic break and short of a justification, the government foolishly decided to quote from intercepted Soviet telegrams decyphered by GC&CS, as public evidence of Comintern's subversive intent. A similar indiscretion in 1923 had had no serious consequences, but this time the Soviet Union reacted intelligently. Realising their codes had been broken, the Soviets swiftly introduced a system of 'one-time pads' for encyphering which completely defied the best efforts of the GC&CS decrypters. As a result, from 1927 until World War II, Britain was unable to read any further Soviet diplomatic traffic. Commander Alastair Denniston, the head of GC&CS, was outraged at the government decision 'to compromise our work beyond question'. Macartney and his Soviet control were arrested later in the year, but this was small compensation for the setback suffered by British signals intelligence – the jewel in the intelligence crown.

In general, as the Macartney case showed, MI5 was still good at the nuts and bolts of counter-espionage. During the 1920s, under the leadership of Captain Guy Liddell, the Special Branch intelligence unit kept up a thorough surveillance of the British Communist Party: its mail was intercepted and its telephone tapped. When Liddell's unit was absorbed into MI5's offices in the Cromwell Road in 1931, this surveillance was linked to Kell's own counter-espionage effort.

MI5 already had its own specialist who ran agents inside the Communist Party. He was a retired naval officer, Maxwell Knight, who was to be responsible for the most successful counter-espionage operation of the inter-war years. Knight was another of the secret world's great eccentrics. As an enthusiastic zoologist – he was later to have a second career making nature programs for

ABOVE: East Enders express their support for the Communist cause in 1928. Such enthusiasts for the Party had little potential as Soviet spies, unless they worked in munitions factories or joined the armed forces. Upper-class recruits would prove of much greater value to the Moscow spymasters.

children's television – Knight kept a menagerie of exotic pets in his flat, including at various times a bear, a baboon, grass snakes, bush babies and a cuckoo. His other enthusiams ranged from cricket to jazz drumming. A bisexual of extraordinary charm he could, according to his assistant Joan Miller, 'make men and women do anything'. But perhaps his greatest love was for the secrecy and mystery of espionage. Known as 'M' to his colleagues, Knight squeezed every drop of glamour and excitement out of the generally rather dull business of surveillance and counter-intelligence.

From his flat in Dolphin Square he ran a network of agents inside the Communist Party and other left-wing organizations. Some of these, such as the future Labour MP Tom Driberg, probably only recounted a few titbits of casual gossip. But others provided more serious intelligence. The key figure in unravelling what became known as the Woolwich Arsenal spy ring was an agent called Olga Gray. Recruited by Knight in 1930 when she was only 19 years old, Gray was instructed to join The Friends of the Soviet Union, and from there she progressed to a secretarial post in a Communist front organization. Gradually she won the trust of Percy Glading, a communist engaged in espionage for the Soviet Union.

In 1937, Glading decided to involve Gray in his secret activities. She was instructed to rent a 'safe house' where she would help photograph secret documents. The documents turned out to be detailed designs of British weaponry 'borrowed' from Woolwich Arsenal. MI5 and Special Branch set 'watchers' to follow Glading and the other agents who visited Gray's flat. They had soon identified two employees at the

Arsenal who were the source of the documents and the Soviet contacts to whom Glading was passing on the photographs.

The only problem for MI5 was to decide when to order Special Branch to move in and make arrests (MI5 itself has never had the power of arrest). Perhaps mistakenly, they allowed the Soviet contacts to leave the country in November 1937, waiting for more of the ring to come to light. The arrest was not made until 15 January 1938, when Glading was nabbed on Charing Cross station in the act of receiving classified documents from a Woolwich Arsenal employee. The rolling up of the spy ring was a considerable feather in Knight's cap, and a sure proof of the value of long-term penetration agents like Olga Gray.

But as in the period before World War I, MI5's counter-espionage successes distracted attention from wider failings. Members of the Communist Party spying for the Soviet Union were small fry. It is hard to see how even the Woolwich Arsenal spy ring, the most substantial uncovered in this period, constituted a real threat to British security. As for the subversive activities of the British and Indian Communist Parties to which so much surveillance was devoted, these were serious only in intent, being almost impotent in practice. Yet, as we now know, at this same period the Soviets were recruiting long-term agents among the educated elite in Britain, totally undetected and, indeed, unsuspected by MI5.

A serious allegation lodged against both

LEFT: A peace demonstration in London in 1931. Although of little danger to the British state such manifestations of popular disquiet were viewed with deep suspicion by MI5.

ABOVE: The Duke and Duchess of Windsor receive a cordial welcome from Adolf Hitler at Berchtesgaden in October 1937. Contacts between Nazi leaders and members of the British establishment were a major source of information for the German intelligence services, but MI5 was powerless – or unwilling – to stop them.

MI5 and MI6 in the inter-war years is that their obsession with the Red Menace distracted them from the more potent threat to Britain's security posed by the rise of Hitler and the rebirth of German militarism. This raises important questions about the nature of recruitment into both secret intelligence and security services, and the political attitudes prevalent among their officers.

Both MI5 and MI6 were very small organizations, with only 20 to 30 officers, many of them involved in work tangential to intelligence and counter-intelligence – for example, maintaining security at War Office buildings. In recruiting officers, MI5 and MI6 were not unlike other areas of the British establishment in their reliance upon the 'old-boy network' – personal contacts with individuals of a 'suitable' social background. But whereas the Foreign Office, for example, tried to snap up the brightest graduates from Oxford and Cambridge universities, MI5 and MI6 had something of a bias against 'intellectuals' – often qualified as 'long-haired'. As Dr Christopher Andrew writes in his book *Secret Service*: 'Amazingly, Soviet intelligence was thus able to begin recruiting in Oxbridge several years before SIS.'

Sometimes MI5 and MI6 recruitment was extraordinarily casual. Dick White, who was to be at different times head of both MI5 and MI6, was working as a schoolteacher in the 1930s when he struck up acquaintance with an MI5 officer during a cruise on an ocean liner and found himself recommended for the service. Mostly recruits were retired army or navy officers, often with some intelligence background from the war, but generally short on brainpower and bemused by the political complexities of the times. Another important source were officers of the British police in India, who had substantial experience of covert surveillance and agent-running in the sub-continent. Kim Philby's unkind characterization of one ex-India policeman, Felix Cowgill, head of MI6's Section V during the war, could apply to many of them:

> His intellectual endowment was slender. As an intelligence officer, he was inhibited by lack of imagination, inattention to detail and sheer ignorance of the world we were fighting in.

Both services believed without question that anyone from the right social set would be trustworthy, but there were additional financial reasons for their narrow recruitment policy. Shortage of funds meant that hardly any money was available for salaries. Even though MI5 and MI6 personnel enjoyed the privilege of not paying income tax, their salaries were little more than pocket money. So only people enjoying a private income, such as an officer's retirement pay, could effectively afford the job.

The political attitudes prevalent in MI5 and MI6 were perhaps even a degree or two more right-wing than those of the social class from which they recruited. There were honourable exceptions – remarkably, Lieutenant Commander Reginald Fletcher of MI6 became a Labour MP – but they were few. Kell himself was a man of trenchantly xenophobic sentiments bordering at times on a paranoid racism. He believed that genuine British people 'are sorry for any of our women folk who marry a foreigner' and was always deeply suspicious of what he termed 'hybrids' – Britons with one foreign parent. It is significant that an MI6 agent who spouted about the threat from 'the International Jews of Russia' received a respectful hearing, instead of being slapped down for anti-semitism.

Was the slowness with which MI5 and MI6 responded to the new German threat in the 1930s due to secret sympathies for Hitler as a natural ally in the struggle against communism? Such views certainly existed in the intelligence community. Admiral Sir Barry Domville, head of naval intelligence from 1927-30, found Hitler 'absolutely terrific' and ended up in Brixton prison during World War II because of his Nazi sympathies. Even Wing Commander Frederick Winterbotham, head of MI6's air section during the 1930s, would have preferred Britain and Germany to unite against what he saw as the real enemy, Soviet Russia. One member of MI5, Mark Pepys, Earl of Cottenham, eventually left the service because he could not accept taking part in a war against Germany. On the whole, though, MI5 and MI6 were no slower than the rest of the British establishment to recognise the new enemy, and neither more nor less split-minded in their response. This is perhaps sufficient condemnation.

MI5 had a relatively small role to play in the anti-Nazi effort up to World War II. A few minor cases of espionage came to light: for instance, a German lawyer, Dr Hermann Goertz, who made sketches of airfields in southern England, and an Irish labourer called Joseph Kelly who stole the floorplan of a Royal Ordnance factory in Lancashire and sold it to the Germans for £30. But the Abwehr, the German armed forces intelligence service, did not carry out a significant espionage offensive against Britain, partly because Germany was hoping to do a deal with the British government and wished to avoid causing annoyance, and partly because they were already well informed about Britain, especially through high-level contacts between the military, diplomatic and business elites of the two countries.

MI5 kept an eye on Sir Oswald Mosley's British fascists and on pro-German organizations such as the Anglo-German Fellowship and the Link, which included such notables as Lord Nuffield, the Duke of Westminster and the Duke of Bedford among its members. But unlike the Communist Party these presented no threat of subversion as MI5 understood it, and until the actual outbreak of war with Germany hobnobbing with leading Nazis did not constitute a crime.

The performance of MI6 in the period between the wars was generally lamentable. As Nigel West writes, MI6 'was spending much time in the 1920s collecting misinformation about Russia; meanwhile, Germany was failing to keep the terms of the 1919 Treaty of Versailles.' Then the service was 'caught napping by the rise of Nazism' and 'was in no position to deliver' intelligence on Germany in the run-up to the war. And this is the judgement of an author who

BELOW: Sir Oswald Mosley, the British Blackshirt leader, addresses his fascist followers at a mass meeting in 1934. MI5 took relatively little interest in British fascists until the late 1930s, regarding them as less of a danger than the communists.

ABOVE: The Nazi persecution of the German Jews led to mass protests in Britain, although many individuals in the British establishment – including MI6 – favoured the Nazi regime.

has been described as the secret service's own (un)official historian!

The failings of MI6 certainly owed something to underfunding. Although the Secret Service Fund rose sharply in the late 1930s to reach £500,000 by 1939, there was still not enough money to equip agents with wirelesses. Too much of the money that was available ended up being misspent, as on buying information from notoriously unreliable Russian emigres, for despite its concentration on the Soviet Union as the principal enemy, MI6's intelligence of events there was extremely inaccurate.

The cover used for MI6 stations abroad also proved to have unexpected drawbacks that hampered efficiency. It grew out of a minor organizational change at the end of World War I, when MI6 had taken over responsibility for issuing visas to foreigners abroad wishing to visit Britain, work that had previously been performed by MI5. It seemed a good idea to use this passport control system to disguise MI6's intelligence-gathering activities, so MI6 station heads took on the cover role of Passport Control Officers (PCOs). PCOs were loosely connected to the diplomatic corps, but did not enjoy full diplomatic status and privileges. If need be, a British ambassador could deny all responsibility for their activities. This was an ideal arrangement from the point of view of the Foreign Office, which wanted nothing to do with espionage and often disapproved of secret service methods and objectives. The PCO cover had the added advantage of bringing in an income from payments for visas which supplemented MI6's otherwise slender budget.

But the drawbacks of this system became only too apparent in the 1930s. Firstly, the PCO cover was a thin disguise. Hostile intelligence services could identify all the MI6 station heads once they had penetrated this one transparent stratagem. The Germans had clearly done so by 1938, when they arrested and interrogated the MI6 station chief in Vienna, Captain Thomas Kendrick, before expelling him for espionage.

Secondly, by a twist of fate, the cover role itself turned into an onerous job. One of the functions of the passport offices was to issue visas to Jews wishing to emigrate to Palestine. As persecution mounted through the 1930s, the trickle of would-be emigrants swelled to a flood, swamping the understaffed passport offices with applications to process – sometimes as many as 2000 or 3000 a month – and leaving the PCOs with little time or energy for intelligence-gathering. The rush of desperate individuals seeking visas also raised financial temptations for underpaid officials. The richer would-be emigrants offered bribes; these were not always refused, and some embarrassing financial scandals occurred as a consequence.

The disasters suffered by MI6 in Holland during the 1930s are the best example of the failures of the PCO system. Major Hugh Dalton, the PCO in the Hague, was a man with an excellent World War I intelligence record, but he succumbed to financial temptations. He had embezzled almost 3000 of passport office money by September 1936, when he committed suicide under pressure from a blackmailer on his own staff, John Hooper. After an investigation, Hooper was dismissed and promptly changed sides to work for the Abwehr. Dalton's successor, Major 'Monty' Chidson did not last long in the job, but long enough to recruit a Dutchman, Folkert van Koutrik, who was almost immediately 'turned' by the Germans to become a double agent.

Chidson was followed as station chief by Major Richard Stevens, an Indian Army officer with no experience of intelligence work outside of the northwest frontier. Stevens himself was astonished to be chosen for such an important post: 'I had never been a spy, much less a spymaster,' he later stated. 'I agreed to go to the Hague as long as my superiors realised that I thought myself to be lacking in experience and training for the assignment and was, in my own eyes, altogether the wrong sort of man for such work.' Poor Stevens took over a station already penetrated by the Abwehr through van Koutrik, and made things worse by absurdly re-employing the blackmailer Hooper, who soon was able to give the Germans the name of one of MI6's best informants in Germany, a naval engineer Dr Otto Krueger (he was arrested in July 1939). As we shall see, Stevens was to be involved in further disasters once war began.

The failings of the MI6 stations in Europe were compounded by poor coordination, analysis and assessment of intelligence in London. The PCOs reported back to case officers in London (known as G officers) who passed their material on to the 'Circulating Sections', which collated it with informa-

ABOVE: The British Passport Control Office in the Hague, scene of a series of disasters for British intelligence.

LEFT: Major Richard Stevens, formerly of the Indian Army, was MI6 Passport Control Officer at the Hague from 1936 to 1939. He was appointed to this crucial post after his predecessor had committed suicide, having fallen prey to financial temptation by accepting bribes.

RIGHT: The German Army marches in to annex Austria to the Reich in March 1938. The MI6 station chief in Vienna was later arrested, interrogated and expelled from the country.

BELOW RIGHT: Hitler watches a flypast by the Luftwaffe. The major goal of British intelligence in the late 1930s was to achieve an accurate estimate of German air strength, but conflicting reports from competing sources only resulted in total confusion.

BELOW: Admiral Wilhelm Canaris, head of the Abwehr, the German Army intelligence service.

tion from other sources such as GC&CS and formulated intelligence briefings for the various ministries and military chiefs. The failure of MI6 to establish a reputation for quality of information meant that it was only one among many intelligence services competing for attention in London. Each of the armed services had its own intelligence branch; there was also the Industrial Intelligence Centre (IIC), headed by Major Desmond Morton, loosely associated with MI6 but producing its own assessments based on economic information; and Foreign Office Under-Secretary Sir Robert Vansittart was running his own network of agents with well-placed contacts inside Germany.

Ironically, there was no lack of good sources for intelligence about Germany, because so many high-placed Germans were either opposed to Hitler or at least desired to avoid a general European war which they thought Germany would lose.

Those prepared to hand over information included a senior official in the German Air Ministry who passed secrets to Group Captain Malcolm Christie, Vansittart's most successful operator, and a senior officer in the Abwehr, Paul Thummel, who initially contacted the Czech secret service and was known by the designation A-54. The head of the Abwehr, Admiral Wilhelm Canaris, was also among those with doubts about Hitler's policies, and passed material to the British, although it remains uncertain to what degree this was a disinformation exercise.

Apart from clearcut espionage, the friendly social relationship between many German and British diplomats, officials and businessmen encouraged indiscretion – both ways. Commander Winterbotham, MI6's chief of air intelligence, had an entree into the highest Nazi circles through his agent Baron William de Ropp – he was even introduced to Hitler – but it is unclear whether Britain or Germany gained the more intelligence from these contacts. Group Captain Christie had several intimate chats with Hermann Goering; this was a far cry from intelligence-gathering by telephone-tapping and opening mail.

Yet because of the confusion of sources and lack of unified intelligence assessment, the information flowing into London served no useful purpose. The Cabinet and the Chiefs of Staff were confronted with numerous contradictory intelligence reports on such crucial issues as the pace of German rearmament, the war-readiness of German forces and the nature of Hitler's intentions. Since they had no grounds for distinguishing genuine information from false rumour, even if an agent came up with pure gold it was indistinguishable from dross and so quite useless. A Joint Intelligence Committee was set up in 1936 to try to produce unified intelligence assessments from the competing agencies, but it had little effect until after the outbreak of war. Perhaps the only source that could have established some absolute credibility and resolved disputes would have been GC&CS. Unfortunately, the cryptographers had no success at all with German traffic, mostly encrypted on the formidable Enigma coding machine.

Through the dramatic period from 1936 to 1939 – the remilitarization of the Rheinland, the Anschluss, the Munich crisis over Czechoslovakia and finally the outbreak of war – British intelligence assessments were consistently wrong on major questions. The size of the Luftwaffe was first underestimated, then exaggerated. The Czech armed forces were wrongly dismissed as worthless, leading to excessive defeatism at

AATSGRENZE
37 Km
ZOLL
DOUANE

161.

ABOVE: British Prime Minister Neville Chamberlain meets Hitler during the crisis over Czechoslovakia in September 1938. The head of MI6, Admiral Sinclair, encouraged Chamberlain in his policy of appeasement and exaggerated the strength of political opposition to Hitler inside Germany.

Munich in 1938. In his briefings to the government, the head of MI6, Admiral Sinclair, actively encouraged the disastrous policy of appeasement. Before the German takeover of Prague in March 1939, information that Hitler was planning a further aggressive move was dismissed by Sinclair as 'alarmist rumours . . . put forward by Jews and Bolshevists for their own ends.' In the run up to the war MI6 was unaware of Nazi-Soviet negotiations for a non-aggression pact and gave exaggerated importance to rumours of domestic opposition to Hitler's war plans.

It was a dismal record. Yet Sinclair did take some positive steps in the pre-war years to prepare for the conflict ahead. In March 1938 he established a new branch of MI6, Section D (for 'Destruction'), headed by Major Laurence Grand, to study techniques for sabotage operations behind enemy lines. More importance was also accorded to counter-intelligence in the last year of peace. The counter-espionage branch of MI6, Section V, under Major Valentine Vivian, cautiously began the expansion that would turn it into a major force after 1940.

Sinclair tried to compensate for the deficiencies of the passport control officer system by accepting a suggestion from Colonel Claude Dansey, formerly PCO in Rome, to set up a completely separate parallel network to spy on Nazi Germany. Dansey was an aggressive and charmless man, but he had extensive contacts in the business world who were prepared to assist the new Z network. They included Alexander Korda, a Hungarian Jew who had become a British movie mogul and allowed his film company to be used as cover by Dansey; William Stephenson, a Canadian millionaire who spied on German industry during trips to the Reich; and a director of the Eno's Fruit Salts company, Frederick Vanden Heuvel. For his Z officers in European cities – the direct equivalent of the PCOs – Dansey chose resident businessmen or journalists, such as Rex Pearson, the Unilever representative in Basle, or Frederick Voight, the *Manchester Guardian* correspondent in Vienna. Pearson had experience of intelligence work in World War I, as had Dansey's man in Holland, Captain Sigismund Payne Best, now an expatriate businessman.

Dansey ran the Z network from an office in Bush House – a building which also housed the Soviet news agency Tass. Security was impressively tight. Sinclair was the only person at MI6 headquarters who knew of the network's existence, and the PCOs were not aware of the Z officers working in their territory. It is doubtful whether the Z network actually provided any vital information during its short life, however, and it certainly contributed to the spectacular disaster which struck MI6 soon after the out-

BELOW: Film producer Alexander Korda (seated) allowed his company, London Films, to be used as a commercial cover for the Z network, Colonel Dansey's top secret intelligence organization.

RIGHT: Captain Sigismund Payne Best, the Z network agent in Holland, an experienced secret operator who nonetheless fell head first into a German trap.

BELOW: Reinhard Heydrich, ruthless chief of the Sicherheitsdienst (SD), the SS intelligence service which competed with the Army's Abwehr. Heydrich gave the order for the kidnapping of British agents Best and Stevens at Venlo in November 1939.

break of war, providing a fitting climax to the debacle of the 1930s.

On 4 September 1939, immediately after the declaration of war, the MI6 station chief in the Hague, Major Stevens, was rather startled when the dapper, monocled Z officer Captain Best, under orders from London, introduced himself as a colleague in MI6 and explained they were now to work together as a team. Best's experience might have made up for Stevens' lack of it, but he too was taken in by German intelligence. The Sicherheitsdienst (SD), the SS intelligence service, had established contact with Best through one of their agents masquerading as a German Catholic refugee in Holland, Dr Franz Fischer. Urged on by Dansey, Best overcame doubts about Fischer's bona fide and was lured into a set-up. Fischer claimed to be able to put Best in touch with German officers plotting to overthrow Hitler and end the war so recently begun. As so often, MI6 believed this because it was what they most wanted to hear.

Through October, a series of meetings were arranged between Stevens and Best and the 'conspirators'. Negotiations started on terms for a peace settlement once the coup had unseated Hitler. The British cabinet devoted valuable time to discussing the finer points of a deal, which were then transmitted to Holland for presentation to the purported leader of the conspiracy, General von Wietersheim. Stevens and Best were to meet Wietersheim in Venlo, on the German border, in early November.

There the trap was closed. On 9 November the two British officers were lured to a cafe between the Dutch and German customs posts, where the meet was supposed to take place. As they waited, a car roared across from Germany carrying men armed with sub-machine guns. Best and Stevens were forced into the vehicle at gunpoint and whisked away across the frontier. A Dutch intelligence officer who tried to stop the abduction was shot dead.

Neither Best nor Stevens put up much resistance to interrogation, and they gave German intelligence a remarkably comprehensive view of MI6's organization. But the Germans primarily exploited the incident for its propaganda value. The two British officers were accused of participating in a plot to assassinate Hitler, and their pictures were splashed across the front pages of German newspapers. The humiliation of MI6 could hardly have been more complete. By strange coincidence, Admiral Sinclair died of cancer just before the Venlo incident, on 4 November 1939. MI6 was leaderless and its prestige at the lowest ebb.

Münchener Ausgabe

VÖLKISCHER BEOBACHTER

Münchener Ausgabe

Kampfblatt der national-sozialistischen Bewegung Großdeutschlands

Verräter Otto Strasser das Werkzeug des englischen Geheimdienstes

Wiederholte Anschläge auf den Führer

Die britische Mordverschwörung

Die große Pleite des Intelligence Service

Strassers Auftrag, den Führer zu beseitigen

ABOVE: A German newspaper report of the Venlo incident. To make maximum use of Best and Stevens, the Sicherheitsdienst should have tried to 'turn' them, employing them as double-agents. Instead their capture was exploited for propaganda purposes and they were publicly accused of involvement in an attempt on Hitler's life.

LEFT: Heydrich's assistant SS-Oberführer Walter Schellenberg, the man who led the SS team that abducted the two British agents at gunpoint.

CHAPTER FOUR

DOUBLE CROSS AND ULTRA

The rapid expansion of the intelligence services at the start of World War II brought an influx of talented recruits from a wide variety of backgrounds, including writers and journalists such as Graham Greene (below) and Malcolm Muggeridge (below right), who both found their way into MI6, and Ian Fleming (far right) who joined Naval Intelligence.

For 20 years from 1919 to 1939, the intelligence community had existed as a small closed circle of long-serving officers, with few new recruits to disrupt established procedures and time-honoured customs. But the demands of total war required that the door at last be thrown open to outsiders. Soon a variety of academics, City businessmen, journalists and lawyers were crowding into the secret corridors, bringing in fresh talents and new attitudes. Many of the recruits were destined later to achieve either fame or notoriety: Graham Greene, Malcolm Muggeridge and Kim Philby in MI6; Anthony Blunt and Victor (later Lord) Rothschild in MI5; Ian Fleming in Naval Intelligence; and Hugh Trevor-Roper (later Lord Dacre) in the Radio Security Service (RSS). Most were at first rather bemused by the world into which they had stumbled – especially by MI6. The old hands in the secret service struck Trevor-Roper as 'by and large pretty stupid and some of them very stupid'. Kim Philby found it hard to believe that the puny organization he had joined was really the British secret service at all:

> It seemed that somewhere, lurking in deep shadow, there must be another service, really secret and really power-

ful . . . But it soon became clear that such was not the case. It was the death of an illusion.

Sinclair's successor as head of MI6, Colonel Stewart Menzies, was cast in the traditional mould of the service. He was a man of no great intellect but exceptionally good social connections – he did not discourage the rumour that he was an illegitimate son of Edward VII, and his mother was a lady-in-waiting at Court. He had a passion for fox hunting and a taste for the smartest London clubs. In short, he was an unlikely person to lead a renaissance of MI6.

Indeed, the performance of the secret service in the first year of the war was disastrous. The Venlo incident demoralized MI6, creating a deep suspicion of any voluntary approaches from the enemy camp. This was especially unfortunate since anti-Hitler elements within the Abwehr were genuinely keen to make contact. As early as 3 November 1939, the MI6 station in Oslo received a package from an Abwehr officer containing ten pages of detailed information about German technological advances, ranging from bomb and shell fuses to the testing of pilotless aircraft at Peenemunde. The material was forwarded to London where it was passed to a research scientist, Dr R V Jones, for assessment. He quite correctly identified the information as of the highest importance, but his opinion was overruled by intelligence officers with no scientific training, who blithely dismissed the 'Oslo report' as a plant.

This error passed unnoticed at the time, but MI6 could not avoid its share of blame

ABOVE: MI6's wartime chief Sir Stewart Menzies enjoys a day out with a society friend. Menzies' social connections were more impressive than his intellect.

RIGHT: Kim Philby, the brightest of MI6's new boys in 1940. Talent, hard work and charm earned him an excellent reputation in the service, and he was one of the few recruits to stay on after 1945.

FAR RIGHT: Colonel Hans Oster, deputy head of the Abwehr, passed secrets to the British during World War II. He was executed for plotting against Hitler in 1945.

LEFT: A jovial Stalin drinks to the camera during one of his wartime meetings with Churchill. Even after Britain and the Soviet Union became allies in 1941, MI5 continued its surveillance of the British Communist Party, although interception of Soviet communications ceased on Churchill's orders.

BELOW: Lord Swinton, head of the Security Executive under Churchill's wartime government. For a period after the dismissal of Sir Vernon Kell in June 1940, Swinton was effectively in control of MI5.

for the military debacle of May 1940. The secret service supported the totally incorrect assessment that the French Maginot Line fortifications would prove a formidable obstacle to German motorized forces. MI6 also failed to provide warning of the imminent German blitzkrieg despite receiving two clear indications: a map of the invasion found in a German aircraft that crashlanded in Belgium, passed on to the MI6 Brussels station by the Belgian police, and a tip-off from no less a person than the deputy head of the Abwehr, Colonel Hans Oster. The map was dismissed as a fake and the warning from Oster disregarded.

It is, of course, much easier to be right with the benefit of hindsight. MI6 officers were faced with a mass of contradictory intelligence reports, most of them false. Spotting the few gems would have required a sure instinct and a good deal of inspiration. Yet it was not MI6 but MI5 that bore the brunt of reform. The debacle of May 1940 coincided with Churchill becoming Prime Minister. Churchill was keener on secret intelligence than any British leader before or since, and had a strong prejudice in favour of MI6, which had unofficially fed him with information right through his 'wilderness years' between the wars. For MI5, however, he had no special respect. On 10 June Sir Vernon Kell was summarily dismissed after 31 years as head of the security service. He died a broken and embittered man two years later.

For an interim period the service was effectively run by the Security Executive, a government committee chaired by Lord Swinton. Then a replacement for Kell was

found in David Petrie, former head of the Indian Political Intelligence Bureau. Petrie was an outsider to MI5 and he was the candidate favoured by MI6 chief Stewart Menzies. To some of the old guard in the security service, it was almost as if their firm had been taken over by its rivals. Petrie introduced business efficiency experts from the City to scrutinize the organization in detail and make suggestions for modernization. The antiquated Registry was overhauled with the introduction of an up-to-date punch-card system; very successfully according to Kim Philby, who described it as a 'place of delight' compared with the 'untidy labyrinth' of MI6's chaotic archives.

As well as being swept with a new broom, MI5 underwent some disruptive geographical moves in the early years of the war. To cope with an expanded staff, the service first moved into the unlikely location of Wormwood Scrubs prison in north London. The sight of the stylish debutantes who staffed the Registry streaming into work at the Scrubs every morning soon destroyed any secrecy surrounding the building's change of use. There were serious drawbacks to working in a prison – for example, the cell doors had no inner handles, so if they were ever closed the staff inside could not get out – but according to Nigel West 'the mixture of wartime conditions, beautiful girls and eligible young men lent something of a party atmosphere to the office.'

The next move was to Blenheim Palace outside Oxford, which became the main Registry building, while MI5's London office was established in St James's Street. The

ABOVE: Sir David Petrie, the intelligence officer from British India brought in to run MI5 in November 1940.

RIGHT AND FAR RIGHT: Blenheim Palace in Oxfordshire and Wormwood Scrubs prison, the two contrasting wartime homes of MI5. The *Illustrated London News* article on 'the War Office works in prison' appeared in November 1939 but was hardly a breach of security – the fact of office workers entering the prison could not be concealed and MI5 was, of course, not mentioned by name.

THE WAR OFFICE WORKS "IN PRISON": AUSTERITIES OF WARTIME DEPARTMENTAL EXPANSION.

INDICATING THE CIRCUMSCRIBED *LEBENSRAUM* OF THE ORIGINAL INMATE: A WAR OFFICE FILING CLERK IN TEMPORARY QUARTERS IN A PRISON.

A SECTION OF THE NEW OFFICES OF ONE OF THE WAR OFFICE DEPARTMENTS, FOR WHOSE USE THE GOVERNMENT HAS REQUISITIONED A LONDON PRISON.

"IN PRISON," PERHAPS FOR THE DURATION: WAR DEPARTMENT OFFICE WORKERS PASSING THE EXERCISE YARD TO ENTER THE PRISON BUILDINGS.

A VIEW OF "B" HALL IN THE REQUISITIONED PRISON, SHOWING THE CELLS OCCUPIED BY CLERICAL STAFF, CONNECTED BY NARROW GALLERIES FORMERLY USED BY PRISONERS.

move to Blenheim was still underway when a German incendiary bomb struck Wormwood Scrubs and a considerable part of the records there was incinerated. Fortunately, MI5 had spent a lot of time and money since the start of the war photographing its records to guard against just such an eventuality. Less fortunately, many of the photos turned out to be over exposed and thus completely useless. Many years later, in the 1950s, Peter Wright would find himself reading through Registry files charred at the edges by the fire. Blenheim Palace proved on the whole a good location for the wartime Registry, although the distance from London posed problems of communication and security. Documents required in the War Office or St James's Street were brought down by motorbike. On one occasion, shortly before the Normandy landings, one of the messengers left the lid of his dispatch box open as he roared down the road to London and secret papers were scattered along the roadside. Yet no breach of security seems to have resulted.

Through these various disruptions, MI5's performance in counter-espionage remained, as in the previous war, impressive. Resemblances to the earlier conflict were numerous. There was the same scare about enemy nationals who might constitute what was now called a 'Fifth Column' in Britain. This led inevitably to the internment of aliens on a substantial scale. Internment was carried out with a sometimes absurd lack of discrimination – among those interned, for instance, were Jewish refugees from Nazi persecution, who were only too keen to aid the British war effort. Many British Nazi sympathizers and Fascists listed on MI5's files were also rounded up, including Oswald Mosley.

As in World War I, an element of absurdity crept in with panic and paranoia. Despite technological advances that had made the radio now a standard espionage tool, pigeons once more came under suspicion as a likely means of carrying messages to Europe. Aircraft from the scant resources of the RAF were devoted to dropping pigeons

BELOW: Foreign nationals resident in Britain were obliged to register as aliens at the outbreak of war. This queue was in the Golders Green district of London where many German and Austrian Jews had taken refuge. These victims of Hitler were initially treated as potential enemies of Britain and 'Fifth Columnists'.

over the Channel in paper bags, in the strange expectation that they would fly to Nazi dovecotes and spread confusion. Lord Tredegar, a well-known falconer, was installed on the south coast with his birds as part of the Falcon (Interceptor) Unit, with instructions to hunt down any suspicious-looking carrier pigeons that might pass by. Lest it be thought this was not a serious part of the war effort, it should be recorded that MI5 had the unfortunate Lord briefly imprisoned in the Tower of London for revealing details of his secret employment to a fellow peer.

It was generally believed that any German invasion would be preceded by the infiltration of thousands of undercover agents into the country. MI5's B Division, responsible for counter-espionage and headed from June 1940 by Guy Liddell, had to cope with an astonishing volume of reports from members of the public who had sighted strange flashing lights, or wished to denounce a neighbour as a German spy, or had seen a parachute landing by night. Almost all these reports were false. Only a very small number of German agents were actually sent into Britain, most of them (about 30) between September and November 1940. They generally landed by parachute in rural areas or from small boats on the coast.

ABOVE: As the military situation worsened through 1940, MI5 organized the rounding up of aliens into internment camps. This clumsy operation caused much suffering to innocent people – although, of course, there was the possibility that the Nazis might have infiltrated their agents amongst these refugees.

The agents' standard of training was low and even in a country teeming with foreign refugees of all descriptions, they managed to attract attention to themselves by their odd behaviour. Carl Meier rowed ashore with two colleagues on 3 September 1940 and promptly tried to buy an alcoholic drink from a village pub at 10 o'clock in the morning, apparently in complete ignorance of the British licensing laws. Not surprisingly, he was soon in the hands of the authorities. Karel Richter, who parachuted into Hertfordshire on 14 May 1941, was picked up by the local police for a violation of the curfew regulations applying to aliens – according to his papers he was a London resident and had no right nor reason to be deep in the countryside as night fell. Josef Jakobs broke his leg parachuting into a field in Huntingdonshire and was discovered there, with his radio transmitter, by a lance-corporal of the Home Guard.

Once arrested, German agents were handed over to MI5 for interrogation. The MI5 interrogation centre was Latchmere House in the village of Ham Common, just outside London. It was run by an irascible hard-drinking ex-officer of the Peshawar Rifles, Colonel 'Tin-eye' Stephens, his nickname presumably a reference to the monocle he wore tightly clenched over his right eye. Stephens was much disliked within the security service for what Nigel West describes as 'his almost Nazi behaviour and vile temper'. His qualifications for his task were not, however, limited to the undoubted ability to terrify both friend and foe; he also spoke fluent German and several other European languages.

BELOW: Colonel 'Tin-eye' Stephens (right), the fearsome commandant of MI5's Latchmere House interrogation centre, accompanies a German agent, Karel Richter, back to the scene of his parachute landing in Hertfordshire on 14 May 1941. After a trial later in the year, Richter was hanged in Wandsworth prison, one of 16 spies executed in Britain in the course of the war.

Latchmere House earned a fearsome reputation in the course of the war. There were several suicides or attempted suicides in its cell blocks and one prisoner was beaten near to death – an incident which merited a severe reprimand from the Home Secretary. But the pressures applied to prisoners were mostly psychological rather than physical. All spies who refused to cooperate with their captors faced certain execution and this fact alone was supremely persuasive.

A total of 16 enemy agents were executed in Britain in the course of the war, 15 of them hanged and one, Josef Jakobs, shot by a firing squad in the Tower of London (Jakobs received special treatment because he was a German officer, not a civilian). But the majority of those who were captured agreed to be 'turned' and work for the British. They became part of one of the most successful secret operations of modern times, Operation Double-Cross.

The origins of double-cross went back to before the war. In 1936, an electrical engineer called Arthur Owens was taken on as an agent by MI6, paid to report back on his business trips to German shipyards. Owens proved to be a very slippery customer, with a genuine talent for intrigue and double-dealing. Routine MI5 counterespionage checks soon spotted that he was working for the Abwehr as well. Unabashed, when confronted with the evidence Owens claimed he had only accepted to serve the Abwehr so he could penetrate the organization on behalf of British intelligence. MI6 refused to have any further dealings with Owens, considering him fundamentally unreliable, but MI5 continued to play along with him, although quite unsure which side he was really working for.

As soon as war broke out, Owens was arrested as a suspected German spy and locked up in Wandsworth prison. There his MI5 case officer, Colonel T A 'Tar' Robertson, paid him a visit and a deal was struck. To avoid prosecution, Owens agreed to use his Abwehr-supplied radio to contact German intelligence and pretend to be still operating as their agent. From his cell, watched by Robertson, he made the first

LEFT: The view from the commandant's office at Latchmere House, showing the barbed wire entanglements of the inner and outer perimeters. The MI5 interrogators had a large measure of success in 'turning' German agents, making possible the 'Double-Cross' system of deception.

BELOW: A radio captured from a German agent parachuted into Britain. Agents who had been 'turned' maintained radio contact with their German controllers as if still at liberty, feeding back false information carefully prepared by the Twenty Committee.

ABOVE: J. Edgar Hoover, the powerful director of the FBI. Hoover was always suspicious of the British and refused to play ball with MI5 when double agent Dusko Popov visited the United States in 1941. Hoover's attitude could have endangered the whole Double-Cross operation – and may have prevented President Roosevelt receiving advanced warning of the Japanese attack on Pearl Harbor.

transmission that his Abwehr control was expecting:

Must meet you in Holland at once. Bring weather code. Radio town and hotel Wales ready.'

With this cryptic message, the double-cross system of deception had begun. At first MI5 were mainly concerned to use Owens (given the codename SNOW) to learn details of Abwehr codes and operational practice, or to uncover espionage networks and receive advanced warning of the arrival of new agents. But as an increasing number of German agents were 'turned', it was realized that double-agents could be used for more important purposes as part of a systematic campaign of disinformation.

The idea was to convince the Abwehr that it had an extensive series of espionage rings operative in Britain sending back high-grade intelligence. The contents of this intelligence would be controlled by the British in order to deceive the enemy whenever there was a critical need to do so. It was a long-term game that involved supplying the Germans with a good deal of accurate non-essential information to build up the agents' credibility. Decoded intercepts of Abwehr traffic supplied by GC&CS provided a check on whether the enemy was actually swallowing the bait.

Although MI5 ran double-cross, the system led to an unprecedented degree of co-operation between different intelligence organizations. MI5 was responsible for turning most of the German agents who became involved. Wulf Schmidt, for example, one of the most successful of all the double-agents, was arrested after parachuting into England in September 1940 and agreed to work for his captors after a couple of unpleasant weeks in Latchmere House, contemplating the prospect of the hamgman's rope. But another leading player in the game, Yugoslav Abwehr agent Dusko Popov, was recruited by MI6 in December 1940 when he contacted the station chief in Belgrade. Security Intelligence Middle East (SIME), a joint MI5/MI6 outfit based in Cairo, ran its own double-agents.

Most essential was the need to assemble and co-ordinate the information – true or false – to be radioed back to Germany by the various participants in the double-cross operation. For this purpose, representatives of MI5, MI6 and the services' intelligence departments met each week from January 1941 onward in what was known as the Twenty Committee (because in Roman numerals 20 is written as XX, a double cross). Chaired by Sir John Masterman, who would later write the definitive history of the double-cross system, the Twenty Committee achieved a remarkable degree of agreement among its diverse members on the strategy for deception, transforming what could have been a series of disparate small-scale operations into a master plan to help win the war.

According to Masterman, British intelligence 'actively ran and controlled the German espionage system' in Britain and was consequently able to make the Germans think what it wanted them to think. There are reasons for moderating this claim with a measure of scepticism. As several authors have pointed out, the Abwehr may well have been, up to a point, willing collaborators with the double-cross system. We have already seen how several Abwehr officers were keen to aid British intelligence, and that the Abwehr chief Admiral Canaris was at least ambivalent in his attitude to the regime he served. The evidence of collaboration over double-cross is sometimes most striking. For instance, in January 1941 Owens was flown to Lisbon to meet his Abwehr controller as part of an elaborate plan which involved another double-agent actually accepting the risk of a brief trip back to Germany. On his return to Britain, the ever-unreliable Owens confessed to MI5 that, under pressure, he had revealed the truth of his betrayal to the Abwehr – yet his fellow double-agent, his cover apparently

blown, was not molested in any way.

Even more explicit was the case of the Yugoslav, Dusko Popov. When Popov made his approach to British intelligence, he claimed that his Abwehr controller, Johann Jebsen, had actually instructed him to act as a double agent. This was apparently confirmed in 1941 as a result of a disastrous period Popov spent in the then neutral United States, where he was ostensibly sent by the Abwehr to establish a German spy ring. Although FBI chief Edgar Hoover was informed by his British opposite number that Popov was in reality working for Britain, he took an instant dislike to the Yugoslav who was something of a playboy and offended his puritan instincts. Hoover not only refused to consider information from

ABOVE: Dusko Popov, the Yugoslav double agent and *bon viveur*, who is believed to have been one of the models for Ian Fleming's fictional spy James Bond.

Popov that might have allowed the United States to predict the Japanese attack on Pearl Harbor, but also interfered with his operations in such a blatant way that the Abwehr almost certainly must have realized their agent had been turned. Yet the Abwehr chose to ignore the oddity of Popov's performance in America, attributing it bizarrely to 'family worries'.

So there was almost certainly an element of 'triple-cross' to the double-cross system, with the Abwehr as participants unbeknownst to MI5. But this is not a cause to deny its successes. In April 1945, as the war in Europe drew to an end and long after Hitler had brutally purged the Abwehr of the officers who had betrayed him, double-agent Wulf Schmidt was still receiving appeals from his German control in Hamburg to keep up the flow of information.

The moment for full exploitation of double-cross came with the elaborate deception plan for Operation Overlord, the Normandy landings of 1944. It was essential to convince the Germans that the Pas de Calais, rather than Normandy, would be the site of the main Allied onslaught. All the resources of double-cross were devoted to this end. One double-agent, Felipe Fernandez (codenamed GARBO), was even made to radio an accurate warning of the Normandy invasion to his controller – but, of course, too late to be of any use to the Germans. With his credit thus enhanced, GARBO then informed the Abwehr that the Normandy landings were only a diversion and the true invasion would still come in the Pas de Calais. Hitler was shown this intelligence report and it may well have influenced his crucial decision to hold back armoured reinforcements instead of sending them immediately to contest the beachheads.

Double-cross was not the only example of successful co-operation between different intelligence services in World War II. Churchill put his formidable weight behind efforts to create a coherent system of intelligence gathering and assessment. The Joint Intelligence Committee (JIC), which before the war had been powerless to impose order on the chaotic intelligence community, came into its own from 1941 onward. Aided by the Joint Intelligence Staff which was responsible for assessing and distributing information from all intelli-

BELOW: Troops wade ashore during Operation Overlord, the Normandy landings of June 1944. Double-Cross may have played an important part in deceiving the Germans about the intended location of the invasion of Europe, thus saving thousands of Allied lives.

gence sources, the JIC created a unified intelligence strategy and tried, with some success, to ensure that it was implemented.

But Churchill's pressure for the creation of a single all-embracing intelligence organization was resisted, and rivalries continued to flourish at the expense of efficiency. MI6 was the main offender, probably because its situation was the most insecure. Hugh Trevor-Roper has contrasted the attitude of the newcomers to the secret service, like himself, who 'regarded the Service as existing to help win the war' and the old hands who sometimes behaved as if they 'regarded the war as a dangerous interruption of the Service'. This is perhaps an excessively jaundiced view, but Menzies and his wartime deputy, Colonel Dansey, undoubtedly devoted much energy to bureaucratic in-fighting – with considerable success.

On the face of it, MI6 had a very poor hand to play. By mid-1941 the sweeping German victories in Europe had forced the closure of MI6 stations everywhere except in the peripheral neutral states – Switzerland, Sweden, Spain and Portugal. No arrangements had been made to leave behind clandestine networks, so MI6 was almost wholly dependent on the secret services of the Allied governments in exile for intelligence from within Nazi-controlled countries. Fortunately, some of these services still had quite efficient contacts in Europe, although their relations with MI6 were frequently stormy, especially in the case of the French. General de Gaulle did not welcome MI6's decision to maintain two separate operations in France, one in alliance with his own Free French, the other through links with the pro-German Vichy regime.

Even in the few neutral states where MI6 still had stations, its activities were often limited. In Spain, the British ambassador Sir Samuel Hoare, himself once a secret service officer but also a leading advocate of appeasement, took action to curtail MI6 operations, on the grounds that they might compromise his efforts to maintain good relations with Generalissimo Franco's pro-German government. In Stockholm, the Swedish security police took a dim view of British espionage activities, and a number of British agents ended up in jail.

But Menzies had been dealt one trump card and he played it to the maximum advantage of his organization. The trump card was Ultra – decoded intercepts of German radio communications. Ultra was unquestionably the best source of intelligence in the whole course of the war. It depended on the ability to break into the codes pro-

The sharp political divisions in wartime Europe created a difficult context for MI6 operations.

LEFT: General de Gaulle (standing, right) reluctantly shakes hands with a political opponent, General Giraud. MI6 offended de Gaulle by maintaining contact with the Vichy government's intelligence service as well as with his own Free French.

BELOW: British ambassador Sir Samuel Hoare (right) with a Spanish fascist dignitary in Madrid. Sir Samuel was so keen to keep on good terms with Franco's government that he blocked MI6 activities in Spain.

duced by the Germans' Enigma encoding machines, used for all top secret radio messages. Through the 1930s, cryptographers of the Polish secret service had worked on ways of decrypting Enigma, developing a primitive computer which they called the 'Bombe' to speed up analysis of the thousands of possible interpretations of each coded word. The results of their work were passed on to the French and British cryptographers.

The codebreakers of GC&CS were installed for the duration of the war at Bletchley Park, a large house some 50 miles from London. Their much expanded wartime complement consisted primarily of brilliant young intellectuals – linguists, classicists, chess players and mathematicians – almost all under the age of 30 and working in an atmosphere of considerable informality. Basing themselves on the progress made by the Poles and French up to 1940, and exploiting a number of intelligence windfalls, such as captured Luftwaffe and Reichsmarine codebooks, they achieved a very high level of success in decoding German radio traffic.

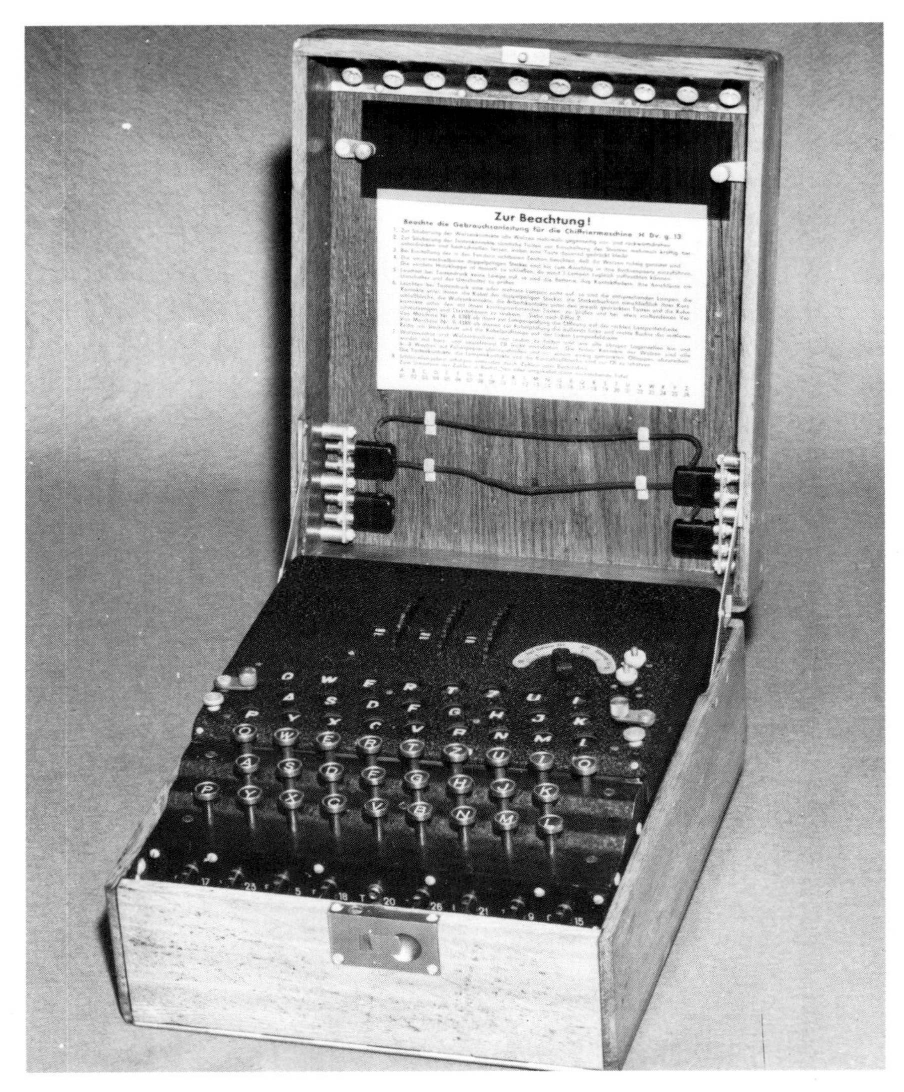

BELOW: A German Enigma encoding machine, a deceptively simple device which its users thought would make decryption impossible. However, with the help of initial information from the Poles and French, the world's first modern computer, captured codebooks and the enemy's simple operating mistakes, Britain's codebreakers repeatedly cracked the German codes during World War II.

Since the secrecy surrounding Bletchley Park was first lifted in 1974, the impact of Ultra on the course of the war has perhaps been exaggerated. Its contribution to Allied victory was limited by certain inherent drawbacks. Firstly, the information was very difficult to use. It was essential to protect the secrecy of the source, or the Germans would change their coding procedures and all advantage would be lost. This meant that most 'customers' for the information, such as officers in the field, would receive the intelligence without knowing whence it came. So the unfortunate General John Lucas, commanding the landings at Anzio in January 1944, was urged by his high command to strike out of his beachhead since only insubstantial enemy forces confronted him. This they knew because Ultra had told them. But Lucas, unaware of their source, considered the intelligence assessment unreliable and stayed where he was, thereby preventing any easy chance of a rapid breakout.

Another problem was that the intercepted messages did not necessarily give a true account of the facts. As Peter Calvocoressi, who worked at Bletchley Park during the war, has written: 'Reading a man's correspondence is not the same thing as reading his mind.' German commanders were liable to exaggerate the weakness of their forces when contacting Berlin to request supplies and reinforcements. Or they might acknowledge an order to do one thing, but choose to do another. In such cases, an Ultra decrypt of a message could be completely misleading. One of the permanent hazards of secret intelligence work is the tendency to believe that a stolen document or a conversation overheard by an eavesdropper will convey the truth. It is not necessarily so.

Still, the successes of Ultra were real enough. In particular, the Battle of the Atlantic might have had a very different conclusion if the cryptographers had failed to break German naval codes. It was a close-run thing. In early 1942 the German navy introduced the Triton code which remained impenetrable for ten months. During that time, the U boats very nearly cut Britain's Atlantic lifeline, inflicting an unacceptable level of losses on merchant shipping. But once the code was broken in 1943, the U boats lost their advantage, their movement being anticipated by the British convoy defences. The Germans never understood why the submarine war had turned against them like this.

Ultra was, of course, not really a triumph for MI6. The GC&CS organization was only

ABOVE: Bletchley Park, Buckinghamshire, the wartime home of the Government Code & Cypher School, whence Ultra intelligence flowed to its government and military customers.

LEFT: General Guderian with his Panzer command signals unit – complete with Enigma machine. If the Germans had always followed strict operating procedures, their radio codes would have been much more difficult to crack, but errors were frequently committed.

ABOVE: A U-boat radio operator with his Enigma machine at his left elbow. The curbing of the U-boat menace was the Ultra codebreakers' greatest single contribution to the Allied victory.

RIGHT: A small portable Mark III transceiver of the kind supplied to French Resistance fighters for contacting London.

administratively subject to the secret service; otherwise it operated as a quite separate body. But Menzies insisted that MI6 have control of the distribution of Ultra material and exploited the chance to grab most of the credit. A package of the best material was sent to the Prime Minister every day, and as often as possible Menzies delivered it in person. Churchill took an almost childlike delight in this arrangement and Menzies' prestige soared.

As well as GC&CS, MI6 gained control of the Radio Security Service (RSS), which specialized in monitoring Abwehr communications. This was originally another MI5 success story. RSS had been set up at the start of the war to try to spot illicit radio transmissions from enemy agents in Britain, but it soon turned its attention to intercepting and decoding Abwehr traffic, which it could do very successfully thanks to information provided by the double-agent SNOW. MI6 was furious that MI5 had begun

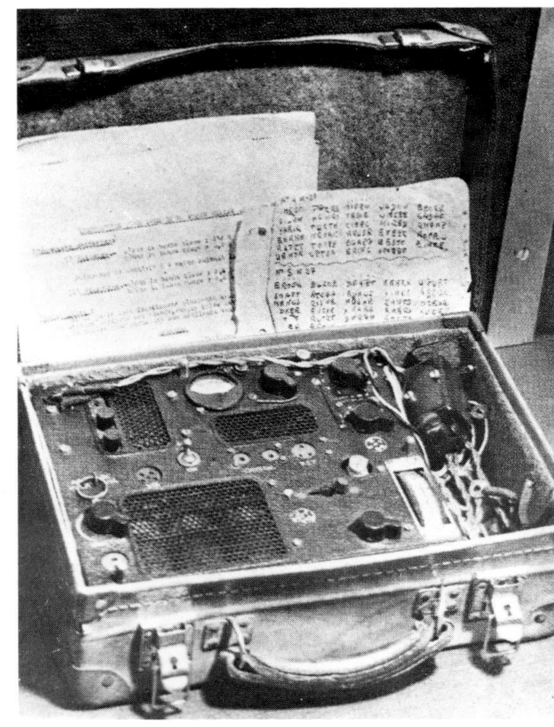

to trespass on territory it considered its own reserve, and in May 1941, after a fierce struggle, control of distribution of RSS material passed from MI5 to MI6's counter-intelligence section, Section V. Colonel Cowgill, the head of Section V, felt the most intense antipathy to MI5 and often preferred to keep RSS intelligence to himself, leaving the rival service in the dark, rather than promoting a free flow of information.

Despite Cowgill's antics Section V was probably the most successful section of MI6 during World War II. Until 1939, counter-intelligence had hardly been regarded as MI6's business – and some within the service, notably Colonel Dansey, continued always to consider it as best left to MI5. Yet the need for stations abroad to counter enemy agents active on their patch was fairly obvious, especially after the disasters experienced in Holland at the hands of the Abwehr and the Sicherheitsdienst. And MI5 needed information on its enemy abroad if it was to resist him successfully at home. Section V began its expansion even before the outbreak of war, and once the Nazi victories of 1940-41 had severely limited offensive intelligence-gathering, counter-intelligence came into its own. With the help of RSS, Section V officers attached to the MI6 stations in Spain and Portugal became especially efficient at identifying German agents operating in Iberia, and either 'turning' them or frustrating their plans.

Another MI6 section that seemed destined for wartime expansion was Section D, set up just before the war to develop ideas for sabotage and subversion in enemy territory. By the summer of 1940, Section D had grown to a strength of 140 officers – bigger than all the rest of MI6 put together. Although various madcap schemes to block German iron ore supplies from Sweden or cut off German oil imports from Rumania with a handful of plastic explosives had come to nought, the section's training establishment – nicknamed 'Guy Fawkes college' by one of its officers, Guy Burgess – was busy running courses for foreign exiles who were to be infiltrated back into Europe to spread subversion.

In July 1940, however, Churchill created a new organization, the Special Operations Executive (SOE), to carry out clandestine offensive action in Occupied Europe. In Churchill's phrase, SOE was to 'set Europe ablaze'. One of its first actions was to absorb Section D from MI6, riding roughshod over Menzies' agonized protests. Although the first operational head of the new organization was Frank Nelson, formerly of Dansey's Z network, the nearest MI6 could get to a share in SOE was the right initially to control its communications.

As one former MI6 officer, Henry Kerby, told a group of journalists in 1967, the conflict between MI6 and SOE became 'the biggest, bitterest internal battle in the history of our intelligence services.' As well as personal animosities, which unquestionably contributed to this troubled relationship, there was a genuine conflict of interest. The two organizations were competing for limited resources, especially transport. Boats and aircraft to ferry agents or arms into Occupied Europe were in very

BELOW: SOE operatives with local Yugoslav partisans. Yugoslavia was the only European country in which a full-scale guerrilla war backed by SOE actually did tie down large numbers of German troops.

FAR RIGHT TOP: One of the converted fishing boats that formed MI6's private fleet under Captain Frank Slocum, used to ferry agents across to Nazi-occupied France.
FAR RIGHT CENTRE: Members of SOE operating in the Dordogne in 1944.
FAR RIGHT BOTTOM: Men of SOE and the French Resistance retrieve supplies dropped in by parachute.

BELOW RIGHT: Niels Bohr, the Danish nuclear physicist spirited out of Occupied Europe in 1943.

BELOW: Colonel Claude Dansey, the Assistant Chief of MI6. His bitter hostility to SOE may have led him to work against its Resistance networks.

short supply. Also, they had conflicting objectives. MI6 was primarily interested in intelligence-gathering; SOE was designed for sabotage. As SOE officer Bickham Sweet-Escott correctly wrote, 'the man who is interested in obtaining intelligence must have peace and quiet . . . But the man who has to carry out operations will produce loud noises if he is successful . . .' It was easy for a cantankerous and obsessive individual like Colonel Dansey to come to believe that vulnerable intelligence sources in Europe were being compromised by enthusiastic amateurs from SOE, blundering about the Continent blowing up trains and factories. It did not improve the temper of MI6 officers that SOE's resistance contacts often came up with better intelligence than their own very depleted networks could produce.

It has been alleged that the bitterness of Dansey's hostility to SOE went so far that he was prepared to connive in the betrayal of a major SOE-run French Resistance network, Prosper, to the Gestapo in the summer of 1943. The evidence is unclear and the truth now probably beyond retrieval. Yet the very fact that such an allegation can be made indicates the extraordinary level of animosity that at times prevailed.

The clandestine operations conducted by SOE and MI6 during the war had the usual element of the comically surreal. Agents were landed from motor gunboats on the coast of Holland by night wearing full evening dress and carrying empty champagne bottles – if questioned, they were to claim to be revellers from a nearby fashionable beachside hotel. When asked for a way of sabotaging the Vemork heavy water plant in Norway, vital to Germany's chances of producing an atomic bomb, MI6 scientists suggested adding castor oil to the water. This resistance workers duly did, to the bemusement of the Germans, but without inhibiting heavy water production.

But the dominant note was tragedy. Many lives were lost – of agents, resistance fighters, non-combatant civilians – for very little gain. Holland provided the worst example. In February 1942 an SOE-trained radio operator, Herbert Lauwers, was captured by the Germans. He agreed to transmit messages to England under Abwehr control, knowing that by omitting a prearranged security check he could tell London that he had been arrested. But astonishingly the missing security check was ignored and both MI6 and SOE continued to communicate with Lauwers as normal. Over the following two years, the Abwehr sustained a superbly managed system of deception, which they code-named NORDPOL. False radio messages lured the British into sending more than a hundred agents into Holland, all of whom found a German reception committee waiting for them. Large quantities of equipment were also delivered straight into the arms of the enemy. Each new radio transmitter that arrived was 'played back' to London by the Abwehr, enlarging the deception system. When two Dutch agents escaped their captors and heroically struggled back to Britain to warn SOE and MI6 of the catastrophe that had befallen their Dutch operations, they were not believed – indeed, both were locked up in Brixton prison for allegedly aiding the enemy. MI6 did not finally realize the terrible truth until the end of 1943. An elementary blunder thus cost the lives of over 100 men and women in Holland and others in France and Belgium, since networks there were also compromised by NORDPOL.

Of course, there were notable successes. The heavy water from Vemork was finally destroyed when the train removing it to Germany was blown up by SOE. MI6 played a part in spiriting nuclear physicist Niels Bohr out of Occupied Denmark. The various national resistance movements welcomed the moral and material support that SOE could offer – it was especially valuable to Yugoslav partisans from 1943 onwards. But even success often had tragic consequences. SOE organized the assassination of leading Nazi Reinhard Heydrich by two Czech agents in May 1942, but a direct result of this action was the destruction of the village of Lidice by the Nazis and the execution of its entire population in reprisal.

In the later years of the war in Europe, the structure of Allied intelligence was further complicated by the arrival on the scene of the United States' Office of Strategic Services (OSS). MI6 played a large part in the creation of the OSS, the forerunner of the post-war Central Intelligence Agency (CIA). In May 1940 Colonel (later Sir) William Stephenson, a Canadian businessman working for MI6, was appointed to the newly established post of British Security Coordinator (BSC) in New York. Stephenson was one of Churchill's friends and his mission went beyond simple intelligence. He was to help bring the United States into the war.

Stephenson's principal contact was William J Donovan, World War I hero, Wall Street lawyer, millionaire and influential friend of President Roosevelt. One of Ste-

ABOVE: 'Wild Bill' Donovan pins a medal on Sir William Stephenson at the end of the war. Appointed British Security Coordinator in New York during 1940, Stephenson used Donovan to make contact with President Roosevelt and influence the United States toward entering the war against Germany. Donovan went on to found the OSS, under careful guidance from Stephenson and MI6.

phenson's first moves was to invite Donovan to London for a first-hand inspection of the British war effort, to counter the defeatist reports Washington was receiving from the US ambassador to Britain, Joseph Kennedy (father of the future president). The carefully stage-managed visit was a great success, and Donovan carried back to Roosevelt an encouraging account of British fighting spirit. This little operation was in itself a triumph of propaganda and helped persuade the president to sign the important Lend-Lease deal with Britain, bringing the United States one step nearer war with Germany.

Stephenson then steered Donovan toward the creation of an American equivalent of MI6. The only civilian intelligence agency in the United States at the time was the FBI, concerned exclusively with internal security. Even with presidential backing, Donovan had a hard struggle to persuade US service chiefs of the need for the OSS, which was finally established only in July 1942, more than six months after the United States had entered the war. All along the way he was guided by Stephenson and MI6, who essentially wanted the material resources the Americans could provide at their own disposal.

The OSS was modelled on MI6 and SOE, although its intelligence and sabotage and subversion sections were united under a single chief, in an attempt to avoid the destructive conflicts that beset the British. American personnel received training and instruction from their more experienced British allies and the center of OSS operations was established in London. In practice, OSS soon came to resemble SOE in its predominant concentration on armed subversion rather than intelligence-gathering – sabotage and guerrilla warfare appealed more to the cowboy instincts of 'Wild Bill' Donovan and much of his staff.

MI6's Section V benefitted greatly from close co-operation with OSS counter-intelligence. Collaboration between the British and the Americans in signals intelligence also became extremely close and was formalized by inter-governmental agreement in 1943. But MI6 did its best to clamp down on all OSS offensive operations. OSS refused to allow MI6 to control its codes and communications, but as it had no transport facilities of its own, it was dependent on the British for any operation that involved putting agents into Occupied Europe. MI6 went to great lengths to block such operations and some OSS officers got into the habit of referring to the British as 'the enemy'. A division of the world into 'spheres of influence' did something to reduce conflict, but there were major overlaps in Europe where both British and American organizations wanted to keep a finger in the pie.

After helping bring OSS into existence, why did MI6 then seem to turn against it? Apart from the sheer cussedness of fraternal rivalry, the British suspected that OSS security was poor – which it was – and believed it was liable to support resistance groups that were politically undesirable. Both MI6 and SOE had been severely embarrassed by the prominence of communists and other left-wing parties in the European opposition to Hitler. Despite bold talk of 'setting Europe ablaze', Britain's aim in the war was to recreate the pre-war status quo, minus Hitler and Mussolini. The maverick decision to support the communist Tito in Yugoslavia split SOE into warring factions.

OSS was in no sense left-wing – many of its operatives were to become leading Cold War warriors and in Yugoslavia it tended to back the monarchists against Tito. But it had no special commitment to the pre-war governments in Europe and in Asia it was positively anti-imperialist, a policy that alarmed Britain and the other old imperial powers. It did not share MI6's caution; it differed from the British both in its readiness to back German left-wingers who were ready to take on Hitler and in the alacrity with which it recruited ex-Nazis after the war.

What, on the other hand, struck OSS most about British intelligence was its seeming reluctance to do anything at all – even to the point of turning down good intelligence. In August 1943 Dr Fritz Kolbe, a convinced anti-Nazi with a post in the German Foreign Ministry, tried to hand over copies of secret documents to Colonel Henry Cartwright, a British intelligence officer in Berne, Switzerland. Suspecting a plant, and apparently convinced that Kolbe's self-confessed theft of documents proved he was an unreliable character, Cartwright had the German thrown out. The next day Kolbe approached Allen Dulles, the OSS man in Berne, who welcomed him with open arms. Kolbe remained a valuable source of intelligence right up to the end of the war. The Americans were astonished that, as the Allied armies closed in around the collapsing Reich in 1945, MI6 did not have a single agent inside Germany and showed no interest in the subject. This was partly because, in the view of MI6, signals intelligence from RSS and GC&CS had made the presence of agents on the ground superfluous. But it was chiefly because MI6 had already changed its focus to look beyond the war. Many officers were eager to turn their efforts back against the traditional enemy, the Soviet Union. In the summer of 1944, a new section of MI6 was formed, Section IX, dedicated to countering Soviet espionage and sabotage. Its first head was one of the brightest of the new recruits brought into the service during the war: Kim Philby.

BELOW: Allen Dulles, the OSS representative in Switzerland during the war, and later for many years director of the CIA. Dulles was one of many US secret agents who were puzzled at MI6's lack of enthusiasm for infiltrating agents into Germany during the last phase of the war in Europe.

LEFT: Pro-Royalist Yugoslav guerrillas and their leader Mihailovic. The British decision to switch support from Mihailovic to the communist Tito caused an open split in SOE.

CHAPTER FIVE

STALIN'S ENGLISHMEN

MI5 and MI6 emerged from World War II with their reputations much enhanced; their standing had never been higher. But this happy state of affairs was not to last. Over the next decade both services were shaken by a series of humiliating revelations, uncovering a hidden history of British security lapses and successful Soviet espionage. While Ultra and double-cross were helping win the war against Germany, Soviet agents had penetrated the top secret Manhattan atom bomb project, the Foreign Office and, the final disgrace, MI5 and MI6 themselves. Worst of all from the point of view of the British establishment, most of the Soviet spies were by birth and education members of the governing elite of the Empire. The British ruling class had rotted away from within. Three questions have recurred with obsessive regularity ever since: Why did so many intelligent and educated individuals betray their class and country? How did they get away with it for so long? And were there other successful 'moles' who to this day remain undiscovered?

The security service's assumption that anyone wearing the right school tie could be trusted with state secrets has occasioned much facile merriment. Yet it is indeed rare for people in the elite of any country to develop an enduring loyalty to a foreign power. There are always the venal or corrupt, those open to blackmail or bribery, who may become the tools of espionage. But such men are unlikely to possess the qualities of intellect or character required to sustain the role of a long-term penetration agent. Only deep divisions of fundamental belief can produce a situation where betrayal of country becomes an ideal to serve. It was the political, economic and social crisis of the 1930s that tore up patriotism by the roots.

Kim Philby, Donald Maclean, Guy Burgess and Anthony Blunt all met at Trinity College, Cambridge in the early 1930s. Their presence at such a prestigious seat of learning marked them out as part of the social and intellectual elite. All came from 'good' public schools, where the values of sportsmanship and Empire were vigorously upheld. Maclean's father was a Liberal MP who rose to be President of the Board of Education; Burgess's father was a naval officer and Blunt's a fashionable cleric.

Philby's background was odder. He was born in British India on New Year's Day 1912. Christened Harold, at an early age he acquired the nickname 'Kim', after the eponymous hero of Kipling's famous Indian novel of espionage and adventure. His father, Harry St John Philby, was an Indian civil servant, but a far from conventional one. After falling out with his superiors, he embarked on a new life exploring the deserts of Arabia, which won him a mild measure of fame. As advisor to the Saudi ruler Ibn Saud in the 1930s, St John Philby helped ensure that valuable oil concessions were awarded to American companies rather than the British. His anti-British posture eventually led him into Nazi sympathies and earned him a spell in a British jail during the war crisis of 1940. With this background, the young Philby was hardly destined to a life of safe conformism. But at Cambridge, with his disarming shyness and habitual stutter, he was the quietest of the future spies. Burgess was a flamboyant homosexual extrovert with a wounding tongue and an outrageous taste for practical jokes. Blunt, also a homosexual, older than the others and already well advanced on the path to a distinguished career as an art historian, introduced Burgess to the prestigious society of aesthetes, the Apostles.

ABOVE RIGHT: Members of the elite Apostles club at Cambridge in 1933, including (third from the right) the youthful Anthony Blunt and (in the open-necked shirt) Alister Watson, a scientist also later to be suspected of espionage. The conversion of so many privileged young intellectuals to communism in the 1930s presented the Soviet Union with a unique opportunity to penetrate the British establishment.

RIGHT: Harry St John Philby (left), father of the famous Kim. Embittered and hostile to Britain, he did not encourage his son to hold conventional patriotic beliefs, although his own politics were right-wing rather than left.

Burgess introduced Maclean to homosexuality. All became communists.

There was a widespread assumption in the 1930s that the existing order of society was doomed – for better or for worse. To Harold Macmillan, then a young Conservative MP and future British prime minister, it was evident that 'the structure of capitalist society in its old form had broken down'. To a young communist like James Klugman, the same perception presented itself in a more excitable form. As he told author Andrew Boyle:

> We simply knew, all of us, that the revolution was at hand. If anyone had suggested that it wouldn't happen in Britain, for say 30 years, I'd have laughed myself sick.

Philby, Burgess, Maclean, Blunt and their fellows grew up in a world of apparently incurable economic depression and mass unemployment. Philby, like many others, concluded 'the rich had had it too damn good for too long and the poor had had it too damn bad'. The Labour Party had shown itself quite incapable of changing society, with the disastrous collapse of its government in 1931. To many intellectuals, the only choice remaining seemed to be the Communist Party. They were attracted by its strict discipline, rigorous analysis and dazzling historical perspective. To choose communism in the 1930s logically meant choosing allegiance to the only socialist state, the Soviet Union, and the leader of world communism, Josef Stalin. After the rise to power of Adolf Hitler in Germany in 1933, the pressure to make some decisive political commitment mounted. Given the feeble response of the bourgeois democracies to Hitler's barbarism, as Phillip Knightley writes, 'the surprise is not that there were so many communist converts in the 1930s who made lifelong commitments to the Soviet Union, but that there were so few.'

The four future spies did not constitute a communist 'cell' at Cambridge, or even a closed ring of friends – Maclean and Philby seem to have been only vaguely acquainted. They were simply four of the

LEFT: Guy Burgess, a notorious camp socialite and practical joker, used his great charm to recruit his friends to spy for Moscow. Despite his apparent frivolity, he was in his younger years a surprisingly dedicated and effective Soviet agent.

BELOW: Hunger marchers demonstrate in Hyde Park in 1932. The grim spectacle of mass unemployment during the Depression years convinced many thinking people that capitalism had failed. Communism – in complete contrast – seemed to offer the only realistic alternative.

ABOVE: Donald Maclean, son of a government minister, was always the most conscience-ridden of the Cambridge spies. Without pressure from Burgess, he would probably have abandoned his espionage career in the 1940s.

many students to espouse communism at that time. Others, such as the poet John Cornford, would die for their beliefs fighting in the Spanish Civil War, or else come to renounce the Marxist faith later in their lives. All the evidence is that Philby, Burgess and Maclean held firm to their intellectual conversion until their deaths. Of the four, only Blunt repented, too late.

Much more remarkable than an outbreak of Marxism among the youth of the British ruling class was the Soviet secret service's quickness to appreciate the unprecedented potential for espionage. One by one, individuals who were party members or of known communist sympathies were discreetly approached, normally by a friend or acquaintance, and sounded out on their readiness to work covertly for the Soviet cause. If they were willing, they were put in touch with a Soviet controller, who instructed them to make a public break with their previous left-wing views and work gradually toward some valuable position in the British establishment. The patience of the Soviet controllers amazed their newly recruited agents, who were often unable to supply any worthwhile intelligence for many years.

Philby seems to have been recruited first. On leaving university in 1933 he volunteered his services to the communist underground in Vienna. There he was a witness of the violent suppression of the socialist party by the right-wing government and its Nazi allies early the following year. By his own account, it was on his return to Britain that he was approached to work for the Soviet Union. With what should have been suspicious suddenness – although no suspicion was aroused – Philby changed into an advocate of the Nazi cause. Soon Burgess became personal assistant to a right-wing Conservative MP prominent in the pro-Hitler Anglo-German Fellowship, and from there made his way into the BBC. Maclean joined the Foreign Office, blandly admitting at his interview that he had not entirely shaken off his previous left-wing views. After 1937, Blunt's writings on art history ceased to follow a Marxist line, although perhaps this was more a result of his own essentially bourgeois approach to aesthetics coming to the fore. And there were others, notably John Cairncross, another Cambridge communist, who unexpectedly dropped both his academic ambitions and his party membership in 1936 to embark on a Foreign Office career. No one in MI5, busy bugging the headquarters of the British Communist Party and pursuing petty espionage at Woolwich Arsenal, paid any attention to this strange pattern of political metamorphosis.

Despite his often clownish behaviour, the insatiably sociable Burgess was the lynchpin of the Cambridge spy ring. He was the only one who was a friend of all the others, giving him a vital role in organization and co-ordination. He was also assiduous at cultivating friends in high places, eventually including Guy Liddell of MI5. But Philby from the start had the more spectacular part to play. He received his baptism of fire as a Soviet agent during the Spanish Civil War, when he was accredited to the forces of General Franco as a war correspondent for *The Times*. This was an excellent position from which to transmit details of military operations to the Soviets, who were backing Franco's Republican enemies. Apparently his performance was regarded as satisfactory by all sides – Franco personally decorated the brave British journalist after he had been wounded by Soviet-supplied artillery.

To have had a medal pinned on your chest by Franco was no doubt a recommendation in some eyes, but there should have been enough odd points about the Cambridge spies to debar them from sensitive employment when war with Germany began. Philby, for example, was actually married to an Austrian communist he had met in Vienna, Litzi Friedmann, who was herself a Soviet agent. Even if a communist past was overlooked as a folly of youth, previous links with the Anglo-German Fellowship were hardly a point in one's favour when Hitler was the enemy. Yet Burgess glided into Section D of MI6 and, in 1940, successfully proposed his old friend Philby for employment by the same rapidly expanding organization. MI5's hurried vetting of Philby, which involved no more than checking his name against the Registry files, produced the bald statement: 'Nothing recorded against'.

Blunt was at first less fortunate. He was rejected by military intelligence in 1939 because of his known Marxist past, although in his conduct and opinions at Cambridge he had been no more explicit than the others (Burgess had openly visited the Soviet Union and met leading officials of the regime). Yet the old-boy network eventually did the trick: Blunt was accepted by the Intelligence Corps and in the summer of 1940 transferred to MI5.

BELOW: Troops in action during the Spanish Civil War. While some of his Cambridge comrades fought and died on the Republican side, Kim Philby worked as a war correspondent with General Franco's forces, his first clandestine assignment as a Soviet spy.

ABOVE: At the start of World War II, Philby (second from left) was sent by *The Times* to Arras as their correspondent accredited to British Army Headquarters in France. With a little help from Guy Burgess, however, he was soon able to leave journalism for a more promising career in MI6.

It must be remembered that this was well before the Soviet Union entered the war against Germany. Indeed, at the time Stalin was virtually in alliance with Hitler. So the failure to block the employment of Philby, Burgess and Blunt had nothing to do with the confusion that developed later in the war, when the Soviet Union became Britain's ally and the official attitude toward communists took on a temporary ambivalence. Only two factors explain the ease with which MI5 and MI6 were penetrated: the inability of MI5's primitive vetting system to cope with the sudden rapid intake of new staff during 1939-40, and the instinctive readiness to accept a recruit from the right social class armed with a personal recommendation.

The relative progress of Philby, Burgess and Blunt inside Britsh intelligence henceforth depended on their differing abilities as intelligence officers. Burgess's career was short-lived. Soon after Section D was taken over by SOE in August 1940, he was sacked by his new bosses as part of a general clear-out of old staff. With his malicious tongue, anarchic sense of humour and carefully cultivated air of irresponsibility, Burgess would never be able to hold down a serious job for very long. He returned to the BBC Talks Department, but this did not prevent him being useful to the Soviet Union: his social contacts were excellent, providing plenty of inside gossip from the corridors of power.

Blunt and Philby, on the other hand, were outstandingly able and laudably serious in their approach to their work. By 1941, deploying his formidable intellect and linguistic abilities, Blunt had established himself as a respected MI5 officer, with the specific task of handling material clandestinely extracted from the diplomatic bags of neutral countries. Philby moved effortlessly across from SOE to Section V, MI6's counter-intelligence division, based at St Albans, outside London. Working in the Iberian sub-section, he impressed everyone with his professional diligence and personal amiability. Philby's wartime colleague, the novelist Graham Greene, remembered 'those long Sunday lunches at St Albans when the whole sub-section relaxed under his leadership for a few hours of heavy drinking . . . If one made an error of judgement he was sure to minimize it and cover it up, without criticism, with a halting stammered witticism. He had all the small loyalties to his colleagues, and of course his big loyalty was unknown to us.' Few officers in the history of MI6 have been as well-liked within the service as Philby was. And his popularity extended beyond his own service, for in striking contrast to the majority of his MI6 colleagues he made assiduous efforts to cultivate good links with MI5. Such a relationship would prove useful in the future as Philby progressed up the intelligence ladder.

The material Philby handled in the Iberian sub-section was not perhaps central to Soviet concerns, but the job opened up other opportunities. Section V was based outside London, in St Albans, alongside the MI6 Central Registry. Philby was able to spend long hours discreetly studying the Registry 'source books', which listed details of MI6 agents throughout the world, including those working against the Soviet Union. He was also a frequent volunteer for night-duty at MI6's main Broadway office, which must have yielded a fruitful harvest of information.

After June 1941, of course, Britain and the Soviet Union were allies. Consequently, the Cambridge spies were in the happy position of being able to work wholeheartedly at their official tasks to help the Allies win the war against Germany, without compromising their clandestine allegiance to Stalin. Both sides, however, recognised the alliance as a temporary marriage of convenience. Although Churchill ordered an end to interception of Soviet radio signals for the duration, Britain had no intention of sharing with Moscow information about intelligence sources or the technical details of weapons development: veteran communist Dave Springhall was sentenced to seven years' imprisonment in 1943 for passing defence information to Britain's Soviet ally. The two main secrets deliberately kept from the Soviets were the atom bomb project and Ultra. About both they were kept admirably informed by their agents.

Stalin's principal obsession between 1942 and 1945 was the fear that the Western Allies might make a separate peace deal with Germany, freeing the German forces to crush the Soviet Union. Despite the official Allied policy insisting on 'unconditional surrender', there were many people in government circles in the West, including MI6 officers, ready to toy with the idea of a separate peace with Germany if Hitler could be removed from the scene. The anti-Hitler elements in the German officer corps and the Abwehr repeatedly tried to set up clandestine negotiations for a deal that would save their country from destruction. The Abwehr chief Admiral Canaris was in contact with the British and Americans via Dulles in Switzerland and even suggested a

BELOW LEFT: The novelist Graham Greene, who worked under Philby in Section V of MI6 during the war.

BELOW: Otto John (left), the Abwehr agent who approached MI6 in 1943 to explore the possibility of peace negotiations between Britain and anti-Hitler Germans. Philby blocked this approach, which in any case would not have found favour with a British government committed to 'unconditional surrender'.

meeting with his British opposite number, Menzies, in neutral Spain.

Stalin's British spies certainly kept him informed of every move in this game, but there is a myth that Philby did much more than that, making him the man who 'kept the world at war'. This is to credit an individual agent with far too much power. Philby did what he could to block discussion of the whole question of the German opposition. When a Lufthansa lawyer called Otto John, working for Admiral Canaris, contacted MI6 in Lisbon in March 1943 to try to open channels for negotiations, Philby dismissed him as 'unreliable'. But this does not add up to much. The Allied leaders were perfectly aware of the possibility of peace feelers from Germany and had already decided to reject them. None of the anti-Hitler German officers was prepared to offer terms that Churchill or Roosevelt would have found even remotely tempting. Despite Stalin's fears, a separate peace was a non-starter.

By 1944 all the Cambridge spies had undoubtedly proved good value for their Soviet controllers. But Philby's appointment as head of the new Section IX for anti-Soviet counter-intelligence in the summer of that year raised the game to fresh heights. Philby recounts the insistence of his Soviet controller that 'I must do everything, but everything, to ensure that I became head of Section IX . . .' Philby was fortunate that his superior officer and the obvious contender for the job, Felix Cowgill, was much disliked, especially by MI5 officers with whom the new head of Section IX would have to liaise. It needed some nimble footwork in office politics for Philby to pull it off, but Cowgill was very effectively out-manoeuvred and shouldered out of the way. Apart from the intrinsic value of having one of their agents in such a post, the Soviets must have realised that there was now no limit to how high in MI6 Philby could go.

Philby's colleagues in espionage were also doing well. In April 1944 Maclean was appointed First Secretary to the British Embassy in Washington, an ideal position from which to keep an eye on the development of atomic policy and moves toward post-war Anglo-American co-operation. In June, Burgess left the BBC for a niche in the Foreign Office press department. Despite constant misdemeanours and a stormy relationship with his superiors, Burgess was to stay in the Foreign Office for the next seven years, enjoying access at times to some choice confidential material. Blunt had climbed to a position on the Joint Intelligence Committee, where he occasionally represented MI5 (as Philby sometimes did MI6), and was attached to SHAEF for the Normandy landings.

But unlike the others, Blunt had decided to quit as soon as he could. Along with most of the academics, lawyers, writers and businessmen who had entered MI5 and MI6 at the start of the war, Blunt left at the war's

BELOW: The Queen discusses art with her Surveyor of Pictures. Blunt's close relationship with the Royal Family was a profound embarrassment to the British establishment once he came under suspicion of being a Soviet agent, and the fear of scandal protected him from public exposure until 1979.

end to return to peacetime pursuits, which in his case was prestigious employment as Surveyor of the King's Pictures. His Soviet controller made no effort to persuade him to stay in MI5. Was this decision, investigators would later ask, because the Soviets had another, even better-placed agent still active inside the security service? Or had they realized Blunt was losing his faith in communism and might become unreliable if pushed too hard?

Blunt retired from espionage just as the going began to get a little tougher for his comrades. The most obvious threat always lay with Soviet defectors, one of whom might be able to point the finger in the right direction. It had almost happened before the war, when Samuel Ginsberg, alias General Walter Krivitsky of Soviet military intelligence, defected. He told his debriefers that there were two Soviet spies in the Foreign Office and that another Soviet agent had covered the Spanish Civil War as a journalist for a British newspaper. Contrary to what is often asserted, the journalist in Spain mentioned by Krivitsky was almost certainly not Philby but his allegations were too close for comfort.

ABOVE: Underneath his shy, charming surface persona, Philby was a dedicated, totally ruthless professional spy. In 1945 he arranged for the 'disappearance' of the would-be defector Volkov, who threatened to reveal the identity of a high-placed Soviet 'mole' inside British intelligence.

ABOVE: Soviet defector Igor Gouzenko, hooded to prevent identification, gives an interview to a journalist at an undisclosed location somewhere in Canada.

ABOVE RIGHT: A nuclear laboratory at Los Alamos, New Mexico, where the atomic bomb was developed. Britain and the United States tried to keep the bomb project a secret from their ally Stalin, but his agents kept him thoroughly informed.

RIGHT: Dr Alan Nunn May, the British physicist arrested in 1946 on the basis of Gouzenko's revelations.

In August 1945 another Soviet agent, Konstantin Volkov, based at the Soviet consulate in Istanbul, contacted an official at the British consulate and announced his intention of defecting. Among the information Volkov claimed to have to offer were the names of two Soviet agents in the British Foreign Office and another agent at the head of a counter-espionage organization in London. In return he wanted money and asylum. As a matter of standard practice, the British diplomatic staff in Istanbul were suspicious of a 'walk-in' agent from the other side and refused to deal with Volkov. Instead, they referred the case to MI6 in London, where Menzies passed it on to his head of counter-intelligence: Philby.

Philby had no doubt that he himself was the leading figure in counter-espionage Volkov intended to name. If the defector was interrogated by a competent intelligence officer it would, in Philby's own ironic phrase, 'put an end to a promising career'. He at once informed his Soviet controller, who in turn contacted his headquarters with the news. British sigint monitors registered a sudden burst of Soviet radio traffic as panic messages rattled back and forth between London and Moscow in impenetrable code.

Philby had to appear to pursue the case with urgency, while in fact delaying progress for long enough to let the Soviets neutralize Volkov. Crucially, Volkov himself had specified that no telegrams should be sent on the subject between London and Istanbul, on the spurious grounds that Soviet intelligence had broken the British cyphers. Thus communication was restricted to relatively slow exchanges by diplomatic bag. Philby persuaded Menzies that the case was important enough to require handling by a senior officer in person, and manoeuvred successfully to land the job himself. Delay followed delay, and by the time Philby at last arrived in Istanbul to meet Volkov, three weeks had passed since the defector's first contact with the British Consulate. Not surprisingly, Volkov was nowhere to be found. Philby had to cable Menzies 'confessing defeat'. Some weeks later, a heavily bandaged figure was rushed on to a Soviet military aircraft making an unscheduled stop at Ankara airport. This may well have been Volkov; nothing was ever heard of him again.

In his official report on the incident, Philby blamed the failure of the operation on Volkov's own insistence on communications by diplomatic bag. As he wrote in his autobiography with heavy irony: 'Another theory – that the Russians had been tipped off about Volkov's approach to the British – had no solid evidence to support it. It was not worth including in my report.'

The Volkov case was closed, but simultaneously another defection was opening new avenues for British counter-intelligence. Just as Philby had been preparing to set off for Istanbul in search of Volkov, news of an important defector in Canada had landed on his desk. This was Igor Gouzenko, a cypher clerk at the Soviet embassy in Ottawa. Gouzenko was under the close protection of the Canadian Mounties, so there was no chance a Soviet hit squad could get to him. Unable to deal with both the Volkov and Gouzenko cases at once, Philby passed on responsibility for interviewing Gouzenko to the director of MI5's F Division, Roger Hollis. The presumed grounds for passing the case to MI5 were that Gouzenko's revelations would concern British internal security. F Division was chiefly responsible for surveillance of the British Communist Party.

Cypher clerks are often one of the weak points in security. Of lowly rank, they are not always subject to the same rigorous selection process as intelligence officers, yet they see all the most secret communications in their place of work. Gouzenko was able to remember many important details of Soviet espionage in North America. Even better, he had brought a briefcase full of secret Soviet files with him when he defected. From interviews with Gouzenko and a study of the stolen files, it proved possible to identify more than 20 Soviet agents operating in Canada and the United States. By far the most important of these, from a British point of view, was the nuclear scientist Alan Nunn May.

Dr Nunn May was yet another of the disillusioned 1930s generation at Cambridge, where he had been a friend of Donald Maclean and had, like him, become a committed communist. Nunn May had made no secret of his beliefs, yet this had not prevented him being employed on the top secret atom bomb project in Canada from 1942 to 1945. He had clandestinely passed on to the Soviet Union all he knew about the bomb, along with samples of the requisite uranium isotopes (Canada was crucial to the development of the bomb because of its large uranium deposits). After a period of surveillance by MI5 watchers, Nunn May was arrested in February 1946 in London, where he had returned to take up a post at King's College. His espionage had been confined to the period of the war when the Soviet Union was Britain's ally, but he was sentenced to ten years' hard labour all the same.

The Nunn May case opened the sad story of the atom spies, which was to obsess Western public opinion in the post-war period. Britain and the United States had been determined to develop the atomic bomb in complete secrecy, without any hint of its existence leaking to their Soviet ally. Yet MI5 had apparently failed to carry out even elementary vetting of personnel engaged on the project. Not surprisingly, it turned out that Nunn May was not alone.

The next revelations of Soviet espionage came not from a defector but from the cryptographers, who scored yet another triumph. The Soviet one-time pad system for encoding radio messages was, if properly carried out, totally impenetrable. From the middle years of the war through to the late 1940s, however, the Soviets laxly took to distributing duplicate sets of pads. This gave American and British cryptographers just an outside chance of breaking into the codes, and they seized their opportunity well. 'Operation Venona' developed into a joint Anglo-American project on a vast

ABOVE: Atom spy Klaus Fuchs (standing, far left) with colleagues at the Harwell atomic research establishment. Fuchs was able to give the Soviets more technical details on the atom bomb than any of their other informants.

RIGHT: MI5 officer Jim Skardon (left) with a colleague at Fuchs's trial in 1950. Skardon was the subtle interrogator who won Fuchs's confidence and induced him to make a full confession.

scale. Britain's Government Communications Headquarters (GCHQ), as GC&CS was now renamed, collaborated tightly with its United States' opposite number, the National Security Agency (NSA), to sift through every possible Soviet radio message on record, looking for repetitions that would let them break into the code. Despite a joint effort that lasted 10 years and used massive resources of manpower and computers, only about one per cent of Soviet radio messages were eventually decrypted even in part. And yet the information gleaned from those frustratingly fragmentary decodes was sufficient to provide unequivocal evidence of widespread Soviet espionage activity against both countries, including penetration of the atomic program and the US State Department.

It was an analysis of Venona material in October 1949 that identified the most important of all the atom spies, Dr Klaus Fuchs. The intercepts revealed regular meetings between a leading nuclear scientist and a Soviet agent. The MI6 station chief in Washington, Peter Dwyer, proved

that only Fuchs's movements fitted the pattern. A brilliant mathematician and physicist, Fuchs had arrived in Britain as a refugee from Nazi Germany in the 1930s. Along with so many other anti-Nazi refugees, many of them left-wingers and some even communists, Fuchs was interned by the British authorities in 1940, but in 1942 he was recruited to work on the atom bomb project, first in England and then at Los Alamos. After the war he returned to Britain to take up a post at the Harwell atomic research establishment, and it was there that Jim Skardon of MI5 first went to interview him in December 1949.

Skardon's deceptively gentle debriefing of Fuchs is generally regarded as a classic of interrogation technique. It extracted a full and detailed confession from a man already worn down by years of living in what he described as a state of 'controlled schizophrenia'. According to Fuchs, as soon as he had learnt the purpose of his work on the atom project, he had 'decided to inform Russia'. He established contact with the German emigre Ruth Kuczynski, codenamed Sonia, who was running a spy ring from Oxford (later in the war her brother and fellow spy Juergen became a colonel in the US Air Force and a respected advisor to the Americans – OSS used him to select Germans suitable for recruitment as agents). When Fuchs moved to the United States, Sonia passed him on to an American controller, Harry Gold. He had also continued to spy on his return to Britain in 1946.

ABOVE: Soviet agent Harry Gold (left) under arrest in New York after Fuchs had identified him as his controller in the United States. The FBI and the CIA were furious with the British for allowing Fuchs and Nunn May to infiltrate the atom bomb project.

Fuchs was formally arrested by Special Branch in February 1950, hastily tried and convicted. As details of the case reached the press, there was an outcry over the failure of the security service to spot Fuchs for so long, or to block his employment in the first place. Only six months earlier, on 29 August 1949, the Soviet Union had exploded its first atomic bomb, four years in advance of the most recent 'best guess' American intelligence predictions. It was widely believed that traitors had handed the greatest weapon of mass destruction ever invented to a brutal enemy who was quite likely to use it. Paranoid hysteria gripped the West, especially the United States, where Senator Joe McCarthy began his notorious crusade to root out communists and fellow travellers from American public life. Two very minor participants in atomic espionage, Julius and Ethel Rosenberg, went to the electric chair – a ritual sacrifice to allay collective fears.

In retrospect, no-one doubts that the Soviet Union would have developed its own atomic bomb without any help from espionage. Soviet scientists had started theoretical work on nuclear weapons as early as 1940. Although their efforts were interrupted by the Nazi invasion and not taken up with any great urgency until after the destruction of Hiroshima, they lacked none of the necessary knowledge or skills to complete the task. The material provided by Fuchs must have been extremely useful to the Soviet atom program. It included a mass of detailed information on the American bomb, ranging from questions of theoretical physics to sketches of components and calculations of blast effects. It may have hastened the explosion of the first Soviet atomic device by a year or so. But as journalist Phillip Knightley has written, attempting to stop the Soviet Union discovering how to make nuclear weapons was 'as futile as trying to keep secret the discovery of the wheel'.

By the time of Fuchs's arrest, Philby had long moved on from his post as head of MI6 counter-intelligence. A new principle had been established within the service that officers should be forced to gain as wide an experience of their trade as possible. Philby lacked any first-hand knowledge of the day-to-day workings of an MI6 station abroad, so in 1947 he was transferred to Istanbul as MI6 station chief – too far from the centre of the action for his own purposes, but a posting he could not be seen to refuse. The next

BELOW: Senator Joe McCarthy (right) pursued a witch hunt against communists and communist sympathisers in the United States in the early 1950s. Like many Americans, he was wrongly convinced that without the atom spies, the Soviet Union would never have been able to explode an atomic bomb.

move was much more to his taste, however. In the autumn of 1949 he was sent to replace Peter Dwyer as head of station in Washington, with a specific brief to forge strong links with the newly formed successor to OSS, the Central Intelligence Agency (CIA).

The Cold War was by now in full swing and the CIA was aggressively committed to a policy of 'rolling back' communism in Europe. It was pouring money into anti-communist organizations in France and Italy, while in western Germany ex-Nazi intelligence officers were recruited in droves to continue their wartime struggle against the Russians. Both MI6 and the CIA were very keen to encourage armed subversion in communist-controlled areas: MI6 had formed a Special Operations Branch and a Political Action Group to take over responsibility for covert action when SOE was disbanded in 1946; CIA sabotage and subversion was the job of the Office of Policy Co-ordination run by Frank Wisner. Projecting their experience of World War II forward into the post-war world, the more excitable Allied intelligence officers tended to regard eastern Europe, the Baltic states and the Ukraine as 'occupied countries', where resistance movements should be provided with arms and encouraged to liberate themselves from their oppressors.

Of course, this strategy had not even worked in the war against Hitler: most of the population of Europe had not been ready to revolt against the Nazis and the occupation forces had proved far too strong and well-organized for the generally small resistance groups. It was even less viable for the war against Stalin. The east European exile movements were riven by political differences and hopelessly vulnerable to penetration by Soviet agents – as was Allied intelligence. The populations in the target areas, even when hostile to communist rule, were mostly cowed and decidedly unwilling to support renewed warfare so soon after the end of a long and bitter conflict that had cost them so dearly. They were also unlikely to identify with exile groups that were in many cases tainted with fascism and Nazi collaboration. An already unpromising situation was not helped by continual political conflicts between MI6 and the CIA – in the Ukraine, for instance, the British insisted on backing the extreme nationalist Stepan Bandera, to whom the Americans were immovably hostile.

All clandestine operations in communist Europe at this time were uniformly disastrous. Typically, small groups of emigres, trained as agents by MI6 or the CIA, would be parachuted back into their native country and never heard from again. Philby wrote chillingly of Bandera supporters dropped into the Ukraine: 'I do not know what happened to the parties concerned. But I can make an informed guess.'

The operation against Albania between 1949 and 1953 was the biggest of all CIA/MI6 attempts at subversion in Europe, and can stand as a paradigm for them all. It was overseen by a four-man Special Policy Committee, initially including Philby as representative of MI6. The political rivalries of Albanian emigres were labyrinthine – royalist supporters of ex-King Zog confronted anti-royalists and a score of personal or regional antipathies further confused the scene. The British and the Americans could not agree who to support and ended up in practice running separate shows.

On the face of it, Albania looked a softer

BELOW: The unfortunate Ethel and Julius Rosenberg, very small fry in the espionage business who went to the electric chair to reassure a paranoid American public. Their contribution to undermining the security of the United States was minimal.

ABOVE: Enver Hoxha (right), the communist ruler of Albania until his death in 1985. MI6 and the CIA thought Albania would be an easy target for subversion and began infiltrating agents into the country in 1949.

option than anywhere in eastern Europe. It was small, its communist government under Enver Hoxha was presumed to be unstable, and it was isolated from the Soviet Union by Tito's Yugoslavia, which had quarrelled with Stalin. Malta was chosen as the base for infiltration – Frank Wisner quipped to Philby: 'Whenever we want to subvert any place, we find that the British own an island within easy reach.' In October 1949 MI6 organized the first landing on the Albanian coast; the agents were picked up by local security forces almost as soon as they came ashore. This inauspicious beginning set the pattern for all that was to follow. The CIA dropped Albanians in by parachute, the British landed them from the sea or infiltrated them across the border from Greece, but the result was always the same. By the end of 1951 MI6 had had enough and the British pulled out. The CIA persisted for another two years, encouraged at last by signs that the agents were surviving and building up networks among the population. The whole business finally came to an end only when the Albanians scornfully revealed how they had turned some of the emigre infiltrators and used them in a classic double-cross to lure others to their doom. None of the networks actually existed. In all several hundred Albanians had lost their lives to no purpose whatsoever.

The failure of the Albanian operation has often been blamed squarely on Philby. It is regularly used as the prime example of his 'wickedness' – the indisputable corpses laid at his door. The intelligence Philby was in a position to provide about this and other attempts at covert action must indeed have been invaluable to the Soviets. Merely to know that an assault on Albania was in the offing and the general form it was going to take, for example, would be extremely useful. Philby almost certainly will not have known the exact times and places of landings or drops, however. And the operation was no more successful after he had left the scene than it had been before.

The precipitate end to Philby's meteoric career was a result of his association with Burgess and Maclean. The Cambridge links that had once been so valuable proved in the end his Achilles heel. In 1948 the tireless labours of the British and American code-breakers working on the Venona material had been rewarded by the discovery that a Soviet agent had been operating inside the British embassy in Washington during the last years of the war. In mid 1945 this agent, codenamed Homer in the Soviet radio transmissions, had been able to leak exact transcripts of messages exchanged between Churchill and President Truman. Philby was briefed on the Homer case by Maurice Oldfield (a future head of MI6, at that time working in counter-intelligence) before his departure for Washington. Of course, Philby knew the identity of the mysterious agent – it was Donald Maclean, First Secretary in Washington from 1944 to 1948.

Maclean had proved extremely useful to Moscow during his time in the United States. Most of the information he provided must have concerned the intricacies of Anglo-American relations during the transition from hot war to cold war, and the true attitudes of the Western governments to the Soviet Union as alliance shifted to confrontation. He was also able to supplement the work of the atom spies through his place on the Anglo-American Combined Policy Committee, responsible for debating the post-war development of atomic weapons. He had a pass to the US Atomic Energy Commission building and frequently used it to pay a visit in the evenings when most of the staff had gone home – although it would be extraordinary if security there was so lax that documents were left lying about on top of desks overnight. Whereas the intelligence Fuchs possessed on the bomb was technical, Maclean could keep Moscow informed on the political decisions about its development and use.

When Philby arrived in the United States, he was relieved to find that the FBI investigation into the British embassy leak was getting nowhere. Instead of investigating diplomatic staff, Hoover's men were concentrating on locally recruited embassy employees, 'sweepers, cleaners, bottle-washers and the rest'. Still, Philby concluded that 'the case would require careful watching'. It could only be a matter of time before the net closed around Maclean.

Philby always made the double life look easy, but in Maclean the terrible strain showed. Even before he left Washington, his heavy drinking – the only characteristic all the spies shared – had begun to get out of control. His next posting was to Cairo. There, whether racked by guilt or simply afraid of discovery, he started to go to pieces. In May 1950 an all-night binge ended with Maclean devastating the flat of

Donald Maclean was a family man (above, with one of his children) riven by conflicting loyalties, addicted to alcohol and homosexual forays. When decrypted Soviet diplomatic traffic revealed a spy at the British embassy in Washington, the anti-British FBI chief J Edgar Hoover (left) was only too willing to sniff out the culprit – but his lines of enquiry led him astray.

BELOW: Guy Burgess photographed in the Soviet Union shortly before his death in 1963. It has always been a mystery why Burgess fled with Maclean instead of simply aiding his escape.

an American ex-patriate, breaking furniture and smashing up the bathroom. There were complaints and Maclean, diagnosed perhaps not inaccurately as the victim of a nervous breakdown, was sent back to London for medical treatment. A sympathetic Foreign Office found him a job in Whitehall as head of its American department.

Burgess's career was also running into a crisis. Two years earlier he had been sacked from a Foreign Office propaganda department; his boss described him to his face as

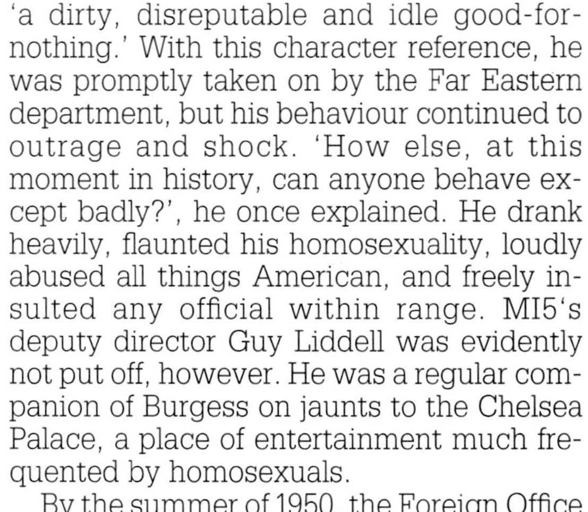

'a dirty, disreputable and idle good-for-nothing.' With this character reference, he was promptly taken on by the Far Eastern department, but his behaviour continued to outrage and shock. 'How else, at this moment in history, can anyone behave except badly?', he once explained. He drank heavily, flaunted his homosexuality, loudly abused all things American, and freely insulted any official within range. MI5's deputy director Guy Liddell was evidently not put off, however. He was a regular companion of Burgess on jaunts to the Chelsea Palace, a place of entertainment much frequented by homosexuals.

By the summer of 1950, the Foreign Office in London had finally had enough of Burgess. They offered him one last chance, if he would accept a posting abroad. They offered Washington. Burgess accepted and sent off a letter to Kim Philby, asking his old friend if he could put him up when he arrived. Philby, perhaps unwisely, agreed. He reasoned that he might have more control over Burgess's increasingly erratic behaviour if he had him under the same roof.

Philby's house was an active centre of sociability for the local intelligence community. Leading lights of the FBI and CIA would drop in for the inevitable drinks. One visitor was James Jesus Angleton, the rising star of CIA counter-intelligence. Philby had taught Angleton his craft in London during the war and the two men were on the friendliest terms. Although it was later claimed Angleton had seen through Philby's disguise, there was certainly no sign of it at the time. Burgess's voluble anti-Americanism was bound to offend visitors to the house, but Philby always showed himself an amiable, if sometimes excessively drunken, host.

All this cosiness was threatened by the cloud hanging over Maclean. He was still drinking heavily and had begun making confessions to strangers in London bars. Meanwhile MI5 had undertaken a fresh examination of the Venona transcripts on Homer. First they established that the Soviet source must have been of second secretary rank or above. Then they uncovered two decisive facts: the spy had been in the habit of visiting New York every fortnight, and in September 1944 his wife was pregnant. Painstaking research revealed that only one diplomat fitted this profile. There was insufficient evidence to prosecute Maclean, but MI5 were almost sure they had found their man. In the spring of 1951 he was put under surveillance, followed around London by Special Branch, in the hope that he might contact his Soviet controller. He was not pursued out to his country home in the evenings or at weekends, when it would have been almost impossible for a watcher to avoid detection, but his home phone was tapped.

Even before these new developments, the Soviets had decided that Maclean must be got out of Britain. Philby attributes this to concern for the fate of an 'old comrade', but there was a more practical motive. If Maclean was ever subjected to interrogation, it seemed most unlikely he would keep silent. A confession would implicate all the Cambridge spies. According to Philby, it was agreed that Maclean would be extracted by the summer of 1951. Burgess would go to London, inform Maclean of the plan and supervise arrangements for his departure.

In March 1951 Burgess was ordered back to Britain by the ambassador, after being booked for speeding three times in one day. By Philby's account, this flagrant breach of diplomatic privilege was deliberately engineered to give Burgess an excuse for returning home. He landed in England on 7 May and with no apparent haste contacted Maclean. The situation was now critical. MI5 were only waiting to complete arrangements with the Foreign Office and the FBI before pulling Maclean in for interrogation. On Friday, 25 May, the Foreign Secretary, Herbert Morrison, gave signed permission for the interrogation to take place the fol-

BELOW: The revelation that two such highly placed members of the establishment as Burgess and Maclean could have been communist spies, fascinated the British public. For several years after their 'disappearance' the press gave head-line coverage to the most trivial of rumours, such as this one of April 1962.

ROOTES COMPREHENSIVE SERVICE FOR Cars & Trucks

Evening Standard

42,872 WEDNESDAY, APRIL 18, 1962 3d.

WEST END FINAL CLOSING PRICES

LES PARFUMS WORTH de Reviens

The runaway diplomats are on the move again and Scotland Yard is ready to pounce

BURGESS - MACLEAN SENSATION

They quit Moscow —No. 1 spy catcher on the trail

Evening Standard Reporters

There was a sensational development this afternoon in the 11-year-old case of the runaway Foreign Office diplomats Guy Burgess and Donald Maclean. Warrants for their arrest were issued at Bow Street Court.

Scotland Yard, giving the news, said:

"*There are grounds for supposing that Donald Maclean and Guy Burgess may be contemplating leaving, or may have left, the USSR for some other territory.*

"In order that they may be arrested should they come in transit or otherwise within the jurisdiction of our courts, warrants have been applied for, and issued, for their arrest for offences under Section 1 of the Official Secrets Act, 1911.

THEY'VE VANISHED

Both men were missing in Moscow this afternoon.

A Moscow telephone operator said: "We always put calls for these two men through to Moscow 465556.

"I've just rung that number and they've asked me to give a message. They say that Burgess is not expected back for two weeks and Maclean is not due back for between one and two weeks.

"The number has refused to accept your call."

The warrants were applied for at Bow Street this morning by Det.-Supt. George Smith, of Scotland Yard's Special Branch.

With him when the warrants were granted by Sir Robert Blundell, the Chief Metropolitan Magistrate, was Mr. Peter Palmes, a barrister from the office of the Director of Public Prosecutions.

Detective-Superintendent Smith, the man who smashed the Lonsdale-Kroger Russian spy ring in 1960, is known as Britain's No. 1 spy catcher.

He returned to Bow Street this afternoon to collect two warrants.

● Page Seventeen, Col. 2

Are they aboard this ship?

THE BALTIKA—due at Tilbury tomorrow.

DONALD MACLEAN—"No reply from Moscow 465556."

GUY BURGESS—"Not expected back for two weeks."

DET.-SUPT. SMITH He smashed spy ring

'150,000 RAIL JOBS IN JEOPARDY'

Mr. Sidney Greene, General Secretary of the National Union of Railwaymen, told the Scottish TUC in Aberdeen today that jobs of about 150,000 railwaymen were hanging in jeopardy because of threatened railway economies.

He said that at discussions with Dr. Beeching on Monday he had the impression that at least one-third of the railway industry was likely to disappear.

Dr. Beeching had taken surveys of traffic and had divided lines into three—those that paid, those that could pay, and those that did not or would not pay

Marples bans lorries in the City
PAGE TWELVE
AIRPORT MEN ACCEPT RISE
PAGE FOURTEEN
Tories brace up for new election shocks
PAGE ELEVEN
Amusements Guide
PAGE TWENTY

EUSTACE WATKINS for WOLSELEY cars
SOLE LONDON DISTRIBUTORS
Distributors for Vanden Plas Princess.
*200 miles only, registered 1962, Wolseley 6/99, o'drive Grey £1135
*1961 Wolseley 6/99, overdrive, 11,000 miles Grey/White ... £975
*1961 Wolseley 15/60, Duo Green, 9000 miles ... £770
*1960 Wolseley 15/60, Grey/White 24,000 miles ... £695
*1961 Wolseley 1500, Black 1500 miles ... £675
*1960 Wolseley 1500, Black 28,000 miles ... £575
1958 Wolseley 6/90, Automatic Maroon, 40,000 miles ... £495
*1961 Morris Mini, Blue 19,000 miles ... £465
1958 Morris 1000 d/l Black 13,000 miles ... £425
1961 Sunbeam Rapier, overdrive, Duo Green 4500 miles ... £925
1962 Ford Anglia Estate, Maroon 1200 miles ... £650
*Under B.M.C. Warranty
Phone, call or write for details of these and other used cars.
Ask about the E.W. personal service scheme available at all branches.
MAYFAIR: 17 Berkeley St., W.1 MAY 5951 CROYDON: 399-401 London Rd., W. Croydon THO 4280
CHELSEA: Chelsea Manor St., S.W.3 FLA 8181 WATFORD: 425-445 St. Albans Rd., WAtford 22311

lowing Monday – intelligence officers apparently preferred not to work at the weekend. That same Friday, in the evening, Burgess picked Maclean up from his house in Surrey, drove him down to Southampton and embarked with him on a ferry to France. His last words, shouted back to the quayside from the deck of the vessel, were: 'We'll be back on Monday.'

The disappearance of Burgess and Maclean thoroughly mystified MI5. It was not until much later that British intelligence was even certain the pair had gone to the Soviet Union. Two aspects of the case have remained a mystery ever since: Who supplied the tip-off that Maclean's interrogation was imminent? And why did Burgess go too? The tip-off might have come from Philby in Washington, although in practical terms it is hard to see how this could have been done; or it might have come from Blunt, who still had excellent contacts in MI5 and had been reactivated by Burgess to help organize Maclean's escape; or there may have been another well-placed 'mole' inside MI5 who gave the warning; or the timing of the disappearance may have been a lucky coincidence. None of these explanations has been satisfactorily validated.

As for Burgess's defection, explanations vary wildly. Was it, as Philby always claimed, Burgess's own spontaneous decision, the freakish act of a totally unpredictable man at the end of his tether? Or did the Russians tell him to leave with Maclean because they thought his position untenable? Or was it simply an accident – had he originally intended just to accompany Maclean to France, only realising after the event that this thoughtless action had

BELOW: Leconfield House in Mayfair is MI5's main London office. It was here that Philby was brought for interrogation on his return from the United States in 1951.

blown his cover, leaving him no option but to continue on to Moscow? The best evidence that Burgess went on his own initiative is the frosty treatment he received in Moscow, noticeably different from that accorded to Maclean or later defectors like Philby and Blake. The best evidence for the 'accident' option, however, is that Burgess left documents in his flat that could have incriminated Blunt and Philby, an inexplicable action unless he intended to return. That these documents were not found was the result of a strange decision by Guy Liddell of MI5, who asked his friend and ex-colleague Blunt to help with the search of Burgess's flat. The wily aesthete quietly pocketed the incriminating documents while Special Branch were occupied in another room.

Still, Burgess's defection inevitably implicated Philby. There was very little to connect Philby with Maclean; had Maclean left on his own, Philby would in all probability have continued his progress toward the top of MI6. But with Burgess unmasked as a Soviet agent, Philby could not avoid the accusation of either treachery or incompetence – for how could a senior counter-intelligence officer have shared his house with a Soviet spy and noticed nothing? Yet the reaction of MI6 was from the very start protective of Philby. They were simply not prepared to believe he could be a Soviet agent. Dick White, the head of MI5's counter-espionage division, felt differently. He insisted that Philby must be interviewed immediately.

Philby was called back from the United States and subjected to two interrogations at Leconfield House in Curzon Street, MI5's post-war headquarters. White put him through a detailed examination of his past career and his friendship with Burgess, but he could not be cracked. Without a confession, there was no evidence to justify a prosecution. Nonetheless, White was convinced of Philby's treachery, and so were the Americans. CIA chief General Walter Bedell-Smith informed Menzies in no uncertain terms that Philby would henceforth be unwelcome in Washington. Reluctantly, MI6 bowed to pressure. Philby was asked to resign from the service.

BELOW: General Walter Bedell-Smith, the head of the CIA at the time of the Burgess-Maclean defection. Philby always feared Bedell-Smith as the man most likely to see through his deceptions; he described the CIA chief as having 'a cold, fishy eye, and a precision-tool brain'.

In November 1951, in a further effort to establish Philby's guilt, he was interrogated by Sir Helenus Milmo, a King's Counsel and former MI5 officer. This 'judicial inquiry' had no better success, however, although Milmo did confront Philby with one new powerful piece of evidence – the GCHQ records of unusually high levels of Soviet radio communications from London in the days after Philby had been told of the Volkov defection, and after he had learnt of the Washington embassy spy investigation. Despite being quite unprepared for an attack from that direction, Philby remained completely unruffled. After Milmo, Fuchs's interrogator Skardon had a go at him, and so, rather half-heartedly, did MI6. It was all in vain. Philby used his great experience of intelligence work in his own defence: he could not be tripped up, trapped or made to confess.

Until 1955, Philby's name remained completely unknown to the general public. The Burgess and Maclean defection had, of course, caused a sensation in the press, and there was recurrent speculation about the identity of the 'Third Man' who had tipped off the other two. Eventually sources inside the CIA and the FBI, eager to see Philby exposed and convinced the British intelligence services were carrying out a cover-up, leaked his name to journalists. The libel laws still kept the newspapers from printing any accusation, but in October 1955 a member of parliament, Colonel Marcus Lipton, was primed to name Philby in a question to the Foreign Secretary, Harold Macmillan, under cover of parliamentary privilege. This clumsy move was entirely to Philby's advantage. It forced Macmillan to make a statement to the House of Commons, and in the absence of any proof of Philby's guilt, the Foreign Secretary was bound to exonerate him. On 7 November Macmillan told MPs that there was no evidence against Philby; the Soviet spy promptly held a televised press conference at which, eyes twinkling with boyish amusement and tongue firmly in cheek, he denied ever having worked for the Soviet Union. It was little short of a triumph.

Both MI5 and the Americans were horrified by what had happened. MI6, on the other hand, reasoned that since Philby had been publicly given a clean bill of health, he could be taken back on the payroll, if only in a limited capacity. Sir John Sinclair, who had become 'C' after Menzies' retirement in 1953, re-employed Philby as a lowly officer in the field, sending him to Beirut with the cover role of journalist. There he remained for the next seven years.

Daily Herald

Clean away—the man who warned Burgess and Maclean

MEN HE AIDED—BURGESS AND MACLEAN

WAS THIRD MAN PHILBY TIPPED OFF?

By W. N. EWER

HAROLD (KIM) PHILBY, journalist and ex-diplomat, was revealed yesterday as the "third man" who helped Guy Burgess and Donald Maclean to flee Britain 12 years ago.

Philby—tipped off Burgess and Maclean

Man who was cleared by Macmillan

By HAROLD HUTCHINSON

'SOMEBODY IS SPREADING RUMOURS'

I'm not a ticket tout, says Pat

MRS. PHILBY

PAT EDRICH

'BULLIED GUARDS' INQUIRY

The world this morning

TWO GIRLS DROWN IN PIT

Astors home

ADVERTISEMENT

Long Range WEATHER FORECAST —may not suit Sinus Sufferers

IRA man freed

Kim isn't here—Burgess

Sport

Chanticleer

WEATHER

BRIGHT BUT COOL

In 1955 Marcus Lipton MP (far left) forced the British government to make a statement on Philby's part in the Burgess-Maclean defection. Lacking solid evidence against Philby, the hapless Foreign Secretary, Harold Macmillan, had no choice but to proclaim his innocence, and the Soviet spy called an impromptu press conference (below) at his mother's flat in Drayton Gardens to celebrate his 'absolution.' Philby's eventual defection to the Soviet Union in 1963 (press report, left) caused a fresh scandal; it was especially embarrassing to Macmillan, by then Prime Minister.

Hard evidence against Philby eventually came from a wholly unexpected direction. In 1962 Flora Solomon, a Jewish pre-war friend of Philby, happened to meet former MI5 officer Victor Rothschild in Israel. She was angry with Philby because he had written articles she considered anti-Israeli, so she told Rothschild that Philby had once tried to recruit her as a Soviet agent. Interviewed by MI5, she stuck to her story. At last doubts about Philby were at an end. Yet the case was still handled very strangely. Nicholas Elliott, a close friend of Philby's and former MI6 head of station in Beirut, was sent out to confront him with the new evidence. Philby immediately admitted to being a Soviet spy, although his 'confession' gave nothing away.

Elliott offered him a guarantee of immunity from prosecution if he would return to England and co-operate fully, naming KGB agents, giving details of operations, and so forth. Not surprisingly, Philby ducked this rather one-sided deal. On 23 January 1963

ABOVE: John Cairncross, another member of the Cambridge Apostles society who spied for the Soviet Union. During the war he was employed by GC&CS at Bletchley Park and passed on Ultra material to the Russians.

he disappeared from Beirut, probably aboard a Soviet freighter. Six months later he surfaced in Moscow. Had the British intelligence chiefs deliberately made his escape possible in the hope of avoiding yet another spy scandal? Or had someone tipped Philby off about Elliott's mission – more evidence for the existence of an undiscovered 'mole' still operating in the upper echelons of British intelligence? The questions remain unanswered.

Philby's defection was another painful blow for MI5 and MI6. As well as the embarrassment of his escape, they now had to face the certain knowledge that Soviet penetration had reached the innermost circles of the secret service – and certain knowledge is very different from suspicion, however well founded. Those officers in MI6 who had believed in Philby's innocence to the last were especially distraught. Once again, the KGB had made fools of the British in public.

Further ramifications of Cambridge espionage soon came to light. In the spring of 1964, an American named Michael Straight revealed that he had been 'talent-spotted' by Blunt in the 1930s. Although MI5 had repeatedly interviewed Blunt about the Burgess-Maclean defection, this was the first really solid piece of evidence to emerge against him. MI5 counter-espionage officer Arthur Martin was authorized to confront him with the new evidence and offer immunity from prosecution if he would co-operate fully with his interrogators. Faced with the probability of public disgrace and imprisonment Blunt confessed and began to name names.

He immediately identified two more of his Cambridge contemporaries as one-time Soviet agents: John Cairncross and a fellow member of the elite Apostles Society, Leo Long. Cairncross had worked at the Treasury until 1940 when he joined GC&CS, with access to Ultra material. In 1944 he had transferred for a brief spell at MI6. He was another person who had come under suspicion at the time of the Burgess-Maclean defection, because a Treasury document provided by him was found in Burgess's flat. He had been put under surveillance and at one point MI5 had believed he was about to meet his Soviet control. No one had turned up to the rendezvous, however, and the matter had been dropped. Now, having been assured that a prosecution was unlikely if he co-operated, Cairncross made a full confession. So did Long, who had worked in military intelligence during the war and had risen to be Deputy Head of Military Intelligence in the British sector of Germany after 1945. He had left the intelligence world in 1952. Both Cairncross and Long had provided the Soviet Union with plentiful secret information, although mostly at a time when Stalin was Britain's ally. Another of the Cambridge Apostles was removed from a post in the Admiralty Research Laboratory as a result of Blunt's testimony, and a number of less sensitively placed civil servants found their careers interrupted.

The knowledge of Blunt's betrayal was a severe embarrassment to MI5. Used to crowing over the failings of MI6, the security service had to face up to the truth of its own vulnerability to Soviet penetration. Blunt had been a friend of Sir Dick White, sequentially chief of both MI5 and MI6, and of Guy Liddell, one-time deputy director of MI5. Even worse, from the point of view of the British establishment, he had enjoyed the confidence and warm respect of the Royal Family – the Queen had bestowed a

BELOW: A haggard Anthony Blunt gives a press conference after the revelation of his espionage activities by Mrs Thatcher in November 1979. Many intelligence officers disapproved of Thatcher's action, since it breached the immunity deal made with Blunt to secure a full confession.

FAR LEFT: Anthony Blunt was the only one of the four main Cambridge spies to lose his belief in the rightness of what he had done, and therefore the only one to feel shamed and humiliated by the public revelation of his guilt.

LEFT AND BELOW: Snapshots of Philby in the Soviet Union. After some difficult years, Philby eventually made a successful adjustment to Soviet life and continued to work for the KGB.

knighthood on the distinguished art historian in 1956. The immunity deal with Blunt was undoubtedly intended in part to elicit more information, but also protected the establishment from revelations it would prefer to avoid.

After the unmasking of Philby as 'the Third Man', journalists never quite lost the scent of 'the Fourth Man' felt still to be lurking in the shadows. There were enough people inside the Anglo-American intelligence community who disagreed with the kid-glove treatment Blunt had received to guarantee that the story would be leaked. By the late 1970s pressure on the government to name 'the Fourth Man' mounted with the publication of Andrew Boyle's book The Climate of Treason, which did everything but identify Blunt by his real name. It is still rather surprising, however, that in November 1979 Prime Minister Margaret Thatcher made a statement to the House of Commons detailing Blunt's activities, thereby reneging on the original agreement – an action that had grave implications for future immunity deals. Blunt was publicly disgraced and stripped of his knighthood. He died four years later.

Burgess had died long before, in 1963, a discontented exile in drab homophobic Moscow, but still a Marxist believer. Maclean eventually adjusted better to Soviet life and even wrote a book offering a Marxist analysis of aspects of British foreign

policy. Philby, after a long period of depression and hard drinking, emerged as a valued advisor to Yuri Andropov, head of the KGB and, briefly, of the Soviet Union. He even appeared on Soviet television and, shortly before his death in 1988, in his last interview with British journalist Phillip Knightley, talked with the same urbane charm and lucidity that had once so endeared him to the colleagues he was secretly betraying.

The importance of the information handed over to the Soviet Union by the Cambridge spies is, literally, incalculable. The impact on Western intelligence of the mere fact of their betrayal is much clearer. It infected both the British and Americans with 'mole fever'. If there was a Fourth Man, why not a Fifth or a Sixth? If Philby could easily have been head of MI6, why not believe the head of MI5 was a Soviet agent? And if British intelligence had been so completely penetrated, why not the CIA?

Worse still, the Cambridge spies and the atom spies spread doubt and distrust between the different components of the Western intelligence community. The Americans were furious at the British both for failing to spot the clear communist associations of men like Fuchs and Nunn May, and for failing to nail spies once exposed. The handling of the Philby case and the prolonged cover-up over Blunt convinced American intelligence chiefs that the British establishment would do anything to protect its own kind, even at the expense of security. The British, in short, were not to be trusted. The already strained relationship between MI5 and MI6 worsened sharply through the dispute over Philby – until 1963 some MI6 officers regarded the whole campaign against Philby as an unjustified MI5 assault, designed to obscure the blunders of the security service in the Burgess-Maclean affair. MI5, not unnaturally, saw MI6 as unprofessional and unreliable.

The whole business also generated an excessive fear of the professional skills of Soviet intelligence. If any Western intelligence officer might be a Soviet agent, then any Soviet defector might be a Soviet plant, any apparent Western intelligence success a deception manufactured by the other side. The Soviets were to be credited with a capacity for operations of phenomenal depth and

BELOW: Philby was buried in Moscow with full military honours in May 1988. He had been a supporter of Mikhail Gorbachev's new policy of *glasnost*, regarding the liberalisation of Soviet politics as a vindication of his lifelong communist beliefs.

THE INDEPENDENT

No 497 SATURDAY 14 MAY 1988 *** Published in London 30p

KGB funeral for the honoured spy

SUMMARY

Clampdown on no-strike agreements

STRICT new rules on no-strike deals to be considered by TUC leaders next week will, if accepted, in effect outlaw controversial agreements being struck by the electricians' union. Papers prepared for the TUC's special review body into future policy-making reflect a considerable hardening of opinion .... Page 2

Deadlock broken

Dublin and London broke a six-month deadlock on procedures for the extradition of terrorist suspects from the republic, but differed in their versions of how agreement had been reached .... Page 2

Clinics warned

The authority which regulates test-tube baby clinics warned against trying to increase success rates by putting more eggs back into the womb ...... Page 3

Market force

Paddy Ashdown, the favourite to win the SLD leadership, signalled a shift towards social market economics......... Page 5

Beirut killings

Syrian troops shot dead five pro-Iranian militiamen in west Beirut, their first intervention in a week of fierce factional fighting .... Page 10

Jerusalem clash

Police fired rubber bullets and baton-charged Palestinian protesters on Jerusalem's biblical Temple Mount on the last Friday of Ramadan.......... Page 10

Regan attacked

George Shultz, the US Secretary of State, came to the defence of America's First Family, and hit out at the memoirs of former White House chief

In death, Kim Philby emerged from the shadowy world of espionage. **Rupert Cornwell** reports from Moscow

Guard of dishonour: Rufina, the Russian widow of Kim Philby, weeping over the body of the spy at his funeral while members of the KGB's border guard stand by.

Philby's tombstone

AN ENGLISHMAN was laid to rest with full military ceremony yesterday: in the dappled sunlight of a Soviet cemetery beneath firs and birches, those eternal emblems of the Russia he had so unswervingly served for the best part of his life.

In the end, Kim Philby's funeral was not the furtive private affair which would have seemed the suitable end to a career spent in the shadows. True, it had its intensely private moments, as his last wife Rufina bent for a full minute over the open coffin to press her face against his cheek.

But the Soviet Union sent one of its greatest spies out in style. Some 200 people came to the graveyard at Kunstyevo, on the western fringes of Moscow. A contingent of 13 uniformed border guards, part of the KGB for which Philby had worked since the 1930s, lined the path as the cortège went by, and fired off a salvo of three shots as the body was laid to rest.

Philby, who was 76, is understood to have died in his sleep in the early hours of Wednesday, after being taken to hospital a fortnight earlier. For two days his body lay in state at the KGB club here.

But only now was the man who had been invisible for 25 years finally at last on show, laid out in a coffin lined with red silk inside and out. The body was clad in a jet-black jacket, a white shirt and a red tie. The rest was obscured beneath a mountain of red carnations and white lilies. Alongside stood nine men, each bearing on a small pink cushion a medal awarded to Philby by a grateful state.

The mourners at the 40-minute ceremony were not just a dozen relatives and friends from the Russian side, uneasily accompanied by a handful of his English family.

George Blake, now the last survivor of two generations of infamous British espionage in exile here, was not to be seen. But 200 others were. They had been swept out to the cemetery on a gentle hill six miles from the city centre in a great motorcade of black Volga limousines and yellow buses, dwarfing the hearse in their midst.

They were people of every age. Some were old, others unidentifiable but surely of the KGB, middle-aged men of a thousand clichés, in dark raincoats or just plain dark suits, shunning contact. And even a few British correspondents managed to get there after a cryptic tip-off, surest sign of all that someone on high did not intend the occasion to go unremarked.

Most striking of all, though, was the younger contingent — many of them not born when the most famous spy of all finally bolted from Beirut in January 1963. But on the brilliant May afternoon of his burial, the process began of turning a man virtually unknown here in his lifetime into a hero and a model for a new generation.

"Kim Philby was a legend," said a Komsomol member chosen to deliver one of the four brief funeral orations from a brown brick rostrum almost opposite the waiting grave where the body would be laid a few minutes later. "He spent much of his last years instructing us. He handed over his strength to us, he was a man of our times."

But some of the 100-odd other young people assembled by the authorities were less sure why they had come. "We were told on Thursday we should come today," said an impassive youth with a Komsomol badge in his lapel. "They said a famous Russian was being buried. He wrote a book once, didn't he — my secret something?"

And truly, Philby yesterday seemed Russian. The four English mourners, including his son John, stayed on the edge of the inner family group. Afterwards they left quickly, on their own. "You know I'm not talking to anyone," was all John Philby would say.

His feelings can only be imagined. A few moments before he had heard his father lauded for his "courage and exceptional qualities", for which the Soviet people would always be thankful. "The name of Philby," an orator declared, "will be linked for ever with Soviet intelligence."

But the speeches, often inaudible in the breeze, were soon over. Four of Philby's Russian relatives and friends walked forward to kiss the body. One, a woman in a blue jacket, wept almost uncontrollably. Then Rufina stepped forward again, to say her last farewell.

The carnations and lilies were re-arranged on the corpse. The band played solemn music and, as the sun disappeared behind a cloud to send a slight chill through the air, a gravedigger in khaki overalls and heavy boots nailed down the coffin's lid.

Then Philby was laid to rest. The three ceremonial shots rang out, and the band struck up to send the Soviet national anthem reverberating though the trees. One by one, the family stepped forward to scatter handfuls of soil upon the coffin. All was suddenly silence, broken only by the scraping of shovels on concrete.

A dozen huge wreaths were cast upon the mound of earth, bearing ribbons of red and white. "From his colleagues," said one. "To a dear husband from a loving wife," said another. "From the son and daughters," ran a third — that, too, in great gold Russian letters.

The band upped its tempo, a platoon of 17 guards marched away at a brisk goosestep. Rufina stayed a few moments, comforted by her family. Then everyone left: the colleagues, the young men from the Komsomol, followed slowly by the relatives and friends. The cemetery was still again.

The KGB general who was Britain's most notorious spy is buried by a path lined with the graves of top Soviet military officers. His neighbour is General Alexei Vladimirsky, who died just three days before Philby.

"He was a nice man, a charming man," said one of the Soviet family mourners, a smartly dressed woman in her sixties, who identified herself only as Irina. "I saw him quite often. He always spoke Russian badly, but I think he was happy here, up to the end." But she, too, like all except a very few, probably never knew the real Kim Philby.

LEFT: By the time of his death, Philby was being described as a 'dinosaur' who had anachronistically survived from the ideological disputes of the 1930s; yet his ghost still haunts the secret world of British intelligence. The paranoia he generated almost tore the secret services apart and all but ruined relations between British and American intelligence officers.

complexity, all common sense abandoned in the search for the most devious explanation of every incident. It was often forgotten that the Soviet penetration had in reality been an operation of great simplicity allied with high professionalism, depending heavily on the amateurism of British counter-intelligence for its success. The real answer to past mistakes was for MI5 and MI6 to discover a new professionalism of their own.

Historian Hugh Trevor-Roper described Philby and Maclean in their Moscow years as 'fossils of the past' – irrelevant relics of a dead era when an ideological commitment to the Soviet Union had seemed a rational option for intelligent and talented individuals. Yet the Cambridge espionage affair has remained the central experience in the history of the British intelligence services, a traumatic loss of innocence from which recovery has been partial and slow.

CHAPTER SIX

THE NEW PROFESSIONALS

ABOVE RIGHT: Sir Percy Sillitoe, the 'honest copper' put in charge of MI5 at the end of World War II. Sillitoe was given a hard time by his subordinates who thought him lacking in flair and imagination.

RIGHT: Dick White, generally regarded as the most brilliant British counter-intelligence officer of the postwar era, had the unusual distinction of becoming successively head of both MI5 and MI6. He epitomised the new professionalism that supplanted the amateur spirit in British intelligence after 1945.

For the British during World War II, the intelligence alliance with the United States involved a simple trade-off. British intelligence had experience but limited resources; the Americans could command almost limitless resources but had little experience. So the British would teach the Americans everything they knew, and in return the United States would provide funding and manpower. When this temporary wartime deal was extended into a permanent peacetime alliance, however, its logic pointed to the long-term dominance of American influence over British intelligence.

This was most apparent in the biggest post-war intelligence growth area, sigint (signals intelligence). Britain's sigint alliance with Washington was formalized in the 1947 UKUSA agreement which also included Australia, New Zealand and Canada (it was later extended to embrace all members of the Nato alliance). The agreement created a worldwide system of listening posts and laid the basis for an explosion of high-technology computer analysis and interception systems. With all its wartime experience, GCHQ, first at Eastcote and then at its present Cheltenham base, was originally the dominant partner, but NSA had the funding and the technology. As the costs of this hi-tech system tended to increase dramatically and Britain fell desperately short of cash, the United States quickly took over the leading role. In 1954 Britain had to fight off an American attempt to take over the running of GCHQ and eventually it was only able to stay in the game by offering NSA facilities in Britain in lieu of a financial stake.

Contrary to some expectations, however, the monitoring of all communications worldwide did not make other forms of intelligence activity irrelevant. Interception on a massive scale and the storing and analysis of material by vast computer banks was not often accompanied by the cracking of enemy codes. So most questions about Soviet intentions and activities remained unanswered, and traditional patterns of intelligence gathering and counter-intelligence, using agents on the ground, continued to flourish. Here the British hoped they could still teach the Americans a thing or two.

MI5 and MI6 had a very mixed record in the first two decades after the war, but in general terms both organizations certainly became more professional and sophisticated than they had been before 1939. There was a marked change in personnel: the old guard of Indian policemen and retired army and navy officers, like Claude Dansey, Maxwell Knight and 'Tar' Robertson, faded from the scene and a new generation of university-educated non-military types rose to the top – men like the formidably intelligent Dick White, recruited in 1936; Martin Furnival Jones, a lawyer who had come into MI5 during the war; Peter Wright, a technical expert recruited in 1949; and Maurice Oldfield, who had not even been to public school and would probably have become an academic historian if the war had not drawn him into the Intelligence Corps. The two services also strove to create a genuine career structure. They were no longer to be staffed by officers and gentlemen living off a pension or a private income. Proper gradings and salaries were introduced with the all the normal financial security associated with government service. In this way, it was hoped, staff of the highest quality could be recruited.

Yet excessive secrecy still hampered this ambition. Unlike the CIA, the British intelligence services could not openly advertise posts that were vacant; after all, they were secret organizations. MI6 ended up recruiting many of its personnel among candidates for the Foreign Office who had failed their entrance examination. At least the Foreign Office was persuaded to accept the legitimacy of secret intelligence gathering as an activity, so the Passport Control Officer cover for MI6 station chiefs could be dropped. Like other intelligence services, MI6 was now able to conceal its officers as ordinary members of an embassy's diplomatic staff – first or second secretaries, for example.

From 1945 to 1951, MI5 had to work under a Labour government, always a potentially difficult situation for the security service. Suspicions were mutual – Labour had never forgotten the Zinoviev letter, perhaps unfairly blamed on MI5. In practice relations soon improved, when the government realised they were under attack from the political left and could use MI5 to counter communists and left-wing trade unionists. Initially, however, Prime Minister Clement Attlee felt the need to assure himself of MI5's loyalty by appointing an outsider to the post of director-general, which fell vacant on Sir David Petrie's retirement in 1946. Guy Liddell, the immensely experienced head of MI5's counter-espionage division, was the obvious candidate to succeed Petrie, but Attlee chose instead a senior Chief Constable, Percy Sillitoe, to fill the post.

Liddell was made deputy director, but he and his colleagues did not take at all kindly to being put under the control of a rather average police officer. Sillitoe was admitted to be an 'honest copper' but dismissed as a 'plodder'. The more intellectual of his subordinates would take delight in confusing him by swapping Latin epigrams or making private allusions he could not understand. Sillitoe later wrote: 'On occasions I felt like a small boy unwillingly let into a prefects pow-wow . . .', an image that admirably captures both Sillitoe's own lack of natural authority and the element of childishness that was a feature of MI5 and MI6 alike.

It was probably a relief to Sillitoe as well as to his enemies inside MI5 when he retired in 1953. Once again, Liddell was passed over, however, this time in favour of Dick White. The defection of his friend Burgess had ruined Liddell's chances of the director-generalship. Once upon a time the friendship between the two men might have been overlooked, but not in the tighter security atmosphere that resulted from the Fuchs case and the Burgess-Maclean affair. MI5

was busy overseeing the introduction of 'positive vetting' in all sensitive areas of government service. This required everyone with regular access to highly classified material to demonstrate their suitability for security clearance. It was, unfortunately, a most unsophisticated procedure, relying almost entirely on self-confession since there was no provision for security officers actually to go out and check statements made. Still, under the circumstances Liddell could hardly be made director-general. He retired to the post of Security Adviser to the Atomic Energy Authority.

White introduced a new structure for MI5, replacing the old 'Divisions' with 'Branches'. Counter-espionage had always been the responsibility of B Division, but now this became D Branch. Most other letter designations remained unchanged. Probably the busiest section of MI5 during the 1950s was E Division/Branch, responsible for operations overseas – that is, in Britain's shrinking Empire. It participated in countering campaigns of subversion and guerrilla warfare in Malaya, Borneo, Kenya and Cyprus. Malaya was the most striking success. Until 1952, it was widely felt that lack of good intelligence was a serious weakness of the counter-insurgency campaign, but the appointment of Arthur Martin, one of MI5's rising stars, to Kuala Lumpur completely reversed the situation. The defeat of the communist insurgency within the next three years is generally put down to first-rate intelligence directing the security forces' efforts. The experience of these colonial wars later much influenced MI5's response to the Northern Ireland crisis in the 1970s.

About the same time that Dick White took over MI5, Sir Stewart Menzies retired and was replaced as head of MI6 by Major General John 'Sinbad' Sinclair, a former Director of Military Intelligence. Sinclair's brief reign as 'C' has since become known in the service, a little unfairly, as the 'horrors'. One source of MI6's setbacks at this time was an over-eager enthusiasm for covert operations of all kinds, including subversion and assassination. This was nothing new – under Menzies MI6 had joined the CIA in futile attempts to subvert communist governments in eastern Europe – but some of the schemes were wilder and more over-optimistic than ever before.

It was perhaps unfortunate that MI6 was first encouraged by a singular success. In Iran a popular nationalist leader, Mohammed Mossadegh, had become prime minister in 1951 and was seeking to nationalize the most powerful economic

OPPOSITE PAGE: During the 1950s, MI5 was heavily involved in counter-insurgency campaigns in Britain's colonies. In Malaya (top), MI5 officer Arthur Martin introduced new intelligence methods that turned the tide against Chinese communist guerrillas. In Cyprus (bottom), sophisticated intelligence techniques led to the capture of many EOKA fighters.

BELOW: Mohammed Mossadegh (right), the popular Iranian nationalist, who was overthrown in a coup masterminded by MI6 and the CIA in 1953.

ABOVE: Egyptian nationalist leader Gamal Abdul Nasser, regarded by the British government as a serious threat to British interests in the Middle East. MI6 even concocted a plot to assassinate Nasser using nerve gas, but it was never carried out.

force in the country, the British-owned Anglo-Iranian Oil Company. Sir Winston Churchill, back at 10 Downing Street after the 1951 elections, wanted to oust Mossadegh by whatever means. Once the American government had been persuaded that Mossadegh was a communist threat, a joint MI6/CIA operation was mounted to restore effective power to the pro-Western Shah. MI6 provided a network of agents inside Iran, built up through a lot of painstaking effort; the CIA supplied two million dollars and quantities of arms. In August 1953, after a masterly campaign of covertly-funded propaganda and straightforward bribery, Mossadegh was duly overthrown by army leaders in the pay of Western intelligence. Kim Roosevelt, responsible for the CIA side of the operation, claimed all of the credit, but MI6's leading contribution was well recognized by the Shah, who always subsequently maintained close links with British intelligence.

When other popular nationalist leaders emerged in Syria and Egypt MI6 was tempted to try covert action again. This suited the British government, which was trying to maintain its worldwide influence with woefully inadequate resources; covert action held out the tempting prospect of cheap victories. The plan for subversion of Syria was so far-fetched, requiring MI6 to orchestrate combined action by Turkey, Iraq and Lebanese Christians, that it stood no chance of realization. The plots against Egypt's Gamal Abdul Nasser, who was threatening British control of the Suez canal, came closer to execution. The CIA was not interested in helping unseat Nasser, but MI6 found an ally in Mossad, the newly formed Israeli intelligence service that was already building up a formidable reputation for skill and ruthlessness.

One conspiracy against Nasser was built up through the recruitment of the head of Egyptian air force intelligence, Mahmoud Khalil, as a double agent. He agreed to organize a group of officers to mount a coup and restore the Egyptian monarchy; as a cover, MI6 fed him with scraps of Israeli secrets to pass on to his customers. In all Khalil was paid around £150,000, but he was not in the last resort prepared to play MI6's game. He eventually betrayed the whole plot to Nasser, along with the complete network of MI6 agents in Egypt.

Another scheme was for an MI6 agent to assassinate Nasser. This idea may have originated with Churchill's successor as prime minister, Sir Anthony Eden. It certainly had his approval. The Porton Down weapons research establishment was experimenting with nerve gasses, drugs and poisons, and it was there that, according to Peter Wright, MI6 sought a tool for the assassination. One of their agents was to introduce nerve gas into the ventilation system at Nasser's headquarters, an act that would undoubtedly have caused appalling casualties. Fortunately the assassina-

BELOW: The conspiracy between Britain, France and Israel to attack Egypt in 1956 provoked widespread protests in Britain and incurred the wrath of the United States. The British government would have preferred to overthrow Nasser by less costly covert action.

Commander Lionel 'Buster' Crabb (above, centre) was a very experienced, if ageing, diver in 1956 when MI6 employed him to inspect the hull of the Soviet cruiser *Ordzhonikidze* in Portsmouth harbour. His disappearance caused a public scandal (right) and led to the resignation of 'Sinbad' Sinclair as head of MI6. What exactly happened to Crabb has never been divulged.

tion plan was cancelled when Eden agreed a combined Anglo-French-Israeli military operation against Egypt instead.

The Nasser assassination plot still did MI6 harm, since Foreign Secretary Selwyn Lloyd was one of the last to hear about it and, assuming Eden could not have authorized such an action, he believed the secret service had taken leave of its senses. What finally sank MI6's reputation, and 'Sinbad' Sinclair with it, however, was the Commander Crabb affair. In April 1956 the Soviet leaders Khrushchev and Bulganin paid a state visit to Britain, landing at Portsmouth aboard the cruiser Ordzhonikidze. The Admiralty was exceptionally keen to know more about this particular ship and asked MI6 to carry out a clandestine survey of the hull underwater. Nicholas Elliott, head of MI6 London Station, accepted responsibility for the mission and entrusted its execution to Commander Lionel 'Buster' Crabb, a veteran frogman well past his prime. Inspecting the hull in Portsmouth harbour should have been a fairly simple task for an experienced diver, yet something went disastrously wrong. Crabb simply vanished; a decapitated corpse was later fished out of the sea, but it was never conclusively established whether this was him or not.

Once it was clear Crabb was not going to return, MI6 London Station contacted MI5 and a damage limitation operation was attempted. MI5 instructed Portsmouth police to visit the hotel where Crabb had been staying and rip out the pages of the visitor's book listing his name alongside that of the MI6 officer accompanying him. But it was to no avail. The Soviets leaked the story to the British press and the Prime Minister was obliged to admit to parliament that the operation had indeed taken place, promising that those responsible would be disciplined. A hurried inquiry reached very unfavourable conclusions about Sinclair's leadership of MI6. The government was convinced that the secret intelligence service needed bringing firmly to heel.

Casting around for a powerful and trust-

Daily Mirror
THURS MAY 10 1956
2D FORWARD WITH THE PEOPLE
No. 16,301

'What was done was done without the authority or the knowledge of Her Majesty's Ministers'—SIR ANTHONY EDEN IN THE COMMONS YESTERDAY

THE FROGMAN BLUNDER

MPs certain it was a Secret Service job

By **WILLIAM GREIG**

ONE guarded sentence by the Prime Minister was taken by M.P.s last night as indicating that the Secret Service DID send frogman Commander Lionel Crabb to Portsmouth, where he made his death dive near the Russian cruiser Ordzhonikidze.

The sentence was spoken during dramatic Commons exchanges on the mysterious disappearance of the frogman during the visit of Marshal Bulganin and Mr. Krushchev.

Sir Anthony Eden, who was being pressed to go beyond the statement he had just made, declared:

"There are certain issues which are the responsibility of the Prime Minister himself."

The only issue which is exclusively one for the Prime Minister and to which the doctrine of Cabinet responsibility does not apply is the work of the various branches of the Secret Service.

Even Ministers whose departments are directly concerned rarely know of its work.

'Not in Public Interest' to Tell

The Premier told M.P.s that it would not be in the public interest to disclose the circumstances in which Commander Crabb is presumed to have met his death.

He said that "what was done was done without the authority or the knowledge of Her Majesty's Ministers," and that "appropriate disciplinary steps" were being taken.

The circumstances of Commander Crabb's disappearance, and the fact that Earl Mountbatten, the First Sea Lord, lunched with Sir Anthony Eden yesterday, are taken as an indication that it was the naval "cloak and dagger men" who were involved, and that it is one or more of them who will be affected by the "disciplinary steps."

I understand that the report which the Prime Minister called for after Commander Crabb's disappearance has not been circulated with the usual Cabinet papers, and that Sir Anthony's colleagues on the front bench were as much in the dark as the back-benchers pressing for information.

Labour May Try to Force Debate

Labour M.P.s who vigorously protested in the House yesterday about the Premier's attitude, were last night discussing means of raising the question again in the hope of getting more information.

One suggestion before the Party leaders was a motion to cut the Premier's salary by £100 — a technical device to force a debate on the issue.

M.P.s are convinced that THE PRIME MINISTER IS AWARE OF WHAT HAPPENED TO COMMANDER CRABB AND THAT IF THE WHOLE STORY WERE TOLD HIS DEATH WOULD BE MORE DEFINITE THAN THE OFFICIAL "PRESUMED."

Reading between the lines of the Prime Minister's statement, M.P.s believe that three other puzzling points have been cleared up:

1—That no foreign Power was involved, or any anti-Russian group in this country.

2—That Commander Crabb was not, as had been suggested in some quarters, engaged on anti-espionage to protect the Soviet ship, otherwise this could have been disclosed.

3—That he was not acting on his own responsibility or on the orders of some minor official, as the police in this case would not have been so speedy in attempting to destroy evidence of his stay in Portsmouth.

"DISCIPLINARY STEPS BEING TAKEN," SAYS EDEN—SEE PAGE 4.

CRABB IN ACTION

THE picture shows Commander Crabb, G.M., in frogman's kit during one of his missions as a Naval diver.

IF he had dived for a close-up look at the Russian cruiser Ordzhonikidze at Portsmouth, what would he have discovered? Here are three theories—

1. He might have seen highly secret radar instruments for detecting submarines.

2. He might have examined equipment for launching underwater guided weapons.

3. He might have found out, with a special detector, whether the ship was carrying an A-bomb. This is unlikely, as Russian leaders were on board.

Advertiser's Announcement

MAKE REAL *Home-Made Cakes* WITH

GREEN'S SPONGE MIXTURE

The High-Quality ingredients to a Famous Recipe are already weighed and carefully blended for you — and for REAL HOME MADE GOODNESS you add your own Eggs.

Try a packet to-day —

It's easy and quick to make and you are sure to become a satisfied and regular user.

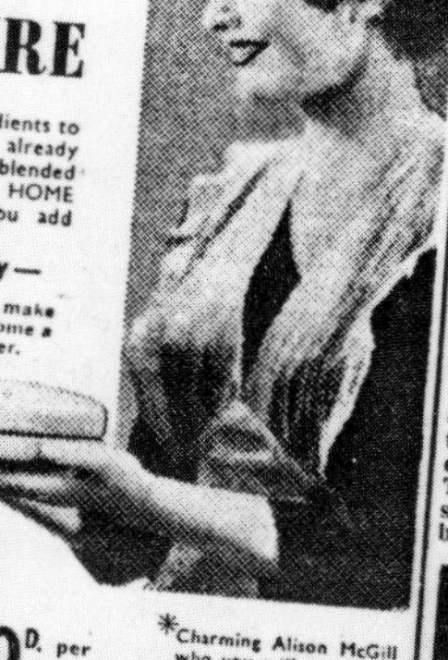

Green's SPONGE MIXTURE

10D. per packet

Chocolate Flavour 11½d.

*Charming Alison McGill who you will see in the Green's Sponge Mixture Film "RISE TO THE OCCASION" at Cinemas throughout Britain.

H. J. GREEN & CO. LTD. BRIGHTON, ENGLAND

WHAT THE 'MIRROR' SAYS—

THE BIG COVER-UP

See Page Two

worthy intelligence officer to replace Sinclair, the Defence Cabinet decided to move Dick White across from MI5. To those steeped in the traditional rivalry between the two services, White's appointment as director-general of MI6 was the ultimate humiliation for the secret intelligence service. Yet in the end MI6 got the better of the deal. White was probably the outstanding counter-intelligence officer of his generation and there was no one of quite the same calibre available in MI5 to replace him. Roger Hollis, White's deputy, was promoted to the director-generalship; apparently a bland administrator, he was to prove the most controversial figure in the history of MI5.

BELOW: George Blake, the Soviet spy who worked for MI6 in Berlin during the 1950s. He is thought to have betrayed about 40 Western agents operating in East European countries.

MI5's loss was MI6's gain. White immediately laid down some new ground rules. All operations would be tightly controlled to avoid fiascos of the Crabb variety. There would be no more assassination plots. MI6 was in the business of intelligence-gathering and analysis, not the subversion of foreign governments through covert action. Thus the British secret service turned back from a path down which the CIA continued merrily to wander through the years ahead. What White could do nothing about was the legacy of Soviet penetration he inherited. Philby had already been re-engaged by Sinclair and sent to Beirut; White was sure of Philby's guilt, but he could not dismiss him again without re-opening the old wound. Another Soviet agent, George Blake, was also operating inside MI6 and would remain undiscovered until 1960.

On the whole, MI5's performance against its main opponent, the Soviet Union, was not especially impressive in the 1950s. The Venona codebreaks had put them on to Fuchs and Maclean, but then that source dried up. The painstaking rituals of counter-intelligence produced little result for enormous effort. The MI5 'watchers' probably had the most laborious task. There were over a hundred of them, keeping the embassies of the Soviet Union and its east European allies under constant visual surveillance and shadowing selected embassy staff around London by car or on foot. Since all the embassies maintained large staffs, many of whom were working for their government's intelligence services, the number of watchers was never adequate. Any unknown person entering or leaving an embassy was photographed and the photo was passed on to the Registry for identification. By co-operation with other Western intelligence agencies, it was possible to build up a complete picture of the movement of Soviet and east European diplomats around the world. This procedure was unlikely to lead to any sensational leads, however. For running its most sensitive agents, the KGB habitually used 'illegals' – officers operating under cover of assumed identities, having no direct contact with any official Soviet body or communist organization. And in any case, the watchers' procedures were undoubtedly well known to the other side.

The long-established tradition of mail intercepts and telephone tapping suffered from the same drawback: the practice was so widely known that no Soviet agent would be caught out by it, although the same was not true of some left-wing British organizations that might not realize they had been

ABOVE: East German officers take Western journalists on a guided tour of the CIA/MI6 Berlin spy tunnel. The tunnel was at the time thought to be an intelligence triumph for the West, allowing them to listen in to supposedly secure landline communications between East Berlin and Moscow. But it is now known that George Blake had told the Russians of the tunnel's existence from the very start.

defined as 'subversive', or might believe they were protected by civil liberties.

In the post-war period both MI5 and MI6 put considerable effort into technical developments, and apart from producing the odd James Bond-style offensive device (the cigarette packet that fires a poisoned dart), they vastly improved the art of bugging. Embassies were once more the focus of attack. Since microphones could now be successfully implanted in walls or window-frames, an embassy under construction or repair could have bugging devices built in. Some MI5 staff became very used to donning white overalls and posing as decorators. If an embassy or consulate was in a terrace, MI5 might gain access – legally or illegally – to the building next door and embed microphones in the party wall. Telephones were also a vulnerable point. The telephone service could be asked deliberately to 'fault' a phone; when the user complained, the repair men sent round would be MI5 operatives, equipped with tiny 'Special Facilities' microphones to conceal in the handset. Peter Wright has described how it was even possible to use a telephone bug for codebreaking. At the time of Suez, Wright and his colleagues placed a device in a telephone next to the enciphering machine in the Egyptian embassy. By listening to the cipher clerk preparing the machine each morning, GCHQ cryptographers were able to work out the day's setting and break into the Egyptian code.

Naturally, Soviet counter-intelligence was as aware of the new potential for bugging as they were of more traditional intelligence techniques. The Egyptians might fall for such ploys, but the Russians were altogether tougher material to crack. They'swept' their embassies electronically to reveal hidden transmitters and were unrelentingly thorough in their general security procedures. The one occasion when Western intelligence really thought they had caught the Soviets out, with the famous 'Berlin tunnel', turned out in retrospect to be more of an own goal.

The tunnel was a joint CIA/MI6 operation to tap the landline communications linking the Soviet military command in Berlin with Moscow. The CIA put up around £25 million to cover the cost of construction, while MI6 took responsibility for actually installing the electronic taps on the Soviet cables. When it was completed in April 1955, the tunnel stretched about 500 metres from the American sector out under the Soviet sector of the city. MI6 sent in Post Office engineers to apply the taps. The intercepts were on such a vast scale that they swamped the Western intelligence agencies' facilities for transcription and analysis. The recorded material was either flown to the United States or to Britain, where an army of Russian emigres was employed to transcribe it. Although the tunnel only functioned for just under a year, the emigres were still working their way through the recordings seven years later.

BELOW: Soviet officers reveal to the assembled pack of Western journalists, the exact positions where the communication cables had been tapped.

In April 1956, Soviet security officers broke into the eastern end of the tunnel, sealed it off from the American side and invited journalists in to inspect this example of perfidious Western behaviour. Coming at the same moment as the Commander Crabb affair, there was some embarrassment in this for MI6, but on the whole the tunnel was still judged to have been a major success. Unfortunately, aiding MI6 Berlin station chief Peter Lunn in this operation was a fluent Russian speaker, officially the station's deputy director of technical operations, George Blake. Since Blake was a Soviet agent, the KGB will have known about the tunnel from the very start. All the messages sent along the landline must either have been cleared by Soviet intelligence as anodyne or deliberately planted as disinformation.

Blake came from a very unusual background for an MI6 officer. He was born in Holland and his mother was Dutch, but his father was an Egyptian Jew with a British passport (Blake's original family name was Behar). During the war Blake fought with the Dutch resistance and then escaped to Britain, where he served as a lieutenant in Naval Intelligence. In 1947 he was recruited by MI6 and given a crash course in Russian, preparatory to a posting overseas. Exactly when he became a Soviet agent has never been made clear, but it may be significant that he spent some time working alongside Guy Burgess in the Foreign Office Far Eastern Department, before being sent to join the MI6 station in Seoul, South Korea, in September 1948. Along with all other British diplomats in Seoul he was taken prisoner when the North Koreans captured the city in 1950. It was once asserted that Blake became a communist through 'brainwashing' during his three years in North Korean hands, but this is now generally discounted (the once notorious Korean 'brainwashing' techniques in fact consisted mostly of classes and lectures on the Marxist version of history and society, which were embarrassingly successful with the less educated American POWs). One of Blake's cousins was a founder member of the Egyptian Communist Party in the 1930s, and it is most probable that his own communist beliefs dated from the same period.

It was in 1955, after a rest to recuperate from his Korean experience, that Blake was posted to Berlin, the spy capital of the world. Nowhere were contacts between

ABOVE: George Blake (extreme left) photographed with other released prisoners on his return from a North Korean PoW camp in 1953. It was once believed that Blake became a double agent after brainwashing by the North Koreans, but in reality it seems certain that his communist sympathies dated back to before the war.

East and West more fluid; agents, double-agents and triple-agents filtered back and forth across the sector boundaries. Blake was able to pass on to Soviet intelligence copies of almost every secret document that came into his hands. He is reckoned to have betrayed more than 40 Western agents operating in eastern Europe. According to some versions of the story, MI6 actually knew of Blake's contacts with the other side but thought he was working an elaborate double-cross, feeding disinformation to his Soviet contacts in return for genuine intelligence. Instead, it was the other way round.

Blake's eventual downfall was due not to the immensely expensive efforts of NSA/GCHQ, hi-tech bugging devices or routine surveillance. Like most MI5 and MI6 successes of the 1960s, it resulted from a deliberate offer of information to the West by an intelligence operative from the East. This was the one simple move in the intelligence game against which neither side appeared to have any defence: straightforward betrayal from within.

The man who pointed the finger at Blake was a senior officer in Polish military intelligence, Michael Goleniewski, who first contacted the CIA in 1959. Initially known to Western intelligence only by the codename 'Heckenschutze' ('sniper' in German), he gave his CIA case officer, Harry Roman, an impressive amount of detailed information that quickly established his credibility beyond any reasonable doubt. In December 1960 Goleniewski defected in West Berlin with his mistress and was flown off to the United States for a lengthy debriefing. Like so many defectors, he proved to be a very strange character – he firmly believed that he was the last of the Romanov dynasty and the rightful Tsar of Russia – but his information was never seriously faulted.

One of Goleniewski's first revelations, passed on by Roman to MI5 and MI6 in April 1959, concerned a Soviet agent operating inside British intelligence. The Poles had copies of MI6 internal documents that could only have come from a double agent in either the Berlin or Warsaw stations. As so often before, however, MI6 was extremely reluctant to admit that it could have been penetrated. All suspects in Berlin and Warsaw, including Blake, were investigated and given a clean bill of health. On rather flimsy grounds, it was assumed the internal documents had been stolen from a burgled MI6 safe in Brussels. There the matter

DAILY EXPRESS

THURSDAY MAY 4 1961 — No. 18,952 — Weather: Showery; bright spells — Price 3d.

42 years' jail: Now the big question: How did Blake work on undetected?

SPY UPROAR EXPLODES

Vast security shake-up on way as MPs protest

By PERCY HOSKINS, DOUGLAS CLARK and ARNOLD LATCHAM

THE nine years of treachery of George Blake, the Foreign Office man sentenced yesterday to an unprecedented 42 years' imprisonment, will set off a tremendous shake-up in the British Intelligence services—and an uproar at Westminster.

For Blake did more damage to Western security and strategy than the diplomats Burgess and Maclean and the naval spies Lonsdale and the Krogers put together.

M.P.s were dismayed last night at the implications of the case. Mr. Macmillan is expected to make a statement on it today.

The Prime Minister is sure to stonewall, saying that in the interests of national security he cannot go into details. That is not likely to satisfy M.P.s, even if heavy pressure is brought on them.

The questions

They want the answer to two questions: 1. How did Blake carry on spying undetected for nine years? 2. What is going to be done about Blake's superiors?

Mr. Richard Marsh (Lab., Greenwich) is first with a question on the Order Paper. He wants Mr. Macmillan to say if he will set up an inquiry.

There is already one inquiry in session—the three-man committee set up under Sir Charles Romer to inquire into the Navy secrets case. But this is not constituted to investigate security weaknesses in the Foreign Office.

The Prime Minister may agree to set up a separate inquiry for this purpose. He is now considering what he can say in Parliament to ease public alarm.

The Labour Front Bench, however, is unlikely to take the matter up as a means of criticising the Government as it did with the Navy case.

Mr. George Brown, the Labour deputy leader, said last night: "I do not propose to raise the matter publicly because of what I understand about the nature of the case. But clearly we shall have to have consultations with the Government."

The sentence

The shutters went up on the glass-panelled swing doors of Court No. 1 at the Old Bailey at 10.40 yesterday. And 59 minutes later, when the court was reopened after a secret sitting, 38-year-old George Blake stood before Lord Parker, the Lord Chief Justice, to await sentence as a spy and traitor.

In a dark grey suit, sober check shirt, and blue tie with red spots, he seemed impassive. His soft blue eyes were steady as Lord Parker began a five-minute speech which ended with the 42-year sentence.

Blake's lips parted slightly at the sentence. Then, composure instantly regained, he turned with a faint smile to the cells below, with Lord Parker's words to remember.

The Lord Chief Justice said that what Blake gave away, "though not of a scientific nature," has "rendered much of this country's efforts completely useless."

"Indeed," he told Blake, "you have said in your confession that 'There was no official document of any importance to which I had access which was not passed to my Soviet contacts.'"

Worst

"When one realises that you are a British subject, albeit not by birth, and were throughout this period employed by your country in responsible positions of trust, it is clear that your case is akin to treason. It is the worst that can be envisaged other than in time of war."

Lord Parker said it was

PAGE TWO, COL. SIX

The nine-year spy—George Blake

POCKET CARTOON by OSBERT LANCASTER

"It looks to me as though the Betjeman of Amman is still stuck for a rhyme for 'Ipswich.'"

DOCK STRIKE ENDS ... WITHOUT GLORY

By TREVOR EVANS

LONDON'S dock strike, which ended yesterday, created more problems than it solved. No one got out of it with glory.

MR. FRANK COUSINS, chief of the Transport Workers' Union, has, say the strike leaders, committed himself to demanding an inquiry.

Yet all the cautious Mr. Cousins promised was that he would "examine the problem."

He advised the men to go back to work "in order that they should allow the constitutional machinery of the union to function."

This is precisely the line he took nearly a week ago. But it was ignored until yesterday.

MR. HARRY WILLCOCKS, the strike committee chairman, threatened yesterday that if the inquiry is not carried out, "we will immediately inform you by calling the requisite mass meetings."

A truce?

This implied that today's return to work is just a truce, and the strike has been merely adjourned.

But the strike leaders became acutely conscious in the last two days that an increasing number of the 15,000 men out were eager to get back to work. A formula for settlement had to be found to avoid a drift back.

But there is likely to be a "jungle fight" to find jobs on the docks this morning.

More than 1,200 dockers were without jobs in the Royal group alone when the strike started. Now many of the ships that were being worked have left for the Continent.

One docks official estimated last night that there may be 3,500 to 4,000 unemployed until the port "settles down" again.

Oysters saved

MERCY NOTE.—Half a million oysters from Portugal, which for 24 hours had been dying of thirst at the London Docks, were unloaded by 30 volunteers yesterday—after an appeal by the Royal Society for the Prevention of Cruelty to Animals.

The oysters arrived at Butley Creek, Orford, Suffolk, last night, and were dumped in the creek by a small army of village volunteers.

Major's wife on theft charge

Mrs. Elizabeth Hill, wife of Major Clement Hill, of Queen Hoo Hall, Tewin, Herts, will appear at Hertford court today accused of stealing goods worth 7s. 7d. from a self-service store.

Major Hill, whose sixteenth-century manor house is open to the public at week-ends, said last night: "She will defend the case, of course."

THE FULL, FANTASTIC STORY OF GEORGE BLAKE, SPY FOR RUSSIA, BEGINS ON PAGE 4

BAN-BOMB SWITCH BY ENGINEERS?

By JOHN GRANT

ON the eve of its vital defence debate, the 1,000,000-strong Amalgamated Engineering Union, long considered certain to reaffirm its ban-the-bomb policy, last night showed signs of a remarkable shift of opinion which could crack the unilateralists within both the union and the Labour Party.

"Unity" has become the key word as tension mounts.

The shopworkers' decision on Tuesday to renounce unilateralism in favour of the compromise plan has had startling effect on the 52 engineering delegates at Eastbourne.

The pro-Gaitskell men, despondent when they assembled 10 days ago, now believe they have a great chance of reversing last year's 38—14 defeat.

Unity plea

Even the powerful Communist faction concedes reluctantly that the switch of a single vote may prove conclusive.

And an appeal today for party unity made by Mr. George Pargiter, A.E.U.-sponsored M.P. for Southall, has added to the hope that though Mr. Gaitskell's line is unlikely to be favoured, the engineers will join the shopworkers to sink Mr. Cousins's unilateralist supporters and call for a compromise.

Defeat at Eastbourne would be the death knell for the unilateralists' hopes of keeping their hold on next October's party conference.

Six boys drowned

NEW YORK, Wednesday.—A 96-ft. sailing ship used as a floating school for American boys was wrecked by a storm in the Gulf of Mexico yesterday, and six of the boys trapped below deck were drowned.

The 93-ton Albatross went down in about a minute, but 13 crewmen, several of them teenagers, succeeded in lowering lifeboats. They were picked up by the 990-ton cargo ship Gran Rio, which is bringing them to Tampa, Florida.—Express News Service.

Bridge fire cuts main line

Ten minutes after a "down" main railway line at Waterloo was cleared following a derailment yesterday morning, a fire on a bridge at Raynes Park, in South-west London, put the main "up" line out of service at 5.45 p.m. Trains were diverted and delays were only slight.

Date in space

CAPE CANAVERAL, Wednesday.—America's first astronaut will be launched into space on Friday, weather permitting.—B.U.P.

RANDOM CHECKS ON WINNERS

Doping: Racing gets a new charter

By CLIVE GRAHAM

PIGGOTT TOLD: IT'S A GIRL

AT RANDOM

REWARD

Among trainers who gave evidence was Sir Gordon Richards whose private inquiries last year brought the matter into the spotlight.

The Duke of Norfolk, whose horses are trained by Gordon Smyth at Arundel, suspected that slowing-up drugs were given to two of his horses, Skymaster and Red Letter, last summer.

A £1,000 reward was offered without avail for any information leading to the conviction of the culprits.

More details—Page 19

Jail-hunt police seek rifle

Police dogs tracking escaped prisoner Arthur Henry Graves switched yesterday to search for a rifle along the River Stour at Durweston, Dorset.

The rifle and ammunition vanished from a shed in the grounds of Portman Lodge, the home of Mrs. Michael Portman, sister-in-law of Lord Portman. Graves, 23-year-old Londoner, escaped from Dorchester Prison on Sunday.

Murder police quiz 7,000

Detectives have visited 7,000 houses in their hunt for the killer of 18-year-old Marion Locke in Blaise Castle Woods, Bristol, a week ago. But they report "little progress."

Last night police said: "We are almost certain that the girl's murderer was a local youth."

65 hurt in 'battle'

NICOSIA, Wednesday.—Sixty-five British soldiers were hurt, nine seriously, during the three-day "Fabulist" Army-R.A.F. exercise which ended in Cyprus yesterday.

JUST FANCY THAT

PASSENGERS on two buses in Brockley, London, watched a fight between the drivers yesterday. One of the men was taken to hospital with a broken leg. The fight is thought to have started because one bus trailed the other—letting the first bus collect all the passengers.

Germans fly in for arms talks

Express Staff Reporter

THREE planes bearing the black Iron Cross of the German Air Force landed yesterday at Manston in Kent, one of the famous Battle of Britain airfields.

LATEST

2 DIE IN WATER MAIN

WORLD CUP — Scotland 3, Eire 1

Hunt for driver

FLEet-street 8000

Salad magic!

Heinz of course

The trial of Blake was yet another embarrassment for MI6 (newspaper report, left). Given a record 42 year jail sentence, he served only five years, escaping from Wormwood Scrubs prison (right) by scaling the walls and jumping down onto the roof of a getaway car (below right).

rested until February 1961, when an accumulation of fresh evidence – including the arrest of one of Blake's main German agents as a Soviet spy – convinced Dick White that MI6 had indeed been penetrated yet again.

By this time, Blake had been posted to Beirut (where Philby was also stationed). White invited him to return to London in April to discuss promotion. The unsuspecting agent fell into the trap. The day after his arrival back in Britain he was interrogated, confessed and was formally charged. The judge at his trial astonished everyone by imposing a sentence of 42 years' imprisonment, the heaviest prison term in modern times.

Blake served only five years of his sentence. In October 1966 he escaped from Wormwood Scrubs prison by climbing the perimeter wall, using a nylon ladder reinforced with steel knitting needles. The fol-

ABOVE: After his escape from prison, George Blake resurfaced in Moscow where he joined the growing band of British spies-in-exile. He is photographed here with his wife and Mr and Mrs Philby enjoying an open-air meal at a dacha outside the Soviet capital. Philby later became godfather to Blake's son.

lowing year he surfaced in Moscow. This is all that is known for certain. An Irish petty criminal called Sean Bourke, a one-time fellow prisoner of Blake in the Scrubs, produced a number of elaborate and contradictory stories of how the escape was managed and of his own part in it, but the truth remains obscure. The KGB must have played a leading role and some observers think the Russians may have used the services of the IRA, with Bourke acting as a linkman – although given the decrepit state of the Irish Republican movement in the mid-1960s, it is hard to see how the IRA could have contributed to such a professional operation. Other reports have attributed the escape plan to left-wing members of the Campaign for Nuclear Disarmament (CND) who met Blake while serving short prison terms for civil disobedience. The only certainty is that Blake's escape was another humiliation for the British authorities, coming only three years after Philby had slipped through their fingers in Beirut. Once more the KGB had shown how it could be relied on to look after its operatives if they ran into trouble.

The unmasking of Blake as a Soviet agent did nothing to improve the public image of British intelligence – the fact that he had operated undiscovered for so long outweighed the fact that he had eventually been caught. But another of Goleniewski's leads opened up a case which could be presented to the public as a notable success, even if the inside story was less clear-cut. Goleniewski said that the Soviets had recruited an Englishman working in Warsaw in the early 1950s. His name began with 'H' and his present employment had some connection with the navy. MI5 soon identified a man who fitted this description – Harry Houghton, an employee at the Underwater Weapons Establishment, Portland. The Registry files revealed, to MI5's acute embarrassment, that Houghton had already been denounced some years earlier. His wife, embittered because her husband was having an affair with another woman, had informed security at Portland that he was making regular visits to London to meet an unidentified foreigner. An MI5 officer had rejected the report as worthless.

In the spring of 1960, Houghton was put under surveillance. The watchers soon struck gold. In July Houghton and his mistress Ethel Gee visited London and were observed exchanging packages with another man, identified as Gordon Lonsdale, a Canadian businessman. Lonsdale was living in a flat overlooking Regent's Park and enjoying a flash playboy lifestyle, with a plentiful supply of casual girlfriends. But it was soon established that he was in fact a Soviet 'illegal' in regular radio contact with Moscow. MI5 occupied the flat next door to Lonsdale's and put bugging devices in the party wall. The watchers kept him under visual surveillance.

In September Lonsdale left for a prolonged trip abroad. Before leaving, he locked a case in a Safe Deposit box at the Midland Bank in Great Portland Street. Armed with a search warrant, Special Branch visited the bank, emptied the box and delivered the case to MI5. To their delight, they found it contained a Soviet spy kit – miniature cameras, a secret writing device and, best of all, a Ronson cigarette lighter with a hollow base containing two tiny one-time code pads. The pads were unglued, every sheet copied, and then the whole thing meticulously stuck back together again, before the items were returned to the bank. GCHQ would henceforth be able to decipher all Lonsdale's radio communications with Moscow.

The operation was now being run by Arthur Martin, the head of D Branch's subsection for Soviet counter-espionage. Martin was worried that in some way Soviet intelligence had found out Lonsdale was blown and had withdrawn him to Moscow. But in mid-October the 'illegal' returned to London, although he did not immediately go back to his own flat. Instead, he lodged in a small suburban house in Cranleigh Drive, Ruislip. His hosts were a New Zealand couple, Peter and Helen Kroger, apparently antiquarian booksellers. The watchers established themselves in the front bedroom of a house opposite to maintain round-the-clock surveillance.

D Branch were convinced there must be a wider network of agents to be uncovered and held off as long as they could in the hope that another lead would eventually emerge. Once Goleniewski defected in December, however, Soviet intelligence was bound to realise Lonsdale was vulnerable. MI5 had to make its move. On 7 January, Special Branch arrested Lonsdale, Houghton and Gee outside the Old Vic theatre, just after secret documents were handed over in a carrier bag. Simulta-

The Portland spy ring: an ex-Royal Navy Master-at-Arms, Harry Houghton (left) was selling secrets on the Underwater Weapons Establishment, Portland, to the Soviets. His contact was KGB officer Konon Trofimovich Molody (above), living in London under a cover identity as Canadian playboy Gordon Lonsdale.

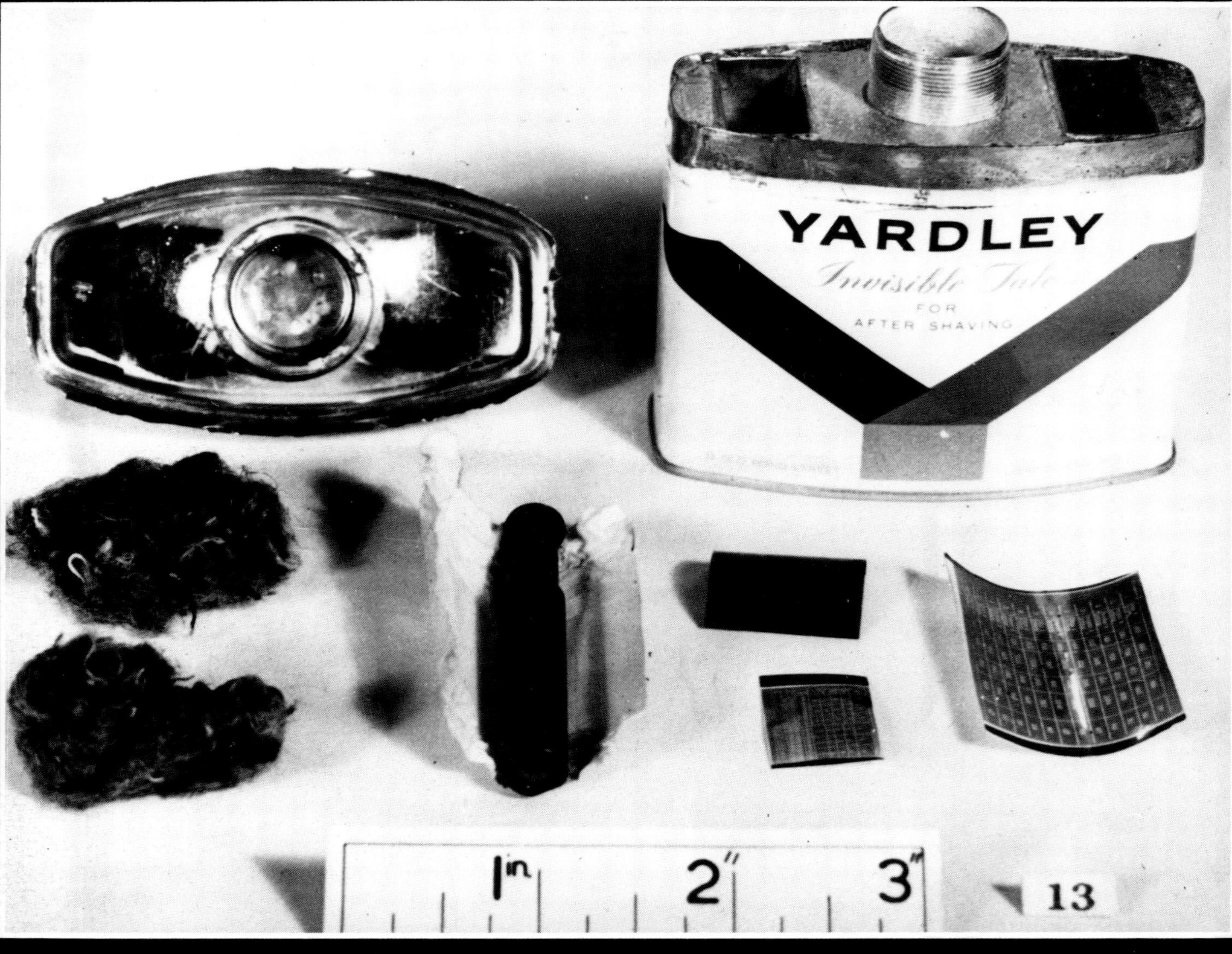
YARDLEY
Invisible Talc
FOR
AFTER SHAVING
1in.
2"
3"
13

Surveillance of Gordon Lonsdale led MI5 to a suburban house in Ruislip, Middlesex (left), the home of Peter and Helen Kroger. After the couple's arrest in January 1961, the house provided a treasure trove of Soviet espionage equipment for MI5 experts to examine, including a talcum powder tin (above left) used for concealing small items such as microfilm, and a shortwave radio transmitter found hidden in a hole under the kitchen floor (right). The Krogers (real names Morris and Lona Cohen) were released in a spy-swap in 1969 (above, leaving Heathrow airport).

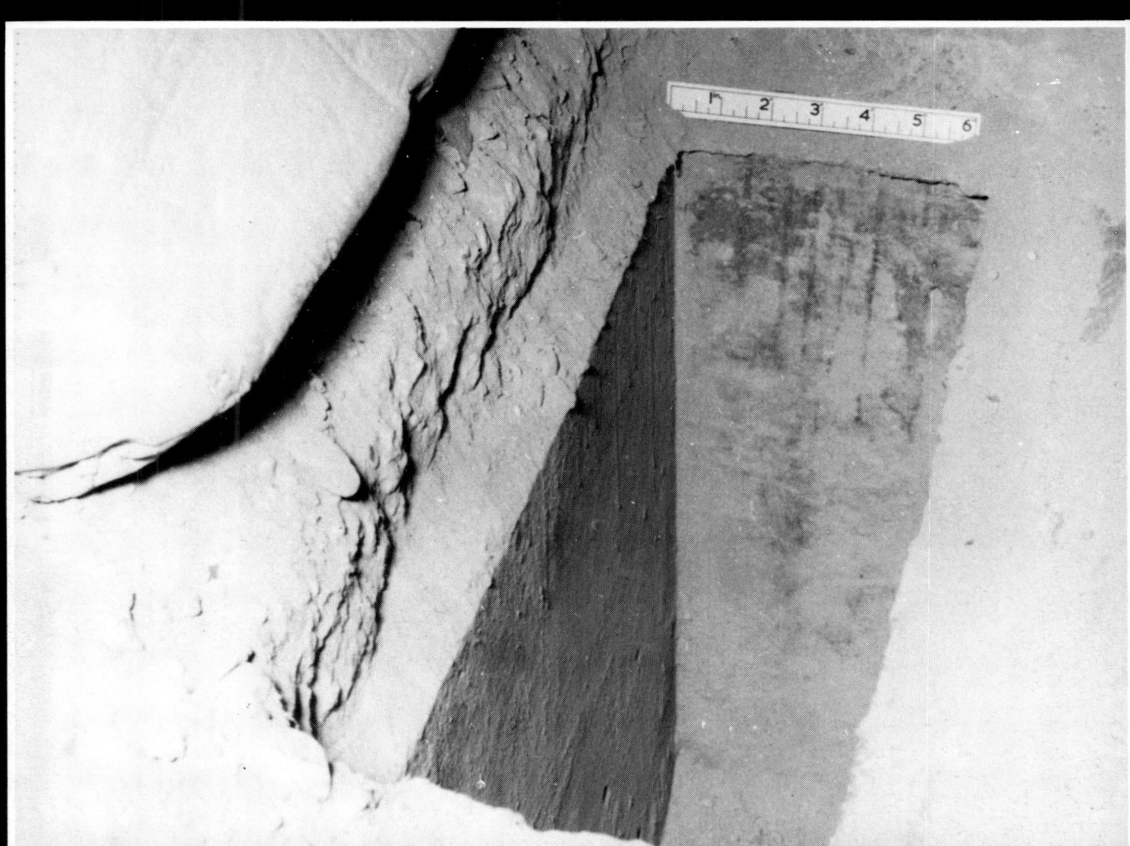

ABOVE: Oleg Penkovsky on trial in the Soviet Union in 1963. Penkovsky was either one of MI6's greatest espionage successes or a Soviet plant who completely fooled Western intelligence agencies.

neously, police raided the Krogers' house in Ruislip. It was a treasure-trove of espionage paraphernalia – false passports, microdot equipment, material for invisible writing. It was nine days before MI5 found the last hiding place, a cavity under the kitchen floor containing cameras and a high-speed radio transmitter (not quite the last hiding place, in fact, since another transmitter was dug up in the back garden 20 years later).

The FBI soon identified the Krogers as Morris and Lona Cohen, Americans who had formed part of Soviet spymaster Rudolf Abel's network in the United States in the 1940s. They had picked up their New Zealand identities somewhere after fleeing New York in 1950. Lonsdale's true identity took longer to establish. He was Konon Trofimovich Molody, a KGB officer who had also worked with Abel in North America.

The British press loved the 'Portland spy ring' story, especially the Ruislip angle, spicing the bland life of London suburbia with a dash of mystery and excitement. But some officers in MI5's D Branch, such as Arthur Martin and Peter Wright, were less than happy. It seemed impossible that Lonsdale and the Krogers had been running only one agent, Houghton. Why had no others been detected during such a lengthy surveillance? Studying the technical details of the case, they became convinced that the KGB must have known Lonsdale was blown from an early stage. But in that case, why was he sent back to London in October 1960 when he could have been safely in Moscow? They concluded that the KGB had 'discarded' Lonsdale and the Krogers to hide a more important asset – a Soviet 'mole' inside MI5. The credibility of the 'discard' theory increased when Lonsdale was 'spy-swapped' back to the Soviet Union in 1964 – the operation had cost the KGB the loss of an experienced officer for a mere three years.

In the early 1960s, MI6 also appeared to win a substantial victory in the spy war, although once again the true final score may have been quite different. The case of Oleg Penkovsky divided opinion in Western intelligence circles from the very start. Penkovsky was an officer in Soviet military intelligence, the GRU, working in Moscow. For reasons that were never convincingly explained, he was desperate to spy for the West. In 1960 he offered his services to the CIA with such fervour that they took him to be an obvious 'plant' and turned him down. He then took to approaching Western businessmen in Moscow, trying to persuade them to accept a package of state secrets that would prove his good faith. Eventually he lighted on Greville Wynne, a British businessman who was doing a bit of espionage for MI6 on the side. MI6 examined the material Penkovsky had to offer and decided he was worth taking on. They invited the CIA to come in on the case.

In April 1961, Penkovsky arrived in London as a member of a Soviet trade delegation. Over a period of more than a fortnight, whenever he was free of official duties, Penkovsky clandestinely met MI6 and CIA officers for exhaustive debriefing sessions. He handed over photographs of more than 10,000 secret documents, includ-

BELOW: Greville Wynne (second from left), the British businessman who provided the initial link between MI6 and Penkovsky. Wynne was arrested shortly after Penkovsky in 1962 while on a business trip behind the Iron Curtain. Here Wynne consults with his lawyers at the trial, which saw him receive an eight-year sentence.

ABOVE: Roderick Chisholm and his wife Janet face the cameras after Penkovsky revealed their role in controlling his espionage activities in Moscow. Since the KGB almost certainly knew Chisholm was working for MI6 and had observed his and his wife's contacts with Penkovsky, there seems little doubt they must have been aware he was handing over secrets.

ing technical details of the latest Soviet missile systems, and listed all GRU officers operating under diplomatic cover in Britain. Penkovsky made several more visits to the West in the course of the year, during which the debriefing routine was repeated. He was also assigned an MI6 controller in Moscow, Roderick Chisholm. At first Chisholm's wife acted as courier, receiving packages from Penkovsky in Moscow parks or at diplomatic functions. Later Penkovsky resorted to a more secure system of dead-letter drops, leaving material to be picked up in a pre-arranged spot, never using the same place twice.

Western intelligence considered Penkovsky's information to be of the highest possible quality. Most importantly, it seemed to show that the Soviet Union was far behind the United States in the development and deployment of nuclear missile systems. This totally contradicted most previous American estimates of the nuclear balance, which had credited the Soviets with a substantial lead – the so-called 'missile gap'. It is generally accepted that Penkovsky had a major impact on American decision-making during the Cuban missile crisis in October 1962, which brought the world to the brink of nuclear war. His technical information allowed the CIA to identify the type of Soviet missiles for which bases were being prepared on the island. But also, crucially, his account of the backward state of Soviet preparedness for a nuclear conflict suggested strongly that Khrushchev was bluffing in his confrontation with the United States – if President Kennedy stood firm, the Soviet Union would have to pull back. This is, of course, what eventually happened. Khrushchev agreed that no missiles would be based in Cuba, in return for a guarantee that the United States would not invade the island to overthrow Fidel Castro.

At the very height of the Cuban crisis, on 22 October 1962, Penkovsky was arrested in Moscow. Two weeks later, the KGB also arrested Greville Wynne in Hungary. After a trial held in a blaze of publicity, Penkovsky was sentenced to death and Wynne to eight years' imprisonment. In 1964, Wynne was freed in exchange for Gordon Lonsdale – a very advantageous swap from the Soviet point of view, since they got an experienced intelligence officer for a British amateur.

Despite what was, from Penkovsky's point of view, an unfortunate end to the operation, Western intelligence was glowing with success and deliberately went public. The CIA hired a ghost writer to produce The Penkovsky Papers and Wynne was allowed to publish his own, almost certainly inaccurate, version of the affair. Although publicly the CIA claimed most of the credit, MI6 had handled the Penkovsky material from the start and privately received warm congratulations from its American counterparts.

Greville Wynne was sentenced to eight years' imprisonment in the Soviet Union, but he was released in 1964 in exchange for Gordon Lonsdale.
ABOVE: The spy-swap takes place at Checkpoint Heerstrasse on the Berlin Wall.
LEFT: Wynne arrives back in Britain. The swap was very advantageous to the Soviet Union, since they received an experienced KGB officer in return for an amateur.

Yet some intelligence officers on both sides of the Atlantic had not entirely shelved their doubts about Penkovsky. They simply could not believe he had survived as a double agent for 18 months undetected by the KGB when his tradecraft was so sloppy. For example, by the start of 1962 the KGB were known to have observed at least some of Penkovsky's very obvious meetings with Mrs Chisholm, and they were certainly aware that Roderick Chisholm was working for MI6. How could they have failed to make the connection? But if the KGB knew Penkovsky was passing secrets to the West, why did they wait so long before arresting him? And why did they finally choose to arrest him right in the middle of the Cuban missile crisis?

Critical versions of the Penkovsky affair were soon in circulation, and they have proliferated over the years. Some critics feel that Penkovsky was originally genuine, but later turned by the KGB. Others think his strange behaviour points to a double-cross from the very start. It has been suggested that retrieving Lonsdale was the whole aim of the exercise – Penkovsky's role was to entrap Wynne so he could be arrested and spy-swapped. More credibly, the case has been directly linked to the Cuban crisis. Perhaps Penkovsky was being employed to convince the West that the Soviet Union did not want a war and that Khrushchev's bragadaccio need not be taken seriously. He could either have been the tool of Soviet factions opposed to Khrushchev and fearful of the consequences of his adventurous foreign policy, or Khrushchev's own game might have been more complex than anyone in the West realised. What if the aim of the Soviet moves in Cuba was simply to head off an American invasion? What if they never had any intention of actually stationing nuclear missiles on the island? In other words, what if it was actually the Soviets who won the showdown? Then Penkovsky's role was firstly to precipitate the crisis by making sure the Americans recognised the bases under preparation in Cuba as Soviet nuclear missile installations, and then to ensure that the Americans would not be panicked into a nuclear attack but would go for a negotiated settlement – allowing Khrushchev to trade the non-existent missiles for a valuable American promise not to invade Cuba. The arrest of Penkovsky would, according to this version, have been designed to raise his credibility in the West to its highest point at the crucial moment.

Peter Wright goes further, seeing the affair as part of a grand design of strategic deception. Wright argues that Penkovsky was used to convince Washington of the Soviet Union's nuclear inferiority so that successive American administrations would become complacent, while secretly the Soviets expanded their nuclear arsenal well beyond the strength of the unsuspect-

BELOW: An American aircraft buzzes a Soviet cargo vessel off the coast of Cuba during the missile crisis. Penkovsky was clearly an important piece in the game between Kennedy and Khrushchev, but whose side was he playing for?

ing West. In all these versions of the story, it is assumed that, far from being executed, Penkovsky was in fact given a new identity and is living somewhere in the Soviet Union.

Whichever side Penkovsky was really working for, one incidental consequence of the case was a spy scandal in Britain that helped bring about the fall of a Conservative government. Penkovsky identified Lieutenant-Commander Eugene Ivanov, a naval attache at the Soviet Embassy in London, as a GRU intelligence officer. This was no news to MI5's D Branch, which had spotted Ivanov's real line of work as soon as he arrived in Britain in 1960. But Penkovsky added the interesting detail that Ivanov had a taste for the high life. A proclivity for smart parties and attractive women might seem innocent enough, but not for a Soviet intelligence officer, especially one as well connected as Ivanov, whose wife was the daughter of a leading official in the Soviet legal system. MI5 saw the possibility of an entrapment.

Entrapment is one of the dirtiest tactics used in the secret war, yet it has proved its effectiveness for both sides on many occasions. A person with access to classified material is lured into some compromising activity or relationship and then blackmailed. They have the choice of either co-operating with their blackmailers or admitting their misdemeanour to the relevant authorities on their own side, to the possible ruin of their careers and marriages. One man who escaped entrapment by coming clean was the British ambassador to Moscow in 1968, Sir Geoffrey Harrison, who confessed to the Foreign Office after being seduced by a chambermaid in the pay of the KGB. Generally, however, blackmail succeeds.

MI5 uncovered the case of a British victim of entrapment in the same period as the Ivanov affair. He was John Vassall, a clerk in the Admiralty with access to a wide range of secret documents. Vassall was a homosexual and had been led into compromising activities during a spell as a clerk at the British embassy in Moscow during the 1950s. Blackmailed by the KGB, he passed on photos of Admiralty documents for six years, from 1956 to 1962. He was eventually identified as a spy after MI5 carried out a careful cross-referencing of information from two defectors, Anatoli Golitsyn and Yuri Nossenko. Vassall was put under surveillance and a listening post was established next door to his flat in Dolphin Square, but no positive evidence of espionage was found until MI5 burgled the flat in September 1962. They found document-

Victims of entrapment: Eugene Ivanov (above), Soviet naval attache and GRU officer in London, was the object of an MI5 plot to involve him in an illicit relationship with Christine Keeler; Admiralty clerk John Vassall (left) was photographed committing homosexual acts while serving in Moscow in the 1950s and then blackmailed into spying for the KGB.

PLANETREE HOUSE

copying cameras in a secret drawer, and Vassall was immediately arrested.

MI5 did not have the success with Ivanov that the Soviets had had with Vassall. Ivanov was discovered to be frequenting the house of a society osteopath, Stephen Ward, who ran a sideline procuring girls for some of his rich clients. In June 1961, MI5 contacted Ward and he agreed to help in a plot to compromise Ivanov. What MI5 did not know was that one of Ward's stable of girls, Christine Keeler, was sleeping with the Secretary of State for War, John Profumo. Inadvertently, MI5 was pushing a Soviet intelligence officer into the proximity of a British government minister. Later

LEFT: The tree in London upon which Vassall would draw a chalk circle in order to contact his Soviet controller.

BELOW: Stephen Ward – putative MI5 agent.

Keeler was to allege that, at Ivanov's request, Ward had asked her to find out details of nuclear weapons deployment in West Germany during her pillow-talk with Profumo.

MI5 soon backed off from the Ivanov entrapment. Ward proved hard to handle and, as the Profumo angle gradually emerged, the risk of unfortunate complications was seen to outweigh any possible advantages. In early 1963, however, Christine Keeler sold her tempestuous life story to the press and the lid came off one of the great political scandals of recent times. Profumo was forced to resign – more because he was believed to have lied about his relationship with Keeler than for any security risk – and

Ward, harried by police and press alike, committed suicide. The affair did enormous harm to the credibility of Harold Macmillan's government and undoubtedly contributed to the defeat of the Conservatives in the 1964 general election.

It is no exaggeration to say that the early 1960s were a disaster for the image of British security. The arrest of George Blake in 1961 and Philby's defection two years later brought the extent of Soviet penetration of MI6 fully into the public gaze. The Vassall case revealed culpably lax vetting in a sensitive government department and, although the Denning report into the Profumo affair cleared MI5 of any blame, it drew an uncomfortable amount of public attention to the seamier side of the intelligence world.

But the image problems would have been much worse if the public had actually known what was going on inside MI5 at that period, for the security service was being torn apart by a 'molehunt'. Some officers had come to believe that the director-general of the service was in fact a Soviet agent. And MI5's problems were only one symptom of a generalized outbreak of paranoia and internecine conflict that infected the whole of the Western intelligence community.

The Profumo scandal discredited the government of Prime Minister Harold Macmillan (far left), as well as leading to the resignation of John Profumo himself (pictured left with his actress wife). It also brought notoriety to the girls involved (below, Mandy Rice-Davies on the left, and Christine Keeler).

CHAPTER SEVEN

MOLEHUNTS AND DEFECTORS

RIGHT: A rare friendly meeting between Soviet and Western intelligence officers – KGB chief Ivan Serov discusses security arrangements with MI5 operatives outside the Soviet embassy in London during a state visit to Britain by Soviet leaders Khrushchev and Bulganin in March 1956.

In a straightforward view of the espionage game, a defector from Soviet intelligence should be the antidote to a Soviet penetration agent or 'mole' in the West. If properly handled by his controller, a Soviet mole would be virtually undetectable by the organization into which he had burrowed. But rumours of his existence were almost certain to have spread through Soviet intelligence circles, whatever efforts were made to restrict access to such information on a narrow 'need to know' basis. Any defector might have seen documents that could only have come from a source deep inside a certain Western organization, or he might have heard a whisper of a codename. Such leads were often enough ultimately to identify the penetration agent, as happened with George Blake.

But in the 1960s, some Western counter-intelligence officers began to have severe doubts about Soviet defectors. They came to the conclusion that most, if not all, Soviet agents who offered their services voluntarily to the West were playing a part in an ultra-subtle Soviet intelligence offensive, an elaborate double-cross designed to spread disinformation and undermine Western intelligence agencies. In short, the defectors and the moles were working for the same side.

The man who did most to promote this disturbing vision of a convoluted Soviet intelligence conspiracy was himself a defector, Anatoli Golitsyn. In December 1961, Golitsyn simply rang the doorbell at the home of the CIA's man in Helsinki and offered to defect to the West. Despite their habitual suspicion of a 'walk-in', the CIA agreed to take Golitsyn on. He was a senior KGB officer who had worked for the First Chief Directorate, the key department responsible for Soviet espionage in the West. As such, he was a prize catch. But in the long run, taking on Golitsyn may have been one of the worst mistakes the 'Company' ever made.

Handling defectors is, at the best of times, a difficult business. Every defector arrives with a certain amount of information to deliver – the price of his ticket to the West. Once this has been unloaded, the lengthy and arduous process of debriefing gets under way. Over a period of years, the defector is repeatedly interrogated in an effort to dredge up every scrap of information from the recesses of his memory. This debriefing is stressful and fraught with problems. The defector may begin to invent material to satisfy his interrogators or maintain their interest – and hence his own importance. The interrogators may begin to uncover inconsistencies and cultivate doubts about the defector's veracity. Under intense emotional strain, defectors' behaviour can become extremely odd. Gouzenko, the cypher clerk who defected in 1945, developed an outsize craving for Western consumer goods, of which he accumulated vast quantities by mail order – at the expense of his hosts. Goleniewski not only came to believe he was the rightful Tsar, but also developed an actively hostile attitude to the CIA, eventually leading to litigation. Golitsyn, however, was without doubt the most difficult of all to handle – in the words of one CIA man, 'a total son-of-a-bitch'.

Part of the problem with Golitsyn was his exaggerated personal fear of moles in the CIA and British intelligence. He refused to talk to any Russian-speaking Western intelligence officer, on the grounds that learning the language could have brought dangerous contact with Soviet intelligence. In 1962, unhappy about his treatment by the

CIA, he insisted on leaving the United States for Britain. There he refused to be lodged in a safe house and instead moved from hotel to hotel at his own volition, only contacting British intelligence when he wished. This British interlude ended abruptly when the CIA leaked news of Golitsyn's presence in the country to the Fleet Street press. Horrified to find himself in the headlines, Golitsyn flew back into the arms of the Americans, even more convinced of the unreliability of MI5 and MI6.

Far worse than Golitsyn's eccentric behaviour, however, was his overwhelming sense of mission. He was convinced that he alone held the key to Soviet plans for world domination. According to Golitsyn, a massive plan of strategic deception was afoot, intended to mislead the West into a false complacency. The Sino-Soviet split of 1961, for example, was not a genuine rift in the communist world but a trick to throw the West off its guard. The same went for the apparent Soviet differences with Yugoslavia and Albania. A major element of the Soviet deception plan was the planting of disinformation through the penetration and manipulation of Western intelligence. Thus every apparent success for Western intelligence was in fact a Soviet double-cross – except, of course, Golitsyn's own defection. Golitsyn claimed that he alone could uncover this plot, and virtually demanded overall control of Western counter-intelligence, with access to all secret files and an absolute right to proclaim who was a Soviet agent and who was not.

The political right-wing in Britain and the United States – to which most intelligence officers at least loosely belong – has always been credulous of communist conspiracy theories. But nonetheless, it is a measure of the demoralization of the Western intelligence services that Golitsyn was taken so seriously. At the simplest, if Philby was a spy, then anything was possible. The true information that Golitsyn provided about Soviet illegals and agents was impressive, but no more so than that of other defectors whom he denounced as Soviet plants. Yet the main counter-intelligence officers who handled the Golitsyn case – James Angleton for the CIA, Arthur Martin of MI5 and Stephen de Mowbray of MI6 – fell for him hook, line and sinker.

One immediate effect that Golitsyn had was to throw doubt on almost all other Soviet sources. The CIA, MI5 and MI6 were devoting a large amount of time and energy to the pursuit of KGB or GRU officers who might be persuaded, by fair means or foul, either to become double agents or to defect. The results in the early 1960s were apparently very encouraging: there was Goleniewski; then Penkovsky; a KGB officer in Geneva, Yuri Nossenko; and two intelligence officers working under diplomatic cover at the United Nations in New York, codenamed Fedora and Top Hat. Only one point about all these men might have seemed suspicious – they all volunteered their services. Not one was obtained through the painstaking recruiting efforts of Western intelligence.

Either directly or by implication, Golitsyn cast suspicion on them all; this was the Soviet disinformation campaign he had predicted. We have already seen how doubts developed about the value of Penkovsky; Goleniewski also came to be regarded as unreliable. But Yuri Nossenko was the centre of the fiercest debate. Nossenko became a double agent in 1962. Even before he chose to defect two years later, Angleton had already decided he was a Soviet plant. His debriefing by the CIA turned into a harrowing ordeal lasting more than three years. He was kept in solitary confinement under brutal conditions worthy of the Lubyanka and subjected to consistently hostile interrogation. Some of his information was undoubtedly genuine – it was his lead that allowed MI5 to identify Vassall as a spy, when an earlier hint from Golitsyn had been too vague. But Angleton was determined to show that some of Nossenko's assertions, which contradicted Golitsyn, were deliberate disinformation. A CIA internal inquiry eventually vindicated Nossenko as a genuine defector, but Angleton remained unconvinced.

On Fedora and Top Hat, at least, a general consensus has emerged. It appears that they really were working for the Soviet side all the time. This did not stop them giving MI5 some genuine leads. In 1963, Fedora claimed the KGB had a spy inside the Atomic Energy Authority, where Fuchs and Nunn May had once worked. From Fedora's information, MI5 was able to identify an Italian physicist, Dr Giuseppe Martelli, as the prime suspect. It was discovered that Martelli had contact with a Soviet intelligence officer and possessed a whole range of espionage tools, but under interrogation he denied ever having handed over any secrets. When the case came to court the evidence proved too thin and, embarrassingly for MI5, Martelli was acquitted.

Top Hat's information, on the other hand, did lead to a successful prosecution. In 1965 he showed his FBI contact photocopies of documents on guided weapons that Soviet intelligence had obtained from Britain. MI5

LEFT: James Angleton, the CIA's chief of counter-intelligence, who fell under the spell of Soviet defector Anatoli Golitsyn and lost himself in the espionage 'wilderness of mirrors'. Angleton became convinced that other Soviet defectors and double agents were part of a sophisticated Soviet deception plan, and that the KGB had penetrated all Western intelligence agencies, including the CIA.

was soon able to identify the source as Frank Bossard, an employee in the Air Ministry. Bossard had been a spy for four years, using a simple but ingenious routine worked out by his controller. He kept a document-copying camera in a suitcase in the left luggage office on Waterloo station. During his lunch break, he would slip some classified documents into his briefcase, pick up the camera from Waterloo, and go to a hotel in Bloomsbury. There he took a room under an assumed name and quickly photographed the documents. Later he would leave the photos in one of a number of dead letter boxes – for example, a broken drainpipe or a hollow tree – and pick up his money from the same place. He knew which location to use by listening for certain pieces of music played on Radio Moscow at a certain time of the evening – 'The Volga Boat Song' meant one thing, 'The Sabre Dance' another. He had met his Soviet contact only once in four years.

Bossard was caught red-handed photographing documents after the MI5 watchers followed him through his lunch-time routine, so this time there was no problem obtaining a conviction. But it was still disturbing that Bossard had not been weeded

FAR LEFT: Frank Bossard, the Air Ministry employee who spied for the Soviets in the early 1960s.

BELOW FAR LEFT: The London pub, the Red Lion in Duke of York Street, where Bossard was first contacted by a Soviet agent.

LEFT: Detectives load items taken from Bossard's flat into a car, ready to be taken to court as evidence in his trial. The ordinary radio set was used to listen for tunes on Radio Moscow, each one corresponding to a pre-established instruction for the spy.

out by positive vetting checks, since it turned out he had a criminal record that he had attempted to conceal. The Martelli and Bossard cases served to reinforce the growing impression in the United States that British security was lax and the British could not be trusted – many of the secrets betrayed by Bossard were *American* secrets. Believers in the fiendish subtlety of Soviet intelligence saw in this the whole point of what Fedora and Top Hat had done. Martelli and Bossard were not just mere 'discards', intended to reinforce the credibility of false double-agents; they were carefully chosen to disrupt the Anglo-American intelligence alliance by sowing distrust between the Allies.

But if the Soviet goal was to undermine Western intelligence by creating a climate of distrust, their chief asset must have been Golitsyn himself. His insistence that the CIA had been penetrated by Soviet agents goaded Angleton into a witchhunt. The internal investigations were so thorough and the suspicions generated so corrosive that whole sections of the Agency became temporarily paralysed. Eventually, Angleton's persistence in these molehunts ruined his

HIGGINS IS LET OFF THE HOOK
— BACK PAGE

DAILY
EXPRESS

THE VOICE OF BRITAIN

Thursday November 27 1986 20p ★★★

Havers: Probe

'Dirty tricks' storm as Attorney General investigates former MI6 chief and ex-Downing St. adviser

Rothschild: Was he the Fifth Man?

Rothschild : Faced interrogation

LABOUR MPs DEMAND AN ANSWER

By PAUL POTTS and DANIEL McGRORY

RETIRED MI5 officer Lord Rothschild was dramatically named yesterday as a suspected Soviet spy and the so-called Fifth Man of traitors inside British Intelligence.

At the same time the Attorney General, Sir Michael Havers, revealed that the activities of Lord Rothschild, an ex-Downing Street advisor, as well as Sir Arthur Franks, the former head of MI6, were under criminal investigation.

Sir Michael dropped his bombshell when he told MPs that, along with Director of Public Prosecutions Sir Thomas Hetherington, he was studying allegations that the millionaire banker and Sir Arthur passed information about State security to spy book writer Chapman Pincher.

Wright: Author

EXPRESS
EXCLUSIVE: Exposed Soviet agent is linked to author Wright
Traitor Blunt's key role in spy book scandal
Prosecute Lord Rothschild, says MP

Yesterday's Express

Pincher: Letters

These latest revelations came as spy fever broke out at Westminster, with Labour MPs determined to unearth another security scandal.

Protected by Parliamentary privilege, they raised suspicions that Lord Rothschild was a Soviet spy and the Fifth Man in the Burgess-Philby scandal.

EXPLOSIVE

Lord Rothschild, who worked closely with former Prime Minister Edward Heath, has emerged as a central figure in the Peter Wright spy book saga unfolding in Australia.

Former MI5 agent Wright has claimed he was put in touch with Pincher by Lord Rothschild and together they worked on the explosive 1981 book Their Trade Is Treachery.

But intelligence expert Nigel West revealed exclusively in the Daily Express yesterday that it was self-confessed traitor Anthony Blunt who acted as a catalyst and helped point an accusing finger at former MI5 chief Sir Roger Hollis as a Soviet mole.

It was also emphasised that although Lord Rothschild was interrogated by the security services he had been cleared.

In a day of fast-moving spy claims and denials, Labour MPs continued to gun for Lord Rothschild and, indirectly, Mrs Thatcher.

She is now under intense pressure to order a major shake-up of the top-secret elite within the intelligence services.

Chapman Pincher meanwhile accused Labour of masterminding a dirty tricks campaign to shame the Government over the bungled Sydney trial.

He said the plan hinged on forcing the Government to prosecute Lord Rothschild and Sir Arthur.

DIRTY

The ammunition for the plot was secretly passed on by Australian lawyer Malcolm Turnbull, who is representing Peter Wright in his bid to publish his memoirs as an MI5 spycatcher.

Mr Pincher said last night: "This has become a very dirty game and someone is going to get hurt."

In a Commons motion the Labour MPs called on Mrs Thatcher "to state whether the security services ever carried out an investigation into suspicions, which surfaced at the time and of which Lord Rothschild was aware, that he was a Soviet spy and the Fifth Man."

They followed up the attack with a

Page 2 Column 2

Clothing clue on Moors

● POLICE searching for the bodies of two missing children on Saddleworth Moor above Manchester last night dug tattered clothing out of the peat. The discovery came as darkness fell and followed a sweep by an RAF photography plane.

● THE clothing was unearthed less than 100 yards from where Moors murder victims John Kilbride and Lesley Ann Downey were found 21 years ago. Ian Brady and Myra Hindley were jailed for the killings.

● Police dogs helped to uncover another substance, which a police spokesman said was not thought to be human remains.

Fatal attraction: See Centre Pages

reputation and contributed to his dismissal, along with the rest of his top counter-intelligence staff, in the stormy aftermath of the Watergate scandal.

The pattern of events in Britain was essentially no different. Some MI5 officers, notably Arthur Martin and Peter Wright, were already half-convinced before Golitsyn's defection that Soviet penetration of British intelligence must have taken place on a substantial scale. They became known as the 'Young Turks' because of their eagerness for a radical clean-up of the intelligence community. Golitsyn could offer them no specific leads to moles inside MI5 or MI6, except for confirming Philby's guilt at a time when this had still not been definitively established. One of the very few personal allegations Golitsyn made was against Victor Rothschild, but MI5 quite properly dismissed this as an example of Russian anti-Semitism (Prime Minister Magaret Thatcher made a statement in the House of Commons officially clearing Rothschild in 1986). The general thrust of Golitsyn's testimony, however, was that Soviet agents were to be found inside all Western intelligence services. And he specifically stated that he had seen original MI5 documents in a safe in Moscow. Under his influence, Martin and Wright found their suspicions raised to the level of certainty. They asked the uncomfortable question: why had no penetration agent been uncovered in MI5? Previously it had been a cause for complacent self-congratulation

FAR LEFT: Mole mania seized the British press in the 1980s. Even Lord Rothschild was briefly suspected; he had been named by Golitsyn as a Soviet agent.

BELOW: Famous and infamous spycatcher Peter Wright in his later incarnation as a Tasmanian livestock farmer.

RIGHT: The molehunters' chief suspect, Sir Roger Hollis, director-general of MI5, wearing what Peter Wright calls his 'Cheshire cat smile'. Above all else a competent administrator, Hollis was an exceptionally bland character with no obvious vices. Very little evidence was ever produced against him.

inside MI5 that, whereas MI6 had been penetrated, the security service had not. But perhaps the only difference between the two organizations was that MI6 had found its mole, while MI5's was still in place.

The evidence for the existence of a mole in MI5 was of two kinds: the apparently inexplicable failure of various operations over the years; and the fragmentary hints provided by defectors or decoded Soviet radio intercepts. Working back through the Registry files and raking up old cases, the Young Turks built up a coherent, if speculative, story stretching back to World War II. In 1945 the defector Gouzenko told how, in Moscow during the war, he had heard of a Soviet agent codenamed 'Elli' who worked in British intelligence – in 'five of MI'. This might have been Section V of MI6, where Philby was employed, but it also could have been MI5. Also in 1945, the would-be defector Volkov referred to a spy in British counter-intelligence, generally assumed to be Philby, but equally possibly a reference to someone in MI5. To the Young Turks it seemed plain: as early as World War II, MI5 had been penetrated – and, for various reasons, Blunt would not fit the bill.

After the war, 'Elli' was responsible for the failure to entrap Soviet intelligence with the same 'double-cross' methods that had worked so well against the Abwehr. He tipped off Burgess and Maclean in 1951, and gave the Soviets prior warning of Commander Crabb's ill-fated diving mission in 1956. It was to protect him that Lonsdale was sacrificed by the KGB in 1961, after he had alerted them to the fact that their Portland spy operation was blown. And finally, it was he who tipped off Philby that the net was closing round him in 1963, allowing the MI6 spy time to arrange his escape from Beirut. When all the ramifications of this story were examined, only two MI5 officers emerged as credible suspects: the deputy director, Graham Mitchell, and the director-general himself, Roger Hollis.

Under normal circumstances, it would have been extremely difficult for a group of officers to launch an investigation of their own superiors, but the presence of Dick White, a former director of MI5 and mentor of Arthur Martin, at the head of MI6, opened the way. In 1963 Martin approached White and laid out the case for him to consider. White backed an investigation of Mitchell (though not of Hollis) and Hollis was obliged to agree. Mitchell was put under surveillance, tailed by a team of MI6 watchers wherever he went (MI5 watchers he might, of course, have recognised) and filmed all day in his office through a two-way mirror. Hollis refused to authorise a tap on his home telephone, however, since this would require political clearance and thus alert the government to the awful state of affairs in MI5.

The investigation of Mitchell went nowhere. Although he was clearly under stress – he had already applied to take early retirement – and often suspicious in his manner or behaviour, nothing solid could be produced against him. By the end of 1963 he had retired and, as far as Hollis was concerned, the case was closed. The MI5 Young Turks and their allies in MI6 counter-intelligence, such as Stephen de Mowbray, found Hollis's desire to prevent further molehunts highly suspicious. They were increasingly convinced that Hollis, not Mitchell, was the Soviet agent.

Hollis had never been popular with his colleagues. His manner was habitually reserved and aloof, and his cool administrative approach to his job had led to conflicts with younger officers who wanted MI5 to pursue a more active line against Soviet influence. He could be quietly authoritarian, a trait which may be explained by his family background – he was the son of a bishop. Educated at Oxford, he had gone to China in the 1930s, where he had joined the British American Tobacco Company. It was hard for even the most hostile investigator to find evidence of early communist sympathies, although Hollis had known one Comintern agent in the Far East, left-wing journalist Agnes Smedley. In 1938 he had returned to England and joined MI5, rising to deputy director in 1952 and director-general four years later. Even his enemies had never thought him an ambitious man; his rapid rise in the service after 1945 was attributed to the fact that he was the only MI5 officer who could stand the plodding post-war boss, Percy Sillitoe. His life had been free of scandal. It was widely known that he was having an affair with his secretary – another very conventional aspect of an exceptionally bland personality. The oddest quirk of behaviour that could be alleged against him was a taste for walking home in the evening instead of taking the car. On the surface at least, few unlikelier candidates for the role of Soviet mole could have been found.

The pursuit of Hollis was complicated by the simultaneous re-opening of the Cambridge spies affair, through Philby's defection in 1963 and the fortuitous unmasking of Anthony Blunt the following year. Blunt's lengthy debriefing led on to Cairncross, Long and many others. Golitsyn insisted that there had been a Cambridge 'Ring of Five', creating a new area of worry since,

even with the Blunt revelations, MI5 could only identify four spies who fitted. And Goleniewski chipped in with an allegation about a 'middle-ranking' spy in MI5, who could not be either Hollis or Mitchell. As these ever widening perspectives opened up, in the autumn of 1964 MI5's D Branch and MI6's Counter-intelligence Division agreed to establish a joint working party, known as the Fluency Committee, to investigate the whole issue of Soviet penetration of British intelligence. The committee was chaired by Peter Wright. Arthur Martin, who had so far made most of the running in the molehunt, was excluded. His behaviour had become increasingly disruptive and eventually Hollis took the drastic step of sacking him – only to see him re-employed immediately by Dick White at MI6.

The disarray of British intelligence did not pass unnoticed on the other side of the Atlantic. If Peter Wright is to be believed, in 1965 President Lyndon B Johnson ordered a clandestine review of British security. A London-based CIA officer conducted two senior American officials around British secret establishments, without informing their hosts of the purpose of these visits. The officials produced a devastating critique of MI5 and MI6 counter-intelligence. Despite angry reactions from British intelligence chiefs when they eventually learnt of the deception practised by the CIA, they had to acknowledge the truth of much of the American criticism.

The Fluency Committee investigations were lengthy. Hollis retired from MI5 at the end of 1965, before the committee had even produced its initial report. His successor as director-general, Martin Furnival Jones, was torn between the desire to curb inquiries that were tearing the service apart and the contrary impulse to clear the air by getting to the bottom of the penetration issue once and for all. When the committee eventually named its prime suspects, he was horrified. Hollis was identified as 'Elli' and Michael Hanley, widely tipped as the next head of MI5 after Furnival Jones, was suspected to be Goleniewski's 'middle-grade' officer.

The case against Hanley was quickly cleared up. He survived a rigorous interrogation and satisfied his fellow MI5 officers that he was completely innocent. When he was appointed director-general of the service on Furnival Jones's retirement in 1972, there were initial protests from MI6, but a swift review of the case once again convinced everyone that he could not have

BELOW: Hollis's successor as head of the Security Service, Sir Martin Furnival-Jones. Although eager to avoid scandal, he allowed the molehunt to continue, but was eventually convinced that Hollis had after all been totally innocent.

LEFT: Vladimir Petrov, the Soviet intelligence officer whose defection in Australia in 1954 caused a media sensation. Peter Wright became convinced that Charles Ellis, formerly of MI6 and at that time an adviser to the Australian Secret Intelligence Service, leaked advanced warning of Petrov's defection to the Soviets.

been a Soviet agent. The question of Hollis, however, was not resolved. The specific pointers against him were all circumstantial. For instance, in 1945 Philby had selected Hollis to debrief the defector Gouzenko. Did this show that the two men were in league? At about the same period a Soviet officer, Lieutenant Skripkin, had tried to defect but had been detected by the KGB and shot. The British intelligence officer handling the case was Roger Hollis. Had he betrayed Skripkin?

In 1968 another reorganization of MI5 created K7, a permanent unit to counter Soviet penetration. Headed by Duncum Wagh and an ex-Marine, John Day, K7 re-examined all the files once again and then proceeded with an interrogation of Hollis. The result was highly unsatisfactory: most of those concerned, including Furnival Jones, considered Hollis innocent, but some officers, Peter Wright prominent amongst them, still thought he was guilty. It proved impossible to reach any consensus. Officially, the case against Hollis was closed.

By the end of the 1960s, the tide was set firmly against the molehunters. Their investigations had earned them plenty of enemies. Few people inside British intelligence were offended by the ruthless persecution of elderly remnants of the 1930s – mostly very minor spies and long since retired – although it precipitated two suicides and served little perceptible purpose. But the feeling of distrust spread within MI5 and MI6 was not easily forgiven. MI6 especially resented the pursuit of one of its former officers, Charles Ellis. He apparently confessed to having passed information to the Germans before World War II but hotly denied ever spying for the Russians. MI5 investigators remained convinced that he had worked for Soviet intelligence while deputy head of British intelligence in Washington during the war and subsequently in Australia at the time of the defection of Vladimir Petrov. MI6 did not appreciate this.digging up of old corpses.

FAR RIGHT: Mrs Petrov, wife of the defector, is forcibly led onto a Soviet aircraft by two KGB 'heavies'. The KGB proved incapable of carrying through this abduction in what developed into a full blaze of publicity, and Mrs Petrov was eventually allowed to stay with her husband in Australia.

Golitsyn's star was on the wane as a new generation of defectors came over with a fresh supply of up-to-date information. The Soviet intervention in Czechoslovakia in 1968 provoked a clutch of defections. Of special interest to MI5 was Josef Frolik, a Czech intelligence officer who had been responsible for espionage in Britain. He was able to identify a large number of agents, most of them inside the British Labour movement.

More spectacular was the defection of Oleg Lyalin. A low-ranking KGB man stationed in London, Lyalin was recruited by MI5 in 1970. He was carrying on an illicit affair with a secretary at the Soviet trade delegation and wished to defect with her. He agreed to spy in place for a time, on condition that MI5 provided him with safe houses where he could make love to his girlfriend. This double life came to an end in August 1971, when Lyalin was arrested for drunken driving on Tottenham Court Road. MI5 rushed in to free him from police custody, prudently armed with antidotes to known KGB poisons, in case Lyalin's drunkenness was not what it seemed. He was spirited away to a safe location and a very fruitful debriefing began. The significant point about the Lyalin case was that his cover had not been blown. If a mole had still been operating inside MI5, he would almost certainly have alerted Soviet intelligence to Lyalin's treachery.

By the 1970s, even the most committed molehunters were convinced that Soviet penetration of British intelligence was a thing of the past. This did not mean, however, that they were prepared to drop the issue. Stephen de Mowbray of MI6 was particularly unhappy, sure that MI5 was being allowed to get away with a cover-up. When the Labour prime minister Harold Wilson came to power in 1974, de Mowbray took the extraordinary step of approaching the government directly over the heads of his superiors. Although by this time Hollis had died, an official inquiry into the affair was

RIGHT: Oleg Lyalin, a KGB man stationed in London, passed information to MI5 for a year before defecting in 1971. The fact that Lyalin remained undetected by Soviet security convinced all but the most extreme molehunters that MI5 was by this time mole-free.

ABOVE: Lord Trend, the civil servant who headed an official enquiry into the Hollis allegations in 1974. He found that the allegations were groundless.

RIGHT: Journalist Chapman Pincher, whose book *Their Trade is Treachery* was largely based on information supplied by molehunter Peter Wright.

conducted by Lord Trend. He concluded by agreeing with all previous investigations: there was no serious evidence to support the allegation that Hollis had been a Soviet spy. The arch molehunter Peter Wright left the service an embittered man in 1975. Still convinced of Hollis's guilt, he primed journalist Chapman Pincher with his version of the affair, which appeared in 1981 as *Their Trade is Treachery* and eventually published an account under his own name, *Spycatcher* – a last revenge on a system he felt had treated him badly.

So in the end, what conclusions can be drawn from this whole affair? There must be a strong possibility that the Soviet Union did once have a mole inside MI5 who has remained undiscovered. It is especially striking that Soviet intelligence made no effort to persuade Blunt to stay in the service at the end of World War II, a surprising omission unless they had another trusted agent in place. There are much more likely candidates than Hollis, however, as a Soviet agent in the immediate post-war period. Guy Liddell, for instance, was a friend of Burgess and Blunt, so why not him as the mole? It is not a very credible allegation, yet Maurice Oldfield of MI6 is said to have been very suspicious of Liddell. There is no real evidence against him, but nor is there against Hollis or Mitchell.

Of course, someone like Liddell would not do for the molehunters because he left MI5 in 1952. Yet the evidence for Soviet penetration after that time is not very strong. For instance, there seems simply no need to think that Philby was tipped off during 1962-63; the way the case was handled by MI6 ensured him the chance to defect if he wished. Again, during the Portland spy case, it did not require a mole to tell the Soviets that Lonsdale was under surveillance. According to Peter Wright's own account, the early stages of the surveillance were carried out so clumsily that Soviet intelligence could hardly have failed to notice. Perhaps by the time the molehunt started, there was no mole.

One way of looking at the 1960s campaign against Soviet penetration of Western intelligence is to ask who gained and who lost by it. The answer is not hard to find. There were small gains to the West in improved security checks – both MI5 and MI6, for instance, began for the first time seriously to apply positive vetting within their own ranks, a quarter of a century after its introduction in other parts of government service. But the real winner was Soviet intelligence, which saw its enemies torn apart by internal conflicts and paralyzed by doubt and mistrust. One CIA internal report concluded that, judging by results, the most likely Soviet mole in the Agency was James Angleton. The same logic would point to Arthur Martin or Peter Wright as playing the Soviet game. Of course, no one was seriously suggesting that Angleton, Martin or Wright were actual Soviet agents. But if the Soviets had an interest in promoting the search for non-existent moles, then the molehunters became their unwitting accomplices.

Peter Wright quotes one of his suspects, Graham Mitchell, as saying: 'In my experience espionage has always been a simple business . . .' Wright and his colleagues rejected this view. Stumbling through a 'wilderness of mirrors' in which no theory was too elaborate or abstruse, any friend might be an enemy, any apparent success part of a devious Soviet double-cross, they too often abandoned all sense of proportion or common sense. Thus Western intelligence lost itself in a maze largely of its own devising.

CHAPTER EIGHT

THE POLITICS OF SECRECY

BELOW: Prime Minister Harold Wilson on a visit to Moscow in 1975. Many MI5 officers were suspicious of Wilson's links with the Soviet bloc and also disliked his socialist policies. However, few accepted CIA counter-intelligence chief James Angleton's view that Wilson might be a Soviet agent.

Between 1964 and 1979, British political life was dominated by the Labour Party and the trade union movement. The Conservative government of 1970-74 appeared as a fragile interregnum, rather than a solid reassertion of traditional centres of authority. The same period saw the rise of international terrorism and the growth of a seemingly ineradicable terrorist movement inside the United Kingdom itself: the Provisional Irish Republican Army (PIRA), often known simply as the IRA. Meanwhile, in the United States, the Watergate scandal led into a wide-ranging public investigation of the CIA that blew apart the secrecy surrounding the Agency and exposed many of its covert operations to denunciation by hostile critics. Although the Thatcher government in Britain and the Reagan administration in the United States succeeded in reversing the political tide in the 1980s, they did so without recreating any durable national consensus. This political background shaped much of the history of MI5 and MI6 over two eventful decades.

With few exceptions, modern British intelligence officers have remained as right-wing in their views as were their predecessors over half a century ago. It is ironic that MI5 indirectly contributed to the defeat of the Conservatives in 1964, since the intelligence community regarded the new Labour prime minister, Harold Wilson, with both distaste and distrust. Wilson was a moderate social democrat, fully committed to continued membership of Nato and the retention of Britain's nuclear forces (a pre-election promise to abandon the Polaris nuclear submarine programme was swiftly jettisoned). Nonetheless, many intelligence officers, both in Britain and the United States, viewed him as a dangerous socialist. MI5 noted that Wilson had links with Soviet bloc countries: he had worked in an East-West trading organization and a number of East European emigre businessmen were among his closest associates.

Wilson's predecessor as Labour leader, Hugh Gaitskell, who enjoyed a much higher reputation among the intelligence community, had died unexpectedly only a year before the general election that brought Wilson to power. He had just returned from a visit to Moscow when he was attacked by a rare tropical disease, lupus disseminata. According to Peter Wright, Gaitskell's doctor asked MI5 whether the Soviets could have administered this disease as a poison, but there was no evidence the KGB had such a capacity. Soon after Wilson became prime minister, however, James Angleton visited London to inform MI5 that, according to sources he refused to name (almost certainly the ubiquitous Golitsyn), Gaitskell had indeed been murdered. Wilson was a Soviet agent and the KGB had removed Gaitskell to open their man's way to the top. To their credit, MI5 officers tended to regard this as more evidence of Angleton's worsening paranoia, but they kept the allegation on file.

The Frolik and Lyalin defections further complicated relations between MI5 and the Labour Party. Frolik's debriefing revealed the extensive range of contacts between Czech intelligence and Labour MPs and trade unionists. Very few of these British socialists could be regarded as Czech 'agents'. Of the MPs, only Will Owen had received substantial payments for information and was prosecuted under the Official Secrets Act. He was, however, acquitted for lack of evidence. John Stonehouse was cleared by MI5 after an investigation (although suspicions resurfaced later when he staged his own disappearance, apparently as a solution to financial and

Czech defector Josef Frolik (above) set the cat among the pigeons by revealing a wide range of contacts between Czech intelligence and members of the British Labour movement. One of those he accused was government minister John Stonehouse (left, surrounded by photographers). MI5 cleared Stonehouse, but doubts resurfaced when he later arranged his own 'disappearance'.

BOEING

marital problems). Another MP, Tom Driberg, had also been employed by MI5 as an information source, but was generally regarded as too unreliable to be of much use to either side. The vast majority of those named by Frolik were, in their own eyes, simply maintaining good relations with eastern Europe. Accepting an expenses-paid trip to Prague or a free meal did not mean they had sold their souls. The Cold War warriors of MI5 were inclined to take a less benign view of such contacts and regarded the Labour movement as having been extensively penetrated by the Soviet bloc.

Lyalin's debriefing brought MI5 investigations closer to Wilson himself. According to the KGB man, one of his colleagues was in touch with Wilson's friend Joseph Kagan, a Lithuanian emigre businessman. MI5 put Kagan under surveillance. By this time Wilson was out of office – it was 1971 – but he got wind of the investigation and reacted furiously to what he saw as an MI5 smear campaign. It would appear that at this time the security service did begin officially to re-examine the question whether Wilson could possibly be a Soviet agent.

It would be wrong to give the impression that the whole intelligence community was hostile to Wilson. Sir Dick White got on well with him and in 1968 Wilson appointed White to the post of Cabinet Intelligence Co-ordinator. But most intelligence officers felt happier with the Conservative prime minister, Edward Heath, and his main adviser on security, Victor Rothschild. After the debriefing of Lyalin in 1971, both MI5 chief Furnival Jones and Sir John Rennie, who had replaced White as head of MI6, thought they had the material for a coup against Soviet intelligence. Many of Lyalin's statements had been extremely wild – he was not widely believed when he alleged that an army of Soviet agents was in place ready to sabotage such targets as the London Underground – but he did give a detailed and uncontrovertible rundown of the KGB order of battle in London.

MI5 had long wanted to reduce the number of Soviet intelligence officers, since maintaining surveillance over so many opponents was a serious drain on limited resources. Armed with Lyalin's revelations, Furnival Jones, backed by Rennie and White, approached the Prime Minister. To

ABOVE: Seventy of the Soviet officials expelled for espionage in 1971 set sail for home on board a Russian cruise ship.

LEFT: Labour MP Tom Driberg, a man who spied on the Communist Party for MI5 but also had links with Czech intelligence. He was probably of little use to either side.

their delight, Heath agreed to the immediate expulsion of 105 Soviet diplomats and members of Soviet trade delegations who had been identified as intelligence officers. Shortly afterward, MI5 briefed Heath on the alleged extensive Soviet penetration of the Labour movement, a controversial move away from the service's traditional stance of at least formal neutrality in party politics.

Under Sir Michael Hanley, who succeeded Furnival Jones in 1972, MI5 became increasingly preoccupied with surveillance of the political left in Britain, rather than with countering Soviet espionage. New Left groups such as the Socialist Workers Party (SWP) and the Workers Revolutionary Party (WRP), which had grown out of the student revolts of 1968, attracted a lot of security service attention, as did the long-established Campaign for Nuclear Disarmament (CND). But the Heath government was most interested in the trade unions, engaged in a series of bitter disputes with their employers and the government. MI5 began to use telephone taps and mail intercepts with unprecedented frequency against trade union activists and other left-wingers.

It is fair to say that by 1974 the British establishment felt less sure of its ability to control the country than at any time since the days of the 'Bolshevik menace' in the aftermath of World War I. An Arab oil embargo had sent inflation spiralling and an IRA bombing campaign was hitting Britain's cities. Heath's government drove headlong into a disastrous confrontation with the mineworkers' union and narrowly lost a general election in February. Wilson returned to power with a more thoroughgoing socialist programme than had been seen in Britain since 1945. The right-wing press filled with rumours of the breakdown of democracy and 'private armies' forming to take on the unions.

It was in this crisis atmosphere that, according to Peter Wright, a group of MI5 officers hatched a plot to drive Wilson from office. Considerable doubt remains to the size of the plot: figures range from 30 down to a few disgruntled middle-ranking officers. The idea was to leak to the press details of allegations against Wilson and other Labour Party members and trade union officials contained in MI5 files. It was to be a repeat performance of the Zinoviev letter affair. If the public knew Wilson was a suspected Soviet agent, he would have to resign; if he fought an election, he would surely lose.

BELOW: Tony Benn addresses a meeting of Concorde workers in Bristol in 1974. The presence of left-wingers such as Benn in the Labour government was totally unacceptable to many MI5 officers. Such was the problem, that left-wing ministers were denied access to information that the Security Service considered highly sensitive.

The plot seems to have aborted because senior MI5 officers would have nothing to do with it. When the affair came rather belatedly to the attention of the head of the service, he reportedly took disciplinary action against some of those responsible. Wilson must have been aware that something was being cooked up against him, without knowing precisely what. After his resignation in 1976 – which seemed to many observers to be related to MI5 pressure but subsequently proved to be unrelated – Wilson made a variety of allegations against MI5 and even contacted the CIA to find out whether any of their operatives might have played a part in plots against him. Until the publication of *Spycatcher*, all this was generally taken as evidence of Wilson's paranoia and weakening grasp of political reality – historian Christopher Andrew, for example, opined that 'a prime minister who . . . entertains suspicions, however improbable, that his own security service is plotting against him scarcely merits confidence in his administration.' Such words would not be written today.

Although Wilson suffered such a bad relationship with MI5, he had a high opinion of MI6. Flying in the face of received

BELOW: Tony Brookes, one of the MI5 officers who handled the Lyalin case. According to Peter Wright, Brookes was one of those later involved in a plot to force Harold Wilson out of office.

ABOVE: Century House, the London headquarters of the Secret Intelligence Service on the south bank of the Thames. Its functional, business-like appearance reflects the modern style of the service, far removed from the cloak-and-dagger antics of the old pre-war amateurs.

opinion, he regarded MI6 as the more professional of the two services. This at least partly reflected a genuine improvement in performance and organization. MI6 had moved to new headquarters at Century House, a modern office block south of the Thames. Its registry was re-organized by Arthur Martin, and Christopher Philpotts, as head of the counter-intelligence section, tightened up internal security – hopefully there would be no more Philbys. The appointment of Sir John Rennie to head the service after Dick White's departure in 1968 was not a popular decision, but in 1973 Rennie resigned when his son was prosecuted for a drugs offence, and MI6 got the 'C' whom most of its officers wanted: Maurice Oldfield. Understandably, but erroneously, believed to be the original for John Le Carre's fictional molehunter George Smiley, Oldfield was the first grammar school product to make it to the top of the service – a social revolution of sorts. A mild-mannered, donnish personality, he reinforced the modern emphasis of MI6 on strictly controlled operations with an absolute minimum use of force. The Sidney Reilly/James Bond style was a thing of the past. Oldfield was also scrupulous in maintaining the duty of MI6 to serve the democratically elected government, believing paradoxically that only a strict adherence to the rules would in the long run protect the service from direct interference by politicians. This was the lesson he drew from the CIA debacle in the mid-1970s.

The objectives of MI6 intelligence-gathering were also widening. There was an increasing demand for economic intelligence – on Britain's EEC partners, the Japanese, the Middle East oil states, and so on. A new government body, the Overseas Economic Intelligence Committee (OEIC), became a major customer for both MI6 and GCHQ. The OEIC would define areas where information was required and then analyse and distribute the material fed to it by the intelligence services. Private British companies were on the distribution list as well as government bodies – MI6 had become a provider of useful tips to businessmen.

Another area where the service became heavily involved was Northern Ireland, after the latest phase of 'the Troubles' erupted

there in 1969. British intelligence had already had a very unfortunate experience in Ireland earlier in the century. On 21 November 1920, during the struggle for Irish independence, IRA gunmen killed 12 intelligence officers in simultaneous attacks on a number of 'safe houses' in Dublin. No trauma on this scale was to occur in Northern Ireland after 1969, but there was to be a disturbing slide away from respect for the rule of law.

As part of the United Kingdom, the Province should have been MI5's exclusive preserve, with MI6 taking responsibility for operations south of the border in the Irish Republic. But, as we have seen, Harold Wilson had a special regard for MI6 and he insisted that the service also adopt a 'watching brief' in Northern Ireland. This role was much expanded under the Heath government from 1971 onward. On past performance, it was hardly to be expected that relations between the two services operating on the same ground would run smoothly, and they did not.

In fact, the intelligence scene in Northern Ireland was especially complex, with the

ABOVE: Sir Maurice Oldfield, mild-mannered head of MI6 from 1973 to 1978, banned most forms of covert action, orienting the service decisively toward a disciplined pursuit of clearly defined intelligence goals.

LEFT: Another view of Century House, home of MI6, depicted alongside the prosaic surroundings of Lambeth North Underground station.

WIMPY

NO
PARKING
SHELL

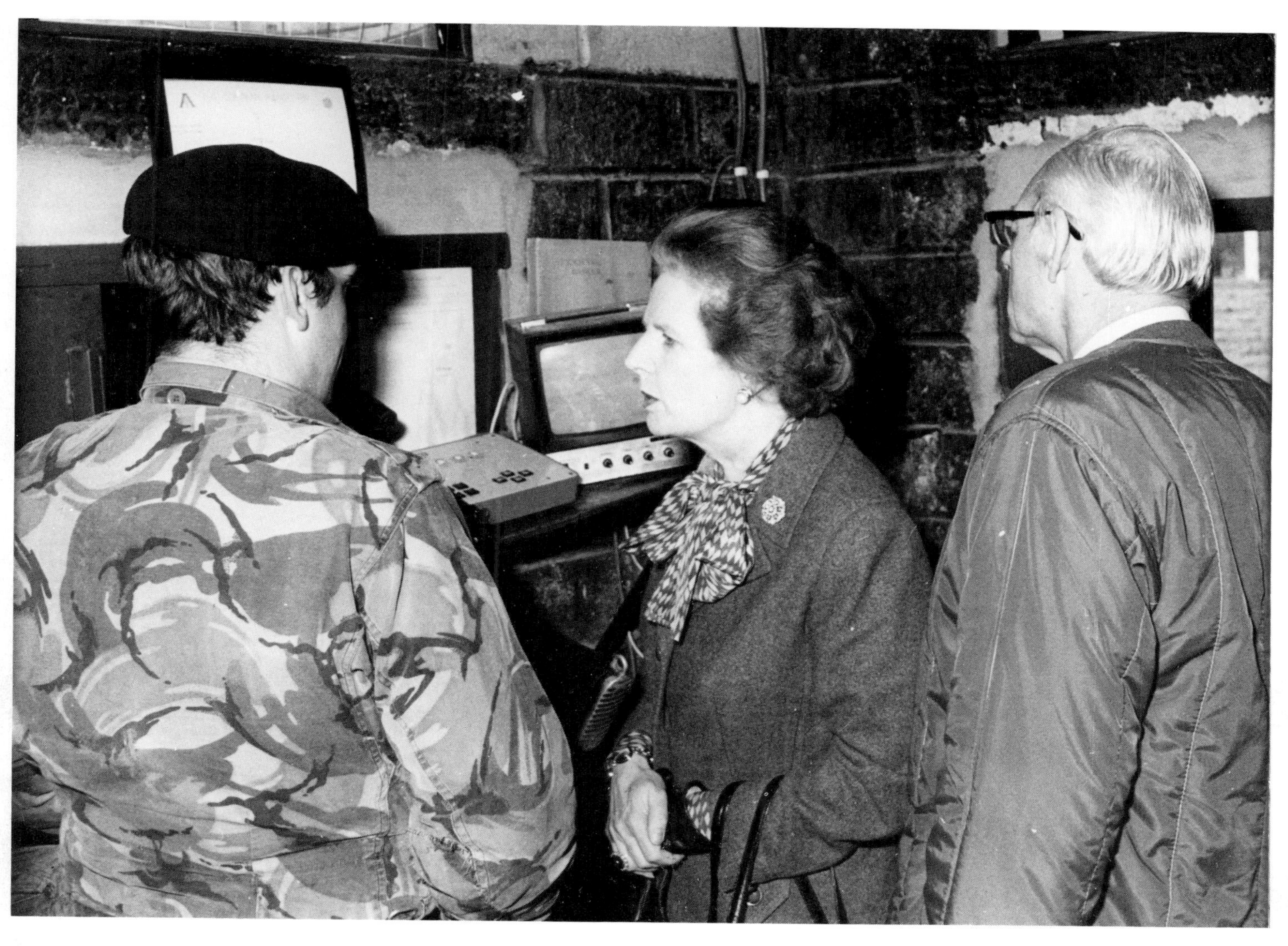

Royal Ulster Constabulary (RUC) Special Branch, British military intelligence and the Special Air Service (SAS) Regiment all playing a part. Their joint aims were to identify terrorists so they could be arrested or eliminated; to maintain a flow of accurate intelligence about the plans, attitudes and organization of terrorist groups; and to influence the political situation through propaganda or 'psyops' – psychological operations. At the same time, MI6 devoted a considerable part of its international resources to tracing IRA links with foreign terrorist organizations, monitoring terrorist contacts with the Eastern bloc and tracking down the IRA's sources of finance and illegal arms supplies.

In all its objectives in Northern Ireland, British intelligence has achieved good results since 1971 (in the earliest years of the crisis, the Province was a mystery to the security forces). Case officers have successfully run agents inside all paramilitary organizations and set up networks of informers. Computer analysis of a mass of information from standard everyday surveillance – random checks on vehicles, for example – has yielded many crucial leads. There have been some spectacular clandestine intelligence-gathering operations, the most memorable being the Four Square Laundry dry-cleaning service run by British intelligence in west Belfast during 1972: an analysis of the clothing collected for cleaning led to a number of important arrests before the deception was rumbled and the driver of the laundry van shot by the IRA. Arms shipments have been repeatedly intercepted, often after being kept under observation from their place of origin right along an international route of some complexity. In mainland Britain, MI5 has a good record of identifying IRA active service units, and co-operation with European security services has resulted in the tracking down of bombers attacking targets on the Continent. During the 1970s, the IRA expressed its recognition of MI5 and MI6 successes with compliments in its own style: a bomb attack on a restaurant beneath an MI5 office in South Audley Street and the attempted bombing of Marsham Court, the London home of Maurice Oldfield.

But British intelligence undoubtedly in-

The IRA terrorist campaign since 1970 has confronted MI5 and MI6 with a serious challenge. ABOVE LEFT: The injured are helped away after a bomb explosion at the Abercorn restaurant in 1972. LEFT: A British soldier patrols the streets of Belfast. ABOVE: British Prime Minister Margaret Thatcher visits an Army post in the Northern Ireland border zone.

ABOVE: The Bogside area of Londonderry, a breeding ground of IRA terrorism. The task of establishing intelligence networks in Catholic areas of Northern Ireland has proved extraordinarily difficult.

Successive prime ministers, Ted Heath (above right) and Harold Wilson (above far right) wrestled unsuccessfully with the Northern Ireland problem. Wilson's poor relationship with MI5 made his chances of success far lower.

RIGHT: An Army helicopter on patrol in Northern Ireland. Advanced military technology has proved less effective against terrorism than the use of small specially trained units on the ground, employing sophisticated intelligence techniques to target terrorists.

RIGHT: Bank robber Kenneth Littlejohn appears on television to claim that his criminal activities were carried out under instructions from MI6.

BELOW: The Protestant Ulster Defence Association on the march in Ballymena. MI5 agent James Miller infiltrated the UDA, but was purportedly ordered to use his position to promote a Protestant workers' strike against British government policy in Northern Ireland.

FAR RIGHT: The wrecked car in which Tory MP Airey Neave was killed by a terrorist bomb as he drove out of the Parliament car park in March 1979.

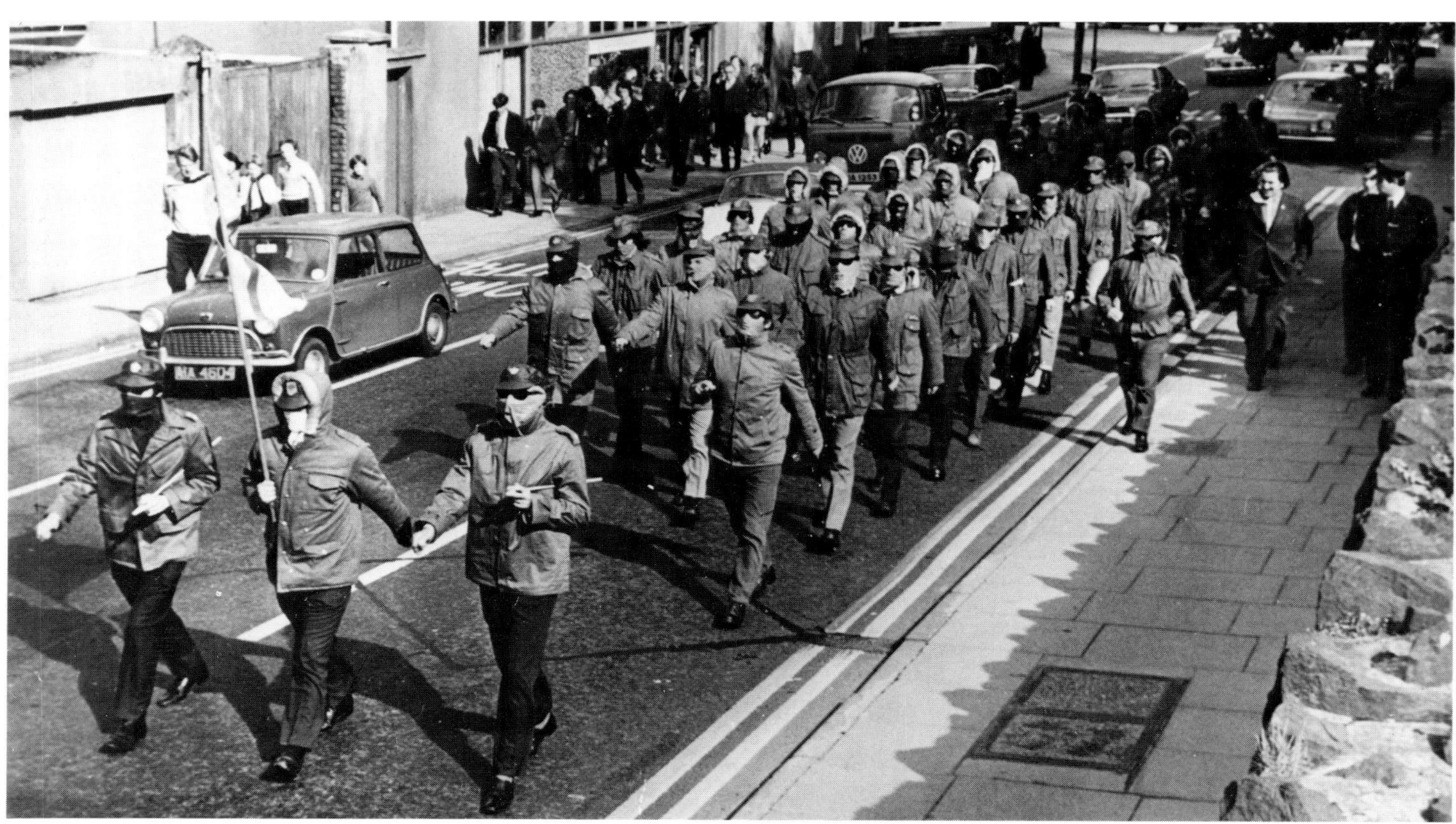

volved itself in some questionable activities that tarnished its successes. The first occasion for concern was the use of 'sensory deprivation' interrogation techniques against 14 men when internment was introduced in Northern Ireland in August 1971. One reason for this exercise, later widely condemned as little short of torture, was simply to experiment with a new interrogation method under real-life conditions. Intelligence agencies are always researching interrogation techniques from two points of view – how to extract information from an enemy and how to train their own operatives to resist interrogation. For example, like the CIA, British intelligence had experimented with the drug LSD as a possible truth-inducer. In the case of sensory deprivation, it was brutal and irresponsible to use as guinea-pigs a clutch of internees – none of whom had even been charged with an offence. All were subsequently paid damages by the British government.

In 1972, MI6 was deeply embarrassed by the infamous Littlejohn affair. The Littlejohn brothers, Kenneth and Keith, were criminals operating in the Irish Republic. They were definitely recruited as informants for MI6 in February 1972 and continued in this role until their arrest for bank robbery the following October. But the rest of the facts of their case are hotly contested. The Littlejohns claimed that MI6 provided them with arms and explosives to carry out bank raids and attacks on police stations in the Republic, knowing that these raids would be blamed on the IRA, and that they had been given a hit list of leading IRA men they were to assassinate. MI6 has always denied this – Oldfield reportedly called the whole staff of Century House to a meeting in the canteen to assure them there was no truth in the

ABOVE RIGHT: An Army control post in Londonderry, an example of the methods forced upon the British security services to ensure civil order in Northern Ireland.

BELOW FAR RIGHT: A propaganda photograph released by the IRA purporting to show IRA members undergoing military training.

Littlejohn allegations. Yet the mud stuck, and the affair contributed to a decision in 1974 to downscale the MI6 presence in Northern Ireland, replacing some of its officers with MI5 men.

MI5 has been the butt of many subsequent allegations of misconduct in the Province. Some of these relate to the vendetta against Harold Wilson and the Labour Party. James Miller was recruited by MI5 in the early 1970s and infiltrated the Protestant extremist Ulster Defence Association (UDA), becoming one of the UDA's leading intelligence officers before his cover was blown and he was forced to flee for his life. Miller now claims that his MI5 controller encouraged him to promote the crucial Protestant workers' strike in 1974 which ruined the Wilson government's Irish policy and personally humiliated the prime minister. There is also evidence that 'black' propaganda – phony political leaflets, forged bank statements and so on – were produced to discredit not only Northern Ireland extremists but also Labour ministers and their policies. With what is known of MI5 attitudes to the government in 1974, it is not difficult to believe these allegations.

There were differences over tactics within the intelligence community. While some intelligence officers from MI6 and military intelligence saw their role as exclusively intelligence-gathering and to this end tried to preserve their contacts inside the IRA, MI5, the RUC and the SAS pursued a more active strategy to eliminate IRA personnel. So an MI6 officer might find that his valued IRA agent had been trapped and shot through the more aggressive efforts of an officer from MI5. And this aggressive approach could easily begin to slide toward the summary execution of suspects. There was also disturbing evidence of close contacts between Protestant extremists and the RUC and MI5. It was obviously good intelligence practice to maintain such con-

RIGHT: Wilson always preferred MI6 to MI5, and it was at his insistence that MI6 first became involved in Northern Ireland. Conflicts between the two services operating on the same territory were often an embarrassment.

LEWIS STREET

The scene of carnage after the Hyde Park bombing which devastated a troop of the Household Cavalry in July 1982. MI5 in general has a good record of identifying IRA active service units operating in mainland Britain, but the service has not been able to prevent the occasional outrage.

ABOVE: Geoffrey Prime under arrest after 14 years spying for the Soviets, latterly inside GCHQ. Prime was not caught through the vigilance of the Security Service; he was denounced by his wife after he had been picked up for sexual offences.

RIGHT: John Stalker, the Manchester policeman appointed to investigate 'shoot-to-kill' allegations in Northern Ireland. Stalker found MI5 uncooperative and was later forced to resign in the face of a concerted campaign to discredit him and his investigation.

tacts, if they were correctly handled. But when it is suggested that, for example, the Ulster Volunteer Force unit that planted a car-bomb in Dublin in May 1974, killing 27 people, was in close touch with MI5 in Belfast, the implications are horrifying.

Sir Maurice Oldfield was widely known to be opposed to illegal methods and strong-arm tactics. He was also inclined to dislike the Protestant extremists even more than their Catholic equivalent. His appointment as Security Co-ordinator for Northern Ireland in October 1979, little more than a year after his retirement from MI6, must have been extremely unpopular with MI5 and the RUC. It was certainly disastrous for Oldfield. The ex-MI6 chief was a homosexual, a fact that was widely known in the intelligence community but that he had not formally stated in his positive vetting – it would have disqualified him from secret work. Apparently, in the spring of 1980 someone complained to the police that a man had made an indecent proposition to him in a Belfast pub; he identified the culprit as Oldfield. The story was extremely unlikely and bore all the hallmarks of a classic 'fit-up'. Nevertheless, Oldfield, his health already failing, was quickly sent back into retirement. He died the following year.

Another person to experience the sad fate of outsiders interfering in the secret world of Northern Ireland security was Manchester police officer John Stalker. In May 1984 he was appointed to head an inquiry into a supposed 'shoot-to-kill' policy being operated by the SAS-trained RUC Headquarters Mobile Support Unit – in other words, police murder. Particularly important was a case in which an innocent 17-year-old, Michael Tighe, was shot dead by an RUC ambush party in a hayshed that had been identified as an IRA meeting place. MI5 had bugged the shed, but Stalker was repeatedly obstructed in his pursuit of the tape made at the time of the killing. Meanwhile a campaign was mounted to have Stalker taken off the inquiry, exploiting his supposed social contacts with known criminals. In May 1986 he was duly removed from the case and soon left the police force altogether. There is no evidence that MI5 had any part in the attack on Stalker, but some observers remain reluctant to believe in coincidence.

Even undoubted intelligence successes against the IRA sometimes left a bad taste in the mouth. The tracing of the IRA unit that intended to explode a car-bomb in Gibraltar in 1988 was a first-rate piece of intelligence work. The first lead was reportedly an innocuous post-card home from an IRA member in Spain, picked out through a routine mail intercept – although this story may be disinformation, covering a sensitive secret source. From whatever small beginnings, MI5 officers were able to identify the whole unit and established effective surveillance in co-operation with the Spanish security authorities. Yet the final gunning down of the three suspects by the SAS suggested disturbingly that the British intelligence community might have come to regard itself as authorised to act with complete disregard for the law. It also had a negative effect on the security situation in Northern Ireland.

Although the relative importance of Soviet counter-espionage declined as other areas such as economic intelligence-gathering and operations against terrorists and 'subversives' absorbed more time and resources, the old battle of wits still went on. In May 1982 British intelligence received one of its periodic shocks with the discovery that Geoffrey Prime, a senior employee in the Joint Technical Language Service sec-

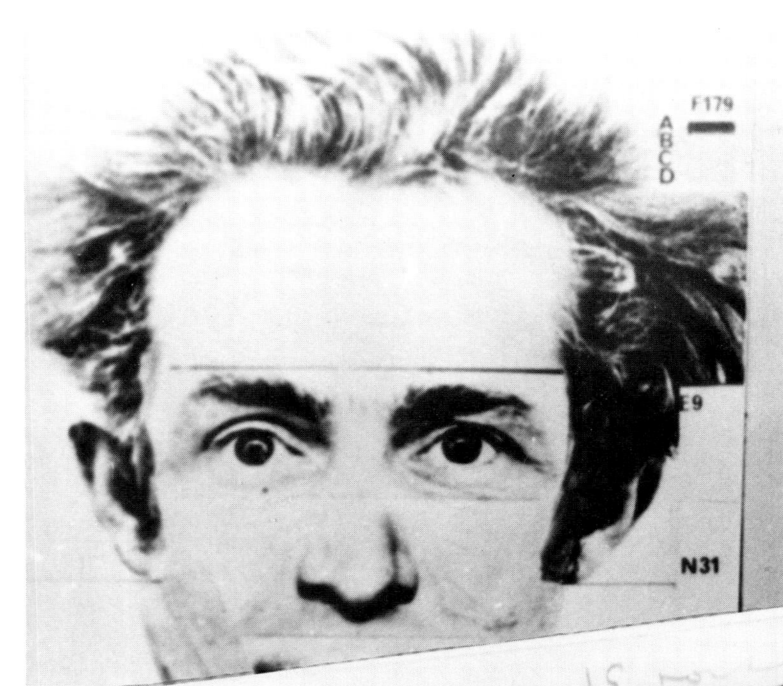

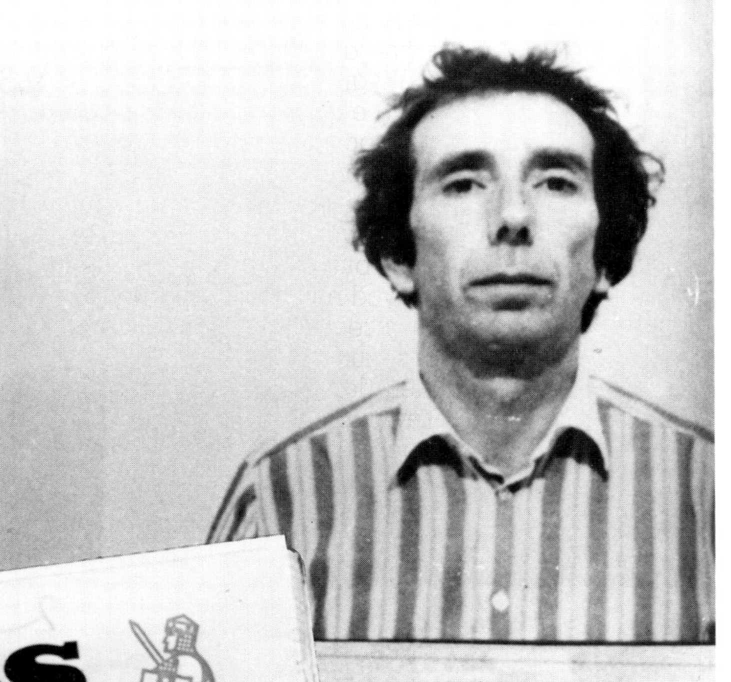

DAILY
EXPRESS
THE VOICE OF BRITAIN

WIN £50,000 PAGE 28

Thursday November 11 1982 • 18p • Weather: Sunny spells

38 YEARS FOR THE MASTER SPY WHO BETRAYED HIS COUNTRY AND HIS WIFE

THE ARCH TRAITOR

THE WIFE: I forgive him, she says after Old Bailey trial

THE SPY: Most important Russian agent, say Americans

By TONY DAWE and RICHARD WRIGHT

GEOFFREY PRIME, sentenced to 38 years' jail yesterday, was rated by the Americans as the most important Russian spy since the war.

He admitted selling secrets for a few thousand pounds over a 14-year spell while working in the RAF, the Foreign Office, and the Government's top-secret communications centre at Cheltenham.

And as Britain's security services came under attack on both sides of the Atlantic

Court story: Pages 2 and 3
Wife's dilemma: Page 7
Life story: Centre Pages

for yet another leak, it was revealed that 44-year-old Prime was caught by accident.

He was arrested for sex offences against young girls and only trapped as a spy when his wife gave him away because of her "Christian principles."

Yesterday, Mrs Rhona Prime, 37, collapsed at the Old Bailey after saying she would forgive her husband and stand by him. They met for 15 minutes in a cell.

Prime's spy masters told him he would be given the rank of colonel and a pension if he ever defected. Twice in 1977 he booked escape flights—but cancelled them to stay with his wife.

At the Old Bailey the details of Prime's treachery were revealed only in secret session. The Lord Chief Justice, Lord Lane, called Prime a ruthless spy who did "incalculable harm to the interests and security of this country and of our friends and allies."

The 38-year term — to "punish and deter" — is the longest ever imposed by a British court apart from spy George Blake's 42 years in 1966.

Today, Mrs Thatcher will make a statement on the case in the Commons—where rumours are rife that Prime's spying endangered British agents' lives.

CHAPMAN PINCHER on Britain's biggest spy scandal: PAGE 6

ABOVE: The photofit picture of the mystery sexual attacker (left) and an actual picture of Prime after his arrest. The identification was not difficult.

LEFT: A newspaper report of Prime's conviction for espionage. His 38-year sentence was the longest imposed since the George Blake trial in 1961.

tion of GCHQ, had been a Soviet spy for 14 years. Recruited while serving with the RAF in Berlin in 1968, Prime had deliberately infiltrated GCHQ so he could give the Soviets first-class information on the latest satellite surveillance of Eastern bloc communications and the effectiveness or otherwise of Western code-breaking. His positive vetting failed to identify his warped sexual tastes which made him an obvious target for Soviet blackmail. MI5 played no part in unmasking him. He was arrested by local police after a series of sexual assaults on young girls and was then denounced as a spy by his wife who knew his secret.

The Prime case outraged the Americans, who threatened to halt the full exchange of intelligence with Britain unless security at GCHQ was tightened. They demanded the introduction of polygraph ('lie-detector') tests for employees and the banning of trade unions at the establishment which opposed this measure. In Britain, one major effect of the Prime case was to attract public attention to GCHQ and its function, until the end of the 1970s a closely guarded secret. In a familiar pattern, the Soviets knew all about GCHQ long before the British public.

British intelligence also had a remarkable success at the expense of the KGB, however. In September 1985 Oleg Gordievsky, the top KGB officer in London, defected. He had first been recruited by Danish intelligence while stationed in Copenhagen in the 1970s, and had worked for MI6 ever since his arrival in London in 1981. It was through Gordievsky that MI6 was immediately informed in 1983 when an MI5 operative, Michael Bettaney, offered his services to Soviet intelligence. MI6 passed on the information to the then director-general of MI5, Sir John Jones, and Bettaney was arrested. The loss of Bettaney disgraced Gordievsky's superior, Arkadi Gouk, allowing MI6's man to replace him as head of KGB London. Gordievsky eventually defected because things were getting too hot for him to stay in place. His betrayal must have been a disaster for Soviet espionage in Britain. Had he succeeded in maintaining his cover, we would not, of course, know of this MI6 success story – a salutary reminder of how much of the intelligence game in recent years still remains hidden.

BELOW: Police demonstrate the 'spy kit' found in Prime's home. It included radios and a briefcase with a hidden compartment. The police's satisfaction was understandable, but neither they nor MI5 would ever have realised Prime was a spy if his wife had not denounced him.

POSTSCRIPT

By the 1980s, the scale of intelligence operations had expanded to a degree that would have astounded Sir Vernon Kell or Sir Mansfield Cumming. According to the best estimates, over 14,000 people were employed in the British intelligence establishment, with a budget of around £300 million a year for MI5/MI6 and the same amount again for GCHQ. All these figures are speculative and probably do not include one-off items of expenditure such as the £250 million reportedly spent on the top-secret Zircon spy satellite program. There is no reason to believe that the rigorous cuts in public spending pushed through by the Thatcher government affected this favoured area.

Large as they were, these budgets shrank into insignificance alongside the grossly inflated expenditure of the CIA and NSA (National Security Agency). Consequently the British were heavily dependent on American intelligence agencies for access to information from the most expensive high-technology sources. In a most unequal relationship, the Americans called the shots. This again was a situation that would have caused the founding fathers of MI5 and MI6 no little astonishment.

Yet in some areas the techniques of espionage and counter-espionage had changed surprisingly little over the years. In theory, the development of satellite surveillance and worldwide monitoring of communications, linked to computers of ever-greater power and sophistication, should have totally revolutionised intelligence work. But the revolution has proved very partial. Firstly, encryption has progressed one step ahead of decryption: Soviet secret communications can be successfully monitored, but they can rarely be read (although Third World countries using less sophisticated codes are usually an open book to Western cryptographers). Satellite photography, apart from problems with bad weather, poses serious difficulties of interpretation. Unsupported from other sources, it is often vulnerable to deliberate deception – dummies are likely to be taken for real objects, real objects easily concealed. The use of bugging devices has expanded to such a degree that most Eastern bloc embassies have more microphones than the BBC, but embassy staff learn the discipline of never discussing confidential material without retreating to a safe place, such as a lead-lined 'Faraday box' built in the middle of a room and electronically impenetrable.

Consequently, much of the intelligence game goes on as before: the running of agents and double-agents, surveillance by the watchers, the painstaking up-dating of registry files (now computerised, of course), mail intercepts and phone taps, the scrupulous combing of publicly available sources – newspapers, journals, magazines, television and radio – and all the sordid business of bribery, blackmail and entrapment. In this sophisticated high-technology age, agents still leave messages for their con-

The contemporary world of espionage depends heavily upon technology. American spy satellites (below left) and spy planes (below, the Lockheed SR-71 Blackbird) are certainly a valuable source of intelligence, made available to Britain, but they are inhibited by cloud cover and liable to deception. They complement, but do not supplant, the agent on the ground.

trollers in hollow tree-trunks; arrange apparently casual meetings on Hampstead Heath or Victoria Station; make sure they are not followed by the 'cinema trick' – entering a cinema, sitting in the back row, then leaving in the middle of the film; use invisible ink and microdots; and receive coded messages in apparently innocent scheduled radio broadcasts or the small ads sections of newspapers. Sometimes espionage still seems a rather dangerous game for children who never grew up.

The Falklands crisis of 1982 presented a classic example of the interlocking elements of modern intelligence in action – and of how intelligence could fail even under the most favourable circumstances. Argentina had a long-standing and frequently reaffirmed claim to the British-owned Falkland Islands. The intelligence task was to tell if and when the Argentinians actually intended to take military action, so that the islands' defences could be reinforced in good time or a naval demonstration organised to deter aggression. In the spring of 1982 British intelligence was in receipt of information from American spy satellites and SR71 spy plane pictures showing Argentinian military preparations, open statements in the Argentinian press proclaiming the imminence of military action, and accurate reports from the well-informed MI6 station in Buenos Aires. In addition, as a junior British minister later rather unwisely revealed to the House of Commons, NSA/GCHQ was reading Argentina's military and diplomatic traffic. All these reports went to the Joint Intelligence Committee (JIC), which included among its members the heads of MI5, MI6 and GCHQ, under a Foreign Office chairman. But the JIC did not warn the British government of the Argentinian invasion until two days before it took place – far too late for effective counteraction.

The failure was clearly one of assessment, rather than input. The JIC had all the evidence it needed of Argentinian military preparations from a wide range of intelligence sources, but was still reluctant to believe the Argentinians really meant business, having formed the firm opinion that the

LEFT: The British government's telephone-tapping headquarters in Ebury Bridge Road, London. The MI5's use of phone-taps to listen in on left-wing political groups and trade unionists has been widely criticised.

LEFT: The Falklands War proved the need for good intelligence at all levels. The destruction of the *Atlantic Conveyor* (above) might have been avoided if the British had better knowledge of the activities of Argentinian naval aviation, while on the other hand, the sinking of the Argentinian submarine *Santa Fé* (below) was in part due to good British intelligence.

ABOVE AND RIGHT: Broadway Buildings, backing on to Queen Anne's Gate, the headquarters of MI6 before its move to Century House. Before World War II, Broadway Buildings also housed GC&CS, the forerunner of GCHQ.

ABOVE: British troops embark on a Wessex helicopter during the Falklands conflict. If British intelligence had drawn the right conclusions from the information available from a variety of sources, the Falklands War need never have happened.

blustering, sabre-rattling military junta in Buenos Aires was incapable of decisive action. The Franks Committee review of the Falklands conflict recommended that the chairman of the JIC should in future be an independent figure, rather than a Foreign Office representative. Whether this would really help with the eternal problem of intelligence assessment seems doubtful. The customers for intelligence will always believe reports that tell them what they want to hear and reject information that runs counter to their prejudices or preconceptions.

During the 1980s, MI5 and MI6 attracted public attention as never before. A veritable flood of books poured from the presses, each claiming more breathtaking revelations than the last. Prime Minister Margaret Thatcher seemed to be ever on her feet in the House of Commons, denying that this person or that was an MI5 mole, admitting that the former head of MI6 had been a homosexual, yet defending again and again the principle of absolute secrecy under which, she asserted, the intelligence services must operate. The long and futile campaign to stop publication of Peter Wright's *Spycatcher* revealed the personal obsession of a prime minister quite capable of imposing her idiosyncratic attitudes as government policy, undeterred by ridicule.

It is reasonable to assume that under any other British government of modern times, the revelations of scandalous plots, illegal activities and gross incompetence would have brought a scathing review of MI5 and MI6, followed by fundamental changes in their structure and accountability. They have survived intact because the Thatcher government was prepared to back them to the hilt, come what may. The cosy relationship between Thatcher and MI5, in particular, had disquieting implications. The events of the Wilson era had highlighted the threat of a security service operating to hamper or overthrow a democratically elected government. But the Thatcher era suggested an equally potent menace: a security service acting illegally at the government's bidding to harass its political opponents under cover of secrecy. MI5

BELOW: Margaret Thatcher on the day of her third consecutive general election victory in July 1987.

As prime minister, Mrs Thatcher (far right) has been dedicated to preserving the curtain of protective secrecy that guards MI5 and MI6 from public scrutiny. Her obstinate efforts to ban Peter Wright's *Spycatcher* (right) proved totally counter-productive, but were no doubt appreciated by the intelligence community. In return, Mrs Thatcher expects the help of the Security Service's F Branch in monitoring the activity of opposition political groupings of which she disapproves, such as the Campaign for Nuclear Disarmament (below).

officer Cathy Massiter quit the service to reveal how she had been pressured to institute illegal phone-taps against members of organizations such as CND and the National Council for Civil Liberties, even though the individuals concerned were not 'subversive' even by the most generous interpretation of the term. Domestic surveillance had become the top priority of MI5 operations.

Although the days when ministers would deny the very existence of MI5, MI6 and GCHQ were long past, there was no progress in opening up a free flow of information that would make the intelligence services accountable to parliament. MPs did not know how much was spent on intelligence, who ran it, what they did, who authorized their operations or how far they succeeded. Unlike any other part of the British bureaucracy, MI5 and MI6 were accountable only to the government – and even then, it would appear, only when it suited them. Far from responding to calls for greater openness and accountability, in 1988 the government introduced a new Offi-

cial Secrets Act that would make the publication of almost any information on secret intelligence or security operations an offence. It could be illegal even to expose illegal acts by MI5, thus completing the iron circle of secrecy protecting this area of state power from any democratic control.

Yet there was an urgent need for decisions about MI5 goals and methods to be determined by public debate. Who was to be defined as a 'subversive' and therefore an object of MI5's attentions? And what were the limits to MI5 operations if it was accepted that the strict letter of the law could not always be observed? Nothing in the history of the service suggested these questions could safely be left for MI5 itself to answer.

In the last analysis, the surprising justification for the massive growth of intelligence agencies in the nuclear age is the need for reassurance. It is essential that governments with their fingers on the nuclear trigger feel confident they know what the other side are doing. The more money they spend and the more operatives they employ, the more secure they feel.

The advent of glasnost under the dynamic Soviet leadership of Mikhail Gorbachev might classically be interpreted as a danger to the interests of the bloated intelligence community. Throughout their history MI5 and MI6 have thrived on threat, and mostly the Soviet threat. Should the mutual secretiveness of East and West decline and confrontation slide into wary collaboration, the intelligence services might be expected to find themselves left high and dry. But in reality, diversification has already taken place. Today MI5, MI6 and GCHQ participate in a multifaceted process of global surveillance that feeds a varied, expanding market for information. There is economic intelligence, technological intelligence, the international campaign against terrorism, the international campaign against drug traffic, as well as the still lively battle against 'world communism' and domestic 'subversion'. Whatever happens to East-West relations, MI5 and MI6 officers are unlikely to swell the dole queues.

In the 1980s, MI5 and MI6 have had to adapt to changing circumstances, finding new goals and priorities. For MI5, surveillance of domestic opponents of government policy (left, police arrest peace demonstrators) has become more important than countering foreign spies. For MI6, the relative rapprochement between East and West (below, Reagan and Gorbachev in a cordial mood) has encouraged a diversification of interests into subjects as different as counter-terrorism and economic intelligence.

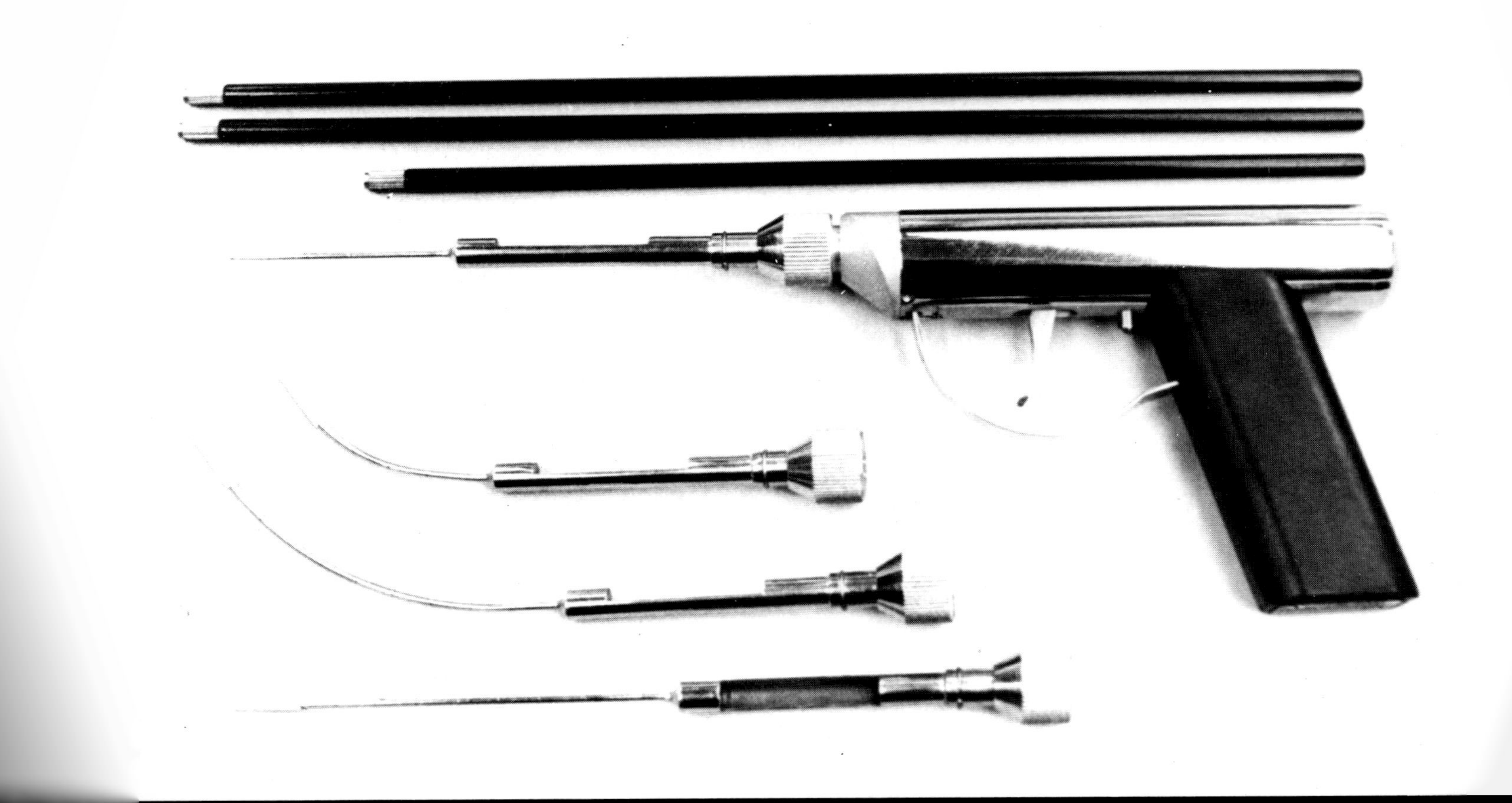

The fascinating and deadly world of spy gadgetry. ABOVE: A pistol with a range of barrels used for firing poison pellets. LEFT: One way of making your telephone conversations secure – tap out the words on a keyboard that automatically encodes the message and transmits it down the line to an identical machine that decodes it for the person you want to communicate with. RIGHT A more old-fashioned set of equipment, the kind carried by an SOE operative on mission in World War II. It includes the classic suitcase radio cameras (standard and miniature), pistol with silencer, knives, and 'secret ink' pens.

SPARES
REACTION
KEY
VOL
Bi-Carbonate de Soude

Director-Generals of MI5 and MI6

MI5

Sir Vernon Kell............................1909-40
Sir David Petrie...........................1940-46
Sir Percy Sillitoe..........................1946-53
Sir Dick White 1953-56
Sir Roger Hollis...........................1956-65
Sir Martin Furnival Jones.............1965-72
Sir Michael Hanley......................1972-79
Sir Howard Smith........................1979-81
Sir John Jones.............................1981-85
Sir Anthony Duff.........................1985-88
Sir Patrick Walker........................1988-

MI6

Sir Mansfield Cumming 1909-23
Sir Hugh Sinclair.........................1923-39
Sir Stewart Menzies 1939-52
Sir John Sinclair..........................1953-56
Sir Dick White 1956-68
Sir John Rennie...........................1968-73
Sir Maurice Oldfield.....................1973-78
Sir Arthur Franks 1979-82
Sir Colin Figures 1982-85
Sir Christopher Curwen 1985-89

Select Bibliography

Andrew, Christopher *Secret Service: The Making of the British Intelligence Community* (Sceptre, 1987)

Boyle, Andrew *The Climate of Treason* (Hutchinson, 1979)

Calvocoressi, Peter *Top Secret Ultra* (Hutchinson, 1979)

Deacon, Richard *A Biography of Sir Maurice Oldfield* (Macdonald, 1985)

Knightley, Phillip *The Second Oldest Profession: The Spy as Patriot, Bureaucrat, Fantasist and Whore* (Andre Deutsch, 1986)

Masterman, JC *The Double Cross System in the War of 1939 to 1945* (Yale University Press, 1972)

Philby, Harold 'Kim' *My Silent War* (MacGibbon & Kee, 1968)

Pincher, Chapman *Their Trade is Treachery* (Sidgwick & Jackson, 1981)

Verrier, Anthony *Through the Looking Glass* (Cape, 1983)

West, Nigel *MI6* (Weidenfeld & Nicholson, 1983)

West, Nigel *MI5* (Bodley Head, 1981)

West, Nigel *A Matter of Trust* (Weidenfeld & Nicolson, 1982)

Wright, Peter *Spycatcher* (Heinemann, 1987)

Index

Figures in *italics* refer to illustrations

ACKNOWLEDGMENTS

Archiv Gerstenberg, pages: 16(bottom), 19(bottom), 51(bottom), 52, 53(top), 56(both), 57(both).
Army Information Services, page: 163
Associated Press, page: 4, 90, 97, 101, 126(top), 139, 145, 151.
Belfast Telegraph, pages: 162(both), 166(bottom).
Bison Books, pages: 111(bottom), 176, 177, 180(both), 182, 188(below).
Bundesarchiv, pages: 53(bottom), 54, 73(bottom), 74(top).
Camera Press, pages: 3(both), 6, 11(top), 12, 19(top), 37, 39(top), 58(right), 59, 60(bottom left), 69, 77(bottom left), 81(bottom), 84, 85, 89, 92(top), 94, 98, 105, 106, 107(both), 109, 111(top), 113, 115, 118, 128, 129, 136-7, 137, 140, 153, 154, 159, 160, 161(bottom), 165(bottom), 169(both), 184(bottom), 186, 187.
Communist Party, UK Picture Library, page: 42.
Courtesy of Mr Harold Dearden, pages: 66, 67(top).
John Fairfax & Sons Ltd, Feature Bureau, page: 149.
John Frost Newspapers, page: 99, 103(top), 108, 117, 122, 144, 174(bottom).
Hoover Institute, pages: 30(top), 33(bottom).
Hulton-Deutsch, pages: 9(bottom), 38, 40, 41, 45, 46, 47, 50, 55, 64, 65, 67(bottom), 71(bottom), 79(right), 81(top), 82, 83, 86(bottom), 97(bottom), 102, 112(both), 119, 120, 121, 123(bottom), 125(both), 126(bottom), 127(both), 130, 133(both), 134, 136, 142(both), 143, 157, 158, 165(top left), 166(top), 168, 170-1, 178-9, 185.
Hulton Picture Company, pages: 13, 14(both), 15, 17, 24, 28(top), 31(top right), 32(both), 33(top), 36, 39(bottom), 58(left), 60(top), 62(bottom), 73(top), 97(top), 103(bottom), 114, 131(both), 155(bottom), 161(top).
Hulton Picture Company/Bettman Archive, page: 91(top).
Robert Hunt Library, pages: 74(bottom), 165(top left), 189.
The Illustrated London News Picture Library, page: 63.
Imperial War Museum, London, pages: 20, 21(both), 27(both), 28(bottom 4), 31(top left), 71(top), 72, 75, 77(right bottom & Middle), 79(bottom), 86(top), 116.
Phillip Knightly, page: 35.
London Express News Service, page: 188(above).
Mail Newspapers PLC, pages: 124(top).
Mansell Collection, pages: 18, 25(top).
MARS pages: 10, 61(top), 70.
Museum of London, page: 25(bottom).
National Army Museum, page: 9(top).
Peter Newark's Historical Pictures, page: 2(Inset right), 30(bottom), 31(bottom), 68, 93(top), 95, 183.
Northern Ireland Housing Executive, page: 164.
Novosti, page: 132.
Pacemaker Press International, pages: 2(main).
Barrie Penrose, page: 104.
Popperfolo, page: 135.
Press Association, pages: 147, 167, 172.
Pippa Temple, page: 16(top).
Topham Picture Library, pages: 2(inset left), 11(bottom), 26, 48, 49, 60(bottom right), 61(bottom), 78, 87, 88, 91(bottom), 152, 156, 172, 174(top), 175(bottom).
Wiedenfeld Archive, pages: 8, 44(top), 62(top), 76, 77(top), 92-93(bottom), 148, 150, 155(top)/Daily Express 44(bottom)/Nigel West 51(top).
Stuart Windsor, pages: 100, 123(top), 181(both).